THESE

are the British

THESE

are the British

BY

DREW MIDDLETON

New York: Alfred · A · Knopf: Mcmlvii

L. C. catalog card number: 57–11164
© *Drew Middleton, 1957*

THIS IS A BORZOI BOOK,
PUBLISHED BY ALFRED A. KNOPF, INC.

FIRST EDITION

This book is dedicated

to the memory

of

ALEX CLIFFORD,

EVELYN MONTAGUE,

and

PHILIP JORDAN

FOREWORD

I T W A S in 1940 that the then Prime Minister of the United Kingdom noted that Britain and the United States would have to be
"somewhat mixed up together in some of their affairs for mutual
and general advantage." This situation has persisted until the present. Yet, despite the closeness of co-operation in the intervening
years, there is among Americans a surprising lack of knowledge
about modern Britain.

This book is an effort to provide a picture of that country—
"warts and all." Such a book must perforce be uneven. There are
areas of British life—the attitude toward religion is one—that have
not been touched. I have tried to emphasize those aspects which
are least well known in the United States and to omit as far as possible consideration of those which are superficial. Ascot, I agree, is
spectacular. But as far as modern Britain is concerned it doesn't
matter a damn. I hope, however, that the reader will find here some
idea of what has been going on in Britain since 1945 and what is
going on there today. This is a modern, mobile society, important
to us as we are important to it. If we look at this society realistically,
we will discern physical and moral strength that the fictions of
Hollywood can never convey.

For one whose roots are deep in his own country, the British are a difficult people to understand. But they are worth understanding. They are worth knowing. Long ago, at a somewhat more difficult period of Anglo-American relations, Benjamin Franklin warned his colleagues that if they did not all hang together, they would assuredly hang separately. Good advice for Americans and Britons today.

DREW MIDDLETON

Bessboro Farm
Westport, Essex County
New York
March 12, 1957

CONTENTS

THESE

are the British

I.   *Britain Today*

They called thee Merry England in old time.
WILLIAM WORDSWORTH

*It was never good times in England since the poor began
to speculate on their condition.*
CHARLES LAMB

TO BEGIN: the British defy definition. Although they are
spoken of as "the British," they are not one people but four. And
of these four, three—the Scots, the Welsh, and the Irish—are
fiercely jealous of their national identity. The English are less concerned. They have been a nation a very long time, and only on
occasions like St. George's Day do they remind themselves, a bit
shamefacedly, that the English are the central force of the British
people. Of course, if there are Scots, Welsh, or Irish in the company, the English keep this comforting thought to themselves.

The variety of the British does not end with nationalities.
There are Yorkshiremen and men from Somerset, Cornishmen and
people of Durham who differ as much as Texans and Vermonters
did in the days before the doubtful blessings of standardization
overtook our society.

Here we encounter the first of many paradoxes we shall meet in this book. Homogeneity in political thought—basic political thought that is not party allegiance—seems far greater in Britain than in France or the United States. Yet, until the present, the resistance to standardization has been much more stubborn. Institutions and customs survive without undue prodding by Societies for the Preservation of This and That, although there are plenty of the latter nesting in British society.

Early in 1954 I was in Inverasdale, roughly five hundred miles northwest of London on the western coast of Scotland. Inverasdale is a small village buffeted by the fierce winds that beat in from the North Atlantic, and its people are independent and God-fearing. John Rollo, a Scots industrialist, had started a small factory in Inverasdale to hold the people in the Highlands, where the population has fallen steadily for a century.

Inside the factory John pointed to one of the workers. "That's the bard," he said. "Won a prize at the annual competition this year."

The bard, clad in rubber boots, old trousers, and a fisherman's jersey, had little of the "Scots Wha Ha'e" about him. But he was the real thing. He had journeyed to the competition on foot and there recited in Gaelic his own composition, a description of his life in Germany as a soldier in the British Army of the Rhine. "I sung of those queer foreign sights and people," he said.

I asked him if he had liked the Germans.

"I did not," he said. He was not a particularly loquacious bard. But he was intensely and unostentatiously devoted to customs and a culture well established before there were white men in America.

The bard was proud of his association with an old and famous race. But, then, all over the British Isles there are groups rejoicing in the same fierce local pride. In Devon you will be told that it was "Devon men" who slashed the Armada to ruins in the Channel. That battle was fought nearly four hundred years ago. In a future century the visitor to London will be told, quite correctly, that it was the near-sighted, snaggle-toothed, weak-chested youngsters from the back streets who held the Germans at Calais until preparation could be made for the evacuation at Dunkirk.

The British often act and talk like an old people because they *are* an old people. Nearly nine hundred years have passed since the Norman invasion, the last great influx of foreign blood. Before that, wide, deep rivers and the absence of natural fortifications near the coast had invited invasion. Celts, Romans, Saxons, and Danes had mingled their blood with that of the ancient Britons. But major invasions ended with 1066.

Consequently, the British are unused to foreigners in large numbers. They make a tremendous fuss over the forty thousand or so Jamaicans and other West Indian Negroes who have settled in the country since 1952. The two hundred thousand Poles and other East European refugees, many of whom fought valiantly beside the British in World War II, are more acceptable. This is true, also, of the Hungarians driven from their homeland by the savage Russian repression of the insurrection of 1956. But you will hear grumbling about "foreigners" in areas where refugees have settled. In rural areas you will also hear someone from a neighboring county, long settled in the village, referred to as a "foreigner."

The Republic of Ireland is the main source of immigrants at present. No one knows the exact figures, for there is no official check, but it is estimated in Dublin that perhaps fifty thousand young Irishmen and Irishwomen have entered Britain in each recent year.

This migration has raised some new economic, social, and religious problems and revived some old ones. It is also beginning to affect, although as yet very slightly, political balances in the western Midlands, for this area is short of labor and its industries gobble up willing young men from across the Irish Sea.

These industrial recruits from a rural background become part of an advanced industrial proletariat. By nature and by upbringing they are foreign to the industrial society that uses them. Their political outlook is far different from that of the loyal trade-unionists beside whom they work. They are much less liable to be impressed by appeals for union solidarity and Labor Party support. They accept the benefits of the Welfare State, but they are not of it. The economic Marxism of the orators in the constituency labor parties is beyond them; besides, have they not been warned that Marx is of the devil? The incorporation of this group into the Socialist proletariat poses a question for Labor politicians of the future.

Despite the lack of large-scale migration into Britain during nine centuries, national strains remain virulent. Noisy and stubborn Welsh and Scots nationalist movements give young men and women in Cardiff and Edinburgh something to babble about. London boasts many local associations formed of exiles from the north or west. Even the provincial English manage to make themselves heard in the capital. Few winter nights pass without the Loyal Sons of Loamshire meeting to praise the glories of their home county and drink confusion to the "foreigners," their neighbors.

If the urbanization of the country has not broken these barriers between Scot and Londoner or between Lancashire and Kent, it has changed the face of England out of recognition. And for the worse.

The empty crofters' cottages around Inverasdale and elsewhere in the Highlands are exceptions, for Britain is crowded. The area of the United Kingdom is 93,053 square miles—slightly less than that of Oregon. But the population is just under 51,000,000, including 44,370,000 in England and Wales, 5,128,000 in Scotland, and 1,389,000 in Northern Ireland.

Since the end of the last century the population has been predominantly urban and suburban. By 1900 about three quarters of the British people were living within the boundaries of urban administrative areas, and the large "conurbation" was already the dominant type of British community. This ugly but useful noun describes those areas of urban development where a number of separate towns, linked by a common industrial or commercial interest, have grown into one another.

For over a third of a century about forty per cent of the population has lived in seven great conurbations. Greater London,

with a population of 8,348,000, is the largest of these. The other
conurbations and their centers are: southeast Lancashire: Manchester; west Midlands: Birmingham; west Yorkshire: Leeds and
Bradford; Merseyside: Liverpool; Tyneside: Newcastle upon
Tyne; and Clydeside: Glasgow. Of these the west Midland area
is growing most rapidly. Southeast Lancashire has lost population
—a reflection of the waning of the textile industry.

The growth of the conurbations, particularly London, has
been accompanied by the growth of the suburbs. Of course, many
of the older suburbs are now part of the conurbations. But the
immediate pre-war and post-war building developments have established urban outposts in the serene green countryside.

Today more than a million people travel into the city of London and six central metropolitan boroughs to work each morning
and return to their homes each night. Another 240,000 come in
from the surrounding areas to work in other parts of greater
London.

The advance of suburbia and conurbia has imposed upon vast
sections of the United Kingdom a dreadful sameness. The traveler
finds himself driving for hours through an endless urban landscape.
First he encounters miles of suburban streets: television aerials,
two-story houses whose differences are discernible only to their
inhabitants, clusters of stores. Then a town center with its buses
and bus center, the grimy railroad station, a cluster of civic buildings, a traffic jam, one or two seventeenth-century relics incon-
gruous amid the jumble of Victorian and Edwardian buildings.
Then more suburbs, other town centers, other traffic jams. Indi-
viduality is lost in the desert of asphalt and the jungles of lamp
posts, flashing signs, and rumbling buses.

On a wet winter day a journey through some of the poorer
sections of the western Midlands conurbation is a shocking experience. As your car moves down street after street of drab brick
houses, past dull, smelly pubs and duller shopwindows, occasionally
coming upon hideous, lonely churches, you are oppressed. The air
is heavy with smoke and the warring smells of industry. Poverty

itself is depressing, but here it is not poverty of the pocket but poverty of the soul which shocks. Remorseless conformity and unrestrained commercialism have imposed this on the lively land of Shakespeare. Can great virtues or great vices spring from this smug, stifling environment?

Yet bright spirits are bred. One remembers people met over the years: a sergeant from the Clyde quoting Blake one morning long ago at Arras; Welsh miners singing in the evenings. Out of this can come new Miltons, Newtons, and Blakes. A Nelson of the skies may be studying now at that crumbling school on the corner.

In September 1945 I was riding in from London airport in a bus crowded with Quentin Reynolds (whose presence would crowd an empty Yankee Stadium) and returning soldiers and airmen of the British Army and the Royal Air Force. As we passed through the forlorn streets of Hammersmith, Quentin, brooding on the recent election, said: "These are the people who gave it to Mr. Churchill."

A sergeant pilot behind us leaned forward. "That's all right, cock," he said, "they gave it to Mr. Hitler too."

To put Britain into a twentieth-century perspective, we must go beyond the Britain many Americans know best: the Merrie England created by literature, the stage, and the movies. This picturesque rural England has not been a true picture of the country for over a century. But the guidebooks and the British Travel Association still send tourists to its shrines, novelists still write charmingly dated pictures of its life, and on both sides of the Atlantic the movies and the stage continue to present attractive but false pictures of "Olde Worlde" England.

The British of today know it is dead. They retain an unabashed yearning for its tranquillity, but the young cynics are hacking at this false front. One morning recently I was cheered to note the advent of a new coffee bar, the "Hey, Calypso," in the self-consciously Elizabethan streets of Stratford-on-Avon. I am sure this would have delighted the Bard, himself never above borrowing a bit of foreign color. And the garish sign corrected the phony ostentation of "Elizabethan" Stratford.

Merrie England has its attractions—if you can find them. There is nothing more salutary to the soul than an old, unspoiled village in the cool of a summer evening. But the number of such villages decreases yearly. The hunt, the landed aristocracy, the slumbering farms are changing, if not passing entirely from the scene.

But—and this is very important—the values of this England endure to a reassuring degree. Indeed, it might be argued that they have revived in the last ten years and that virtues thought dated in two post-war Brave New Worlds have been triumphantly reasserted. However, physically, Merrie England, the country Wordsworth tramped and Constable painted, is dead. The schoolteacher from Gibbsville or Gopher Prairie will find the remains nicely laid out.

Despite the blight of suburbia, the countryside retains a compelling charm for the visitor from the United States. There is that hour in a winter evening when a blue light gathers in the shadows of the wood, when the smoke rises straight from cottage chimneys, when you hear the sound of distant church bells. I remember walking once in 1944 with Al Paris, a young captain of the United States Air Force, through just such a scene. "It's funny," he said, "I walk this way two, three times a week, and I feel like I'm coming home. It's different from anything at home. Yet I feel I know it."

But the important Englands or, rather, Britains are very different. There is the dynamic, bustling industrial Britain of the Midlands, the Northeast, and the Lowlands of Scotland. There is the great commercial Britain of London, Bristol, Glasgow, Southampton, Liverpool—the Britain of traders, middlemen, agents, and bankers, the Britain whose effect on the political development of the country and world has been tremendous.

Out of these Britains have come the machines and the men who have kept the country in business and twice helped to smash the military power of Germany. The steel plants of South Wales, the engineering factories of Birmingham, the banks of London, the shipyards of the Clyde—these are the real modern Britain. They are not so attractive as the old villages sleeping in the afternoon sun. But from the standpoint of Britain, and from that of the United States as well, they are much more satisfying and reassuring than Merrie England.

For this is the Great Britain that is not satisfied with the past or the present, that dreams great and necessary dreams of the industrial uses of atomic energy, that strives to expand the three great groups of industry: metals and metal-using, textiles, and chemicals. It is the combination of this Britain and the character of the old England that provides a basis for faith.

Is Britain's long and glorious story nearly done? Will the political, technological, and social changes of the first half of the twentieth century—changes in which Britain often pioneered—combine to eliminate Britain as a world power? Is the country's future to be a gradual and comfortable decline into the position of a satellite in an Atlantic system dominated by the United States and Canada? Or will Britain withdraw slowly, under force of circumstance, into the unambitious neutrality of Sweden?

These are questions that Britons who care about their country must ask themselves. But because of the confidence that is still so strong in British character, such questions are seldom debated openly. In the spring of 1956, when the leaders of the government and of industry were only too gloomily aware of the magnitude of the problems facing the country in the Middle East, in competitive exporting, in gold and dollar reserves, the British Broadcasting Corporation began a television series, "We, the British," with an inquiry: "Are we in a decline?" No one was greatly excited.

This seeming obliviousness to harsh facts, this innate confidence, is one of the most arresting features of the national character. We will encounter it often in this book as we seek answers to the questions about Britain's future.

Consideration of Britain in the world today, and especially of her relation to the United States and to the Soviet Union, must take into account the historical fact that the country's present situation is not altogether novel to Britons.

For Americans it is unusual, and hence disturbing, to live in the same world with a hostile state—the Soviet Union—that is larger and more populous than their own country. Enmity has burst upon us suddenly in the past. We have been told by generations of immigrants that the whole world loved and admired us. It has taken Americans some time to make the psychological adjustment to the position of world power.

The British situation is different. The British have *always* been inferior in strength of numbers to their great antagonists: the Spain of Philip II, the France of Louis XIV and Napoleon, the Germany of Wilhelm II and Hitler, and, today, the Soviet Union. British power has rested not upon numbers but upon combinations of economic stability, political maneuvering, and the exercise of sea, land, and, latterly, air power. The world abroad has always appeared harsh to the Briton. Except for the second half of the last century —a small period in a thousand years of national existence—the British have always seen on the horizon the threat of a larger, more powerful neighbor. The balance has been restored in many a crisis by the ability first of the English and then of the British to attain in war a unity of purpose and energy which in the end has brought victory.

Unity often has restored the balance between Britain and her enemies. To many of us who were in Britain in 1940 the miracle of that memorable year was not the evacuation of Dunkirk or victory in the Battle of Britain or the defiance under bombing of the poor in London, Coventry, and Birmingham, but the national unity of purpose which developed at the moment when all the social upheavals of the thirties pointed to division, faltering, and defeat.

Ability to achieve a national unity remains a factor in Britain's world position. And it is the lack of this unity which makes Britain's position so perilous today.

The country must make, and it must sell abroad. It must retain access to the oil of the Middle East or it will have nothing to make or to sell. It must be able to compete on even terms with the exports of Germany and Japan. These are the ABC's of the British position.

The leaders of the present Conservative government recognize the country's situation; so do the Labor Party and the Trades Union Congress, although each has its own interpretation of the causes. But there is still an unwillingness or an inability on the part of the general public to grasp the realities of the situation.

Yet such a grasp is essential. The people of Britain must adjust themselves to a condition of permanent economic pressure if they are to meet the economic challenge of the times. Such an adjustment will involve re-creation of the sort of national unity which produced the miracles of 1940. Otherwise, John Bull, better paid, better housed, and with more money (which has less value) than ever before, can follow the road to inflation which led to disaster in Germany and France in the thirties.

This return to unity is a factor in answering the question of where the British go from here. But it is only one of many factors. Before we can arrive at an adequate answer we must know more about the British, about their institutions and who runs them today, about what the people have been doing since 1945, and about how they face and fail to face the problems of the second half of the century.

Repeatedly in the course of this inquiry we shall encounter a national characteristic not easily measurable in commercial and industrial values but deeply established and enormously important. This is the ability of the British to adapt themselves to a changing world and to rule themselves with a minimum of serious friction. Stability and continuity are essential in politics if Britain is to meet and answer the challenge of the times. The British enjoy these essentials now. Their demonstrated ability to change with the times is the best of omens for national success and survival as a great power in the tumultuous years that lie ahead.

II.   *The Monarchy*

Kings are not born; they are made by universal hallucination.

GEORGE BERNARD SHAW

A land where kings may be beloved and monarchy can teach republics how they may be free.

VILDA SAUVAGE OWENS

THE MONARCHY is the crowning anachronism of British society. It stands virtually unchallenged at the summit of that society. In this most political of Western nations, one eternally bubbling with new ideas on the ways and means by which men can govern themselves, the thousand-year-old monarchy is admired, respected, or tolerated, but is seldom attacked. A people who on occasion can be as ruthless and cynical as any in the world preserve close to their hearts a mystic symbol that asks and gets an almost childlike loyalty from millions.

This tie between Crown and people is the basis for the monarchy's existence. Yet, like so many other things in Britain, the tie is almost indefinable. Its strength is everywhere and nowhere.

History is one of its foundations, and the sense of history—a reassuring sense that worse has happened and that the nation and
the people have survived—is very strong in Britain. Yet the present
institution of monarchy has little in common with the monarchy
of 1856 and still less with that of 1756. And the extreme popularity of the royal family has developed only in the last eighty
years.

The reasons for the monarchy's popularity today are far different from those of the past. It is regrettable but true that some
of the most popular monarchs earned their popularity as much by
their vices as by their virtues.

By our American standards the British monarchy is very old,
although it does not compare with the same institution in Iran, for
instance, where kings reigned seven centuries before Christ. Certainly the age of monarchy, linking modern Britain with the
forested, lusty, legendary England of the Dark Ages, contributes
to its popularity. Age in an institution or a person counts in
Britain.

Queen Elizabeth II is in direct descent from Egbert, King of
Wessex and all England, who ascended the throne in 827. The
blood of all the royal families of Europe flows in her veins. Among
her ancestors are some of the great names of history: Charlemagne,
William the Conqueror, Alfred the Great, Rodrigo the Cid, the
Emperor Barbarossa, and St. Louis, King of France. This notable
lineage is unknown to millions who adore the Queen. The visible
expressions of adoration and loyalty to the royal family can be
profoundly moving, but there is nothing to suggest that the crowd's
memory stretches back much further than George V, the present
Queen's grandfather.

Is "profoundly moving" too strong? I doubt it. London was
a gray and somber city in November 1947 when Princess Elizabeth married the Duke of Edinburgh. A long war with Germany
and two years of austerity had left their mark. The crowds, the
buildings were shabby and tired. Yet the Crown evoked in these

circumstances a sincere and unselfish affection such as few politicians can arouse.

What did it? The pageantry of the Household Cavalry, restored to their pre-war glory of cuirass, helmet, and plume, scarlet and blue and white? The state coach with the smiling, excited, pretty girl inside? The bands and the stirring familiar tunes? There is no single convincing answer. Yet the affection was there: the sense of a living and expanding connection between the people and the throne.

But some aspects of the connection can be embarrassing, to Britons as well as to Americans. The doings of the royal family are recounted by popular British newspapers and periodicals in nauseating prose. Special articles on the education of Prince Charles or on Princess Margaret's religious views (which are deep, sincere, and, to any decent person's mind, her own business) are written in a mixture of archness, flowery adulation, and sugary winsomeness.

The newspapers are full of straight reporting (the Queen, asked if she would have a cup of tea, said: "Yes, thank you, it is rather cold") but this does not suffice to meet the demand for "news" about the royal family. Periodically the Sunday newspapers publish reminiscences of life in the royal household. Former governesses, valets, and even the man who did the shopping for the Palace write their "inside stories." These are as uninformative as the special campaign biographies that appear every four years in the United States, but the public loves them. I have been told that a "royal" feature in a popular magazine adds 25,000 or 30,000 in circulation for that issue. The *Sunday Express* is said to have picked up 300,000 circulation on the Duchess of Windsor's memoirs. Like sex and crime, the royal family is always news—and the news is not invariably favorable.

The interest in royal doings is all the more baffling because the Queen is generally held to be powerless politically. This view is accepted in Britain and also in the United States, save among those surviving primitives of Chicagoland who regard all British monarchs as reincarnations of George III ready to order the Lobsterbacks to Boston at an insult's notice. The accepted picture is of a monarch who is a symbol with little or no influence on politics.

Superficially the picture is accurate. But in the last century and in this there have been occasions when the Crown exerted power beyond the functions assigned it by the constitution. These functions include the summoning, proroguing, and dissolution of Parliament, the dismissal or appointment of a Prime Minister, the granting of pardons, and the conferring of peerages and honors. To become the law of the land, a bill passed by Parliament must receive the royal assent.

All very impressive. But in practice these functions are restricted by the principle that the monarch is responsible to the government of the day even though it is styled "Her Majesty's Government." To take one example, if the Queen wants to make Lord Tomnoddy a duke and the Prime Minister says no, Lord Tomnoddy does not become a duke. The monarch retains the right of conferring certain honors, such as the Order of the Garter, without ministerial advice. But when Chancellor Adenauer of Germany receives the insignia of the Grand Cross of the Order of St. Michael and St. George the inspiration comes not from Buckingham Palace but from Downing Street.

The principle of responsibility to the government guides the conduct of the monarch. In rare cases the sovereign can express disapproval of a policy. In the present circumstances the idea of the young Queen rejecting the advice of her Prime Minister is unthinkable. Without being romantic, we can wonder if this will always be so.

George V twice exercised his discretionary powers in choosing from among alternative candidates the man he regarded as best suited to be Prime Minister. Of course, in each case the candidate chosen had to have the support of his party in the House of Commons.

We need not go back that far. George VI, the father of the

present Queen, once made a decision that profoundly affected the history of the world.

When in May 1940 a tired, unpopular Neville Chamberlain resigned as Prime Minister there were two candidates for the post: Winston Churchill and Lord Halifax. The King knew that a large section of the Conservative Party distrusted Churchill and admired Halifax. Its views were conveyed to him in plain language.

According to *The Gathering Storm,* the first volume of Sir Winston Churchill's *The Second World War,* Lord Halifax told both Churchill and Chamberlain that his position as a peer outside the House of Commons would make it difficult for him to discharge the duties of Prime Minister. Ultimately a National Government including representatives of the Labor and Liberal parties was formed, but, according to Churchill, the King made no stipulation "about the Government being National in character."

Lord Halifax certainly doubted his ability to discharge his duties as Prime Minister. But apparently the question of whether he could form a National Government did not arise. In any event, the King, fully cognizant of the views of a considerable section of the Conservative Party on the relative merits of the two men and aware that it would have been possible to form a Conservative government under Halifax, sent for Churchill instead of Halifax and asked him to form a government. History may record this as a signal example of the remaining powers of the Crown.

Sir William Anson explained in *The Law and Custom in the Constitution* that the real power of the sovereign "is not to be estimated by his legal or his actual powers as the executive of the State.

"The King or Queen for the time being is not a mere piece of mechanism, but a human being carefully trained under circumstances which afford exceptional chances of learning the business of politics."

The monarch is not isolated from great affairs. The Queen sees from the inside the workings of government, knows the individuals concerned, and often has a surer sense of what the people will or will not accept than some politicians. So, Sir William reasoned, the sovereign in the course of a long reign may through experience become a person whose political opinions, even if not enforceable, will carry weight. Continuity in office, wide experience in contact with successive governments, and, finally, the influence that the monarchy exercises through an ancient and well-established tie with the people can confer upon the sovereign an influence far greater than is generally realized.

Queen Elizabeth II has twice used the royal prerogative of choosing a Prime Minister. On April 6, 1955, she chose Sir Anthony Eden to succeed Sir Winston Churchill. On January 10, 1957, she chose Harold Macmillan to succeed Sir Anthony. The second selection occasioned sharp political outcry. The "shadow cabinet" or Parliamentary Committee of the Labor Party, meeting in secrecy and dudgeon, reported that the Queen's choice had raised serious questions of a constitutional nature. It argued that the Conservative Party, by asking the sovereign to choose between Mr. Macmillan and R. A. Butler, had involved the Queen in partisan politics. The Tories, Labor said with a touch of self-righteousness, should always have a leader and a deputy leader of the party ready to assume the highest office when called.

(This raised the contingency, pleasing to Tories at least, of James Griffiths, the present deputy leader, as Prime Minister instead of Aneurin Bevan in the event of some serious accident to Hugh Gaitskell.)

The Socialists' argument that the Queen was forced to choose between Mr. Macmillan and Mr. Butler reflected a certain ignorance of what had been going on within the Conservative Party. It was apparent on the night of Sir Anthony Eden's resignation that Mr. Butler did not command the support of a majority of the Tory Members of the House of Commons. It was also apparent, or should have been apparent, that the Queen would be advised by the retiring Prime Minister, Sir Anthony Eden, and the two foremost figures in the party, Sir Winston Churchill and the Marquess of Salisbury. Anyone aware of the currents within the Conservative leadership during the last three months of 1956 could not possibly have thought that any one of these three would advise the Queen to choose Mr. Butler.

There was a good deal less to the high-minded Socialist protest than met the eye. The shadow cabinet made the tactical mistake of coupling the protest with a demand for a general election. One need not be cynical to emphasize the connection. But the spectacle of Mr. Bevan and his colleagues protesting like courtiers over the Queen's involvement in politics and quoting an editorial in *The Times* as though it were Holy Writ added to the gaiety of the nation.

The Queen may have opinions on national and international affairs which differ from those of her ministers. To date there has been no reliable report of such differences. But her grandfather, George V, was seldom backward in expressing opinions contrary to those of his ministers. He told them, for instance, that the conduct of the 1914–18 war must be left to military "experts," which meant Haig and his staff, rather than to politicians. He opposed the dissolution of Parliament in 1918. He refused outright to grant a convenient "political" peerage. This opposition, it should be emphasized, was not directed at court functionaries. On many occasions George V took issue with David Lloyd George, a wartime Premier then at the height of his prestige and power, and a brilliant and tenacious debater.

The present royal family invites comparisons with that of a century ago. Philip, Duke of Edinburgh, is, like Albert, the Prince Consort of Victoria, an exceptional person. He is a man of industry and intelligence. Like Albert, he understands both the broad outlines and the nuances of a new industrial age into which Britain is moving. He has a wider acquaintance with the world of science, so essential to his country, than any other member of the royal family. The techniques of industry and invention really interest him. He understands, perhaps better than some of his wife's ministers, the importance to Britain of such developments as the industrial use of nuclear energy. Finally, the Duke of Edinburgh has one matchless qualification for his role. As a young officer of the Royal Navy he became aware of the way the Queen's subjects, as represented by the lower deck of the Navy, think and feel. He has in fact what the admirers of the Duke of Windsor claimed for him when he was Prince of Wales: an intimate knowledge of the people of Britain.

These qualities are not universally admired. A trade-union leader told me he did not want "well-intentioned young men like Philip mucking about with industrial relations." At the other side of the political spectrum, the *Sunday Express,* Lord Beaverbrook's newspaper, tut-tutted at the Duke's interest in this field.

The reasoning behind both attitudes is obvious. Industrial relations are politics. The union movement is the Fourth Estate of the realm, and "royals" should leave them alone.

There is an obvious parallel. The Prince Consort when he died had established himself at the center of national affairs. But for his death, Lytton Strachey wrote, "such a man, grown gray in the service of the nation, virtuous, intelligent, and with the unexampled experience of a whole lifetime of government," would have achieved "an extraordinary prestige."

Disraeli saw the situation in even more positive terms. "With Prince Albert we have buried our sovereign. This German Prince has governed England for twenty-one years with a wisdom and energy such as none of our kings have ever shown. . . . If he had outlived some of our 'old stagers' he would have given us the blessings of absolute government."

The parallel may seem far-fetched. Of course present-day Britain is not the Britain of 1856. It is hard to think of Sir Anthony Eden or Hugh Gaitskell being moved politically, at the moment, by the views of the Queen or the Duke of Edinburgh as Lord Clarendon was, and as Lord Palmerston was not, by Victoria and Albert. But, to borrow Napoleon III's incisive phrase, in politics one should never say never.

Not long ago a diplomat who had returned from a key post abroad encountered the Queen at what should have been a perfunctory ceremony. He expected a few minutes' conversation. What he got was forty minutes of acute questioning about the situation in the country he had just left. The Queen impressed him with the width of her knowledge, her accurate memory, and the sharpness of her questions. He, a tough, skeptical intellectual, departed with heightened respect for his sovereign's intelligence.

What will be the Queen's influence a quarter of a century hence? By then some politician, now unknown, will be Prime Minister. How much will the wisdom and experience of the Queen, gained as the repository of the secrets of successive governments, affect the government of the day? Monarchy, we Americans are taught, is an archaic symbol and an obsolete form of government. History has moved away from constitutional monarchies and, of course, from one-man rule. But has it? Will the movement continue?

By 1980 the British monarchy may be a memory. But let us suppose that by that year the royal house is represented by an infinitely experienced Queen and a consort who knows the country's problems as well as most of her ministers. Prince Philip is a nephew of Earl Mountbatten, one of the most striking Englishmen of today. What will this infusion of determination, energy, and intelligence do for the fortunes of the monarchy?

The British are cautious in discussing any indications of the influence of the Crown on the day-to-day conduct of government. But occasional comments and indiscretions indicate that this influence is a factor in decisions. For instance, early in 1956 I was talking to an important civil servant about a government decision that was to be announced in the next few days. The government was busy making certain, he said, that "the Palace" wouldn't "make a row about it." I said I was surprised that he should ascribe so much weight to the Palace's view on a matter that involved the cabinet and the House of Commons. His answer was that in a country such as Britain under a Conservative government, influence is not exerted solely through the House or government departments. "What people say to each other counts," he said. "And when the Queen says it, it counts a great deal. Of course, she couldn't change a decision. Nor would she ever attempt to. But it can be awkward, you know."

To guess at the future power of the monarchy we must examine it as it is today. What lies behind its popularity and how is that popularity maintained? What keeps strong this tie between a largely working-class population, highly progressive politically, and an aristocratic institution that has outlived its power if not its influence?

To understand, we must watch monarchy operate within the limitations imposed upon it by the constitution. The principal functions are the public performances of the duties of the Crown—what the British press calls "royal occasions." They range from a state opening of Parliament to a visit to an orphanage.

These take place in an atmosphere fusing formality and enthusiasm. Protocol calls for dignity, friendliness, and a certain aloofness on the part of the Queen. Those who make the arrangements for royal occasions are mindful of Walter Bagehot's warning against allowing too much light to fall on the institution of monarchy. But from the standpoint of popular reaction, the Queen's appearances are most successful when she stops to say a few words to someone in the crowd. Written reports of such encounters usually endow the Queen with a celestial condescension. The fact is that the Queen, though shy, is friendly, and her awed subjects are likely to report that "she talked about the baby just like she was from down the street."

Of course, the Queen is not like someone just down the street. But the essence of a successful display of the monarchy is a combination of this friendliness with the serene dignity displayed on great occasions of state. The men and women in the crowd want to believe that the Queen is, or can be, like them. As long as they do, the monarchy, no matter how rich its members and how expensive its trappings, is relatively safe.

To the people in the streets the Queen is paramount. The Duke of Edinburgh is popular. So are the Queen Mother and Princess Margaret. But it is the Queen who combines all those elements of tradition, affection, and mysticism which contribute to the Crown's unique place in public life.

The crowd does not care much about other royalties. To the man in the street there is little difference between, say, Prince Rainier of Monaco and Aristotle Onassis. The British nurse at their hearts a snobbish isolationism toward foreign crowns. Only their own Queen and royal family really matter.

One reason is that Britain's Queen and the monarchial institution she heads are kept before the people to a far greater degree than is customary in the monarchies of Holland or Sweden. Official political and social appearances in London are augmented by visits to various parts of the country. The Queen and the Duke are the chief attractions, but other members of the family perform similar duties.

Careful planning and split-second timing are the key to successful royal visits. So familiar is the pattern that a skeptic might think the effect negligible. When the Queen comes to Loamshire, however, she is *there* in Loamshire. Everything she does is familiar, but now she is there directly before the crowd's very eyes, rendering a personal service.

The Queen and the Duke arrive in Loamshire for a three-day visit. Their car is a huge, glittering Rolls-Royce flying the royal standard. Thousands of people, most of them women and children, are on the sidewalks and in the windows of the buildings around the town hall of the county town of Loamshire. As the Queen gets out of the car there is a wave of cheering, strong and unaffected. (It is well to balance this enthusiasm against the inattention paid "God Save the Queen" when it is played at the end of the program in a provincial movie theater.)

The Mayor, sweating freely in his excitement, welcomes the Queen and delivers an appropriate address. In a country divided almost evenly between the Conservative and Labor parties, a large number of mayors are Socialists. But, with rare exceptions, the Socialists and their wives are as eager as the Tories to welcome royalty.

The Queen and the Duke are introduced to the dignitaries of Loamshire, with the Lord Lieutenant of the county in attendance. The Queen inspects a guard of honor which may be drawn from the Royal Loamshire Light Infantry or from the local Girl Guides. There is lunch, usually a pretty bad lunch. Then the royal party is off to lay the cornerstone of a new hospital or press a button to start a new power plant or unveil a war memorial. At any such occasion the Queen reads a short speech of blameless sentiments.

Then on to the next town, to more cheering in the streets and waving of flags, more loyal declarations and another mayor and council. This may go on for two or three days. Every step the Queen takes, every action is noted by newsreel and television cameras. Every word she utters is taken down. Every person with whom she talks is interviewed afterward.

Back in London there are more ceremonies. There are also ambassadors to be received, state papers to be read, decorations to be awarded, distinguished visitors to be met.

It is often said that the Queen is just like anyone else of her age, an idea much favored by the spun-sugar biographies in the popular press. Of course it is nonsense. The Queen cannot, because of her birth, upbringing, and station, be like anyone else. Certainly she has a private life not unlike that of other wealthy young women, but her private life is severely restricted.

She and the Duke may like to eat their supper off trays and watch a popular comedian on television, but they seldom get an opportunity to do so. The Queen must be wary of what plays she sees and what amusements she patronizes. As head of the Church she is an inviting target for sorrowful criticism by the bluenoses. The Queen's love of horse racing and the Duke's love of polo are often attacked by puritanical elements. The League Against Cruel Sports periodically reproves her for attending "the sporting butchery" of fox-hunting.

What sort of woman is she? Forget the cloying descriptions of courtiers and the indiscretions of "Crawfie" and her friends, and the portrait is rather an appealing one. Elizabeth II in person is much prettier than her photographs. Her coloring is excellent. Her mouth, a little too wide, can break into a beguiling smile. She is slowly overcoming her nervousness in public, but still becomes very angry when the newsreel and television cameras focus on her for minutes at a time. Her voice, high and girlish on her accession, is taking on a deeper, more musical tone. Years of state duties, of meeting all kinds and classes of people, have diminished her shyness. She was almost tongue-tied when she came to Washington as Princess Elizabeth, but her host on that occasion, President Harry S. Truman, was surprised by the poised and friendly Queen he met in London in 1956.

All her adult life the Queen has been accustomed to the company of the great. Aided by a phenomenal memory and real interest, her acquaintance with world politics is profound. She is intelligent but not an intellectual. She does a great deal of official reading—so much, in fact, that she reads little for pleasure.

The Queen's pleasures and those of her immediate family are so typical of the middle class that intellectuals are often offended. They would prefer more attendance at cultural events such as the Edinburgh Festival and less at race meetings. But the deep thinkers, worried because the cultural tone of Buckingham Palace is pitched to the level of Danny Kaye rather than T. S. Eliot, overlook the fact that attachment to such frivolity strengthens the popularity of the royal house. There is no evidence that the British admire or desire intellectual attainments in a monarch. Nor does history indicate that such lusty figures as Charles II and George IV were less popular than the pious Victoria or the benign George V. Thus, when the Queen spends a week at Ascot to watch the racing, as millions of her subjects would dearly love to do, or attends a London revue, her subjects, aware of the burden of her office, wish her a good time. And the descriptions of such outings, with their invariable reports on what the Queen wore, what she ate and drank, and what she was heard to say, are read avidly by a large percentage of her people.

The people are flattered when the Queen appears at a polo

game in sensible shoes and a print dress, accompanied by her children and her dogs. They are equally flattered when they see her in tiara and evening dress, regal and coldly handsome. When the newspapers printed pictures of the Queen and her royal hosts at a state ball during her visit to Sweden, the popular reaction was: "Doesn't she look lovely, a real credit to the country."

Racing is the Queen's favorite sport. When she was returning from her world tour in 1953–4, one of the first messages the royal yacht *Britannia* transmitted as it neared British shores was an inquiry on the result of a race held the day before.

For Elizabeth, racing is more than a sport; it is an enthusiasm. She knows blood lines and past performances, and her acute judgment of form sometimes conflicts with her personal attachment for one of the royal stable's entries. She likes to watch show jumping and polo, although at polo games she is continually worried about the Duke of Edinburgh, an enthusiastic player. But horse racing: the magic moment when the barrier goes up, the bright silks on the back stretch, the lovely sight of the field rounding the last turn into the stretch—that's her sport. As it is also the sport of millions of her subjects, the sneers of the puritans have little effect.

She is a young woman of determination, having inherited some of her grandfather's temper and his forthright outlook on events. In moments of family crisis she is likely to take what the British call "a strong line." During the row over the romance of Princess Margaret and Peter Townsend, it was reported that the first communication from Buckingham Palace on the situation had been written by the Queen. I find this credible. The announcement certainly had all the faults of a communiqué drafted in anger.

Finally, Elizabeth is religious, very conscious of the importance of her role in British society, and, as she grows older, somewhat censorious of the gay young things enjoying a freedom she never knew.

The monarchy is costly. The Queen is a very wealthy woman in her own right, but, in addition, she receives £60,000 (about $168,000) a year from the Civil List. This is granted to the sovereign by Parliament on the recommendation of a Select Committee. The Civil List not only "pays" the Queen but pays her expenses, which are high. For instance, the salaries of the royal household, secretaries, equerries, servants, and the like, total £185,000 or $418,000 a year, and the running expenses come to £121,800 or $341,040.

Payments charged to the Consolidated Fund maintain the other members of the family. The Duke of Edinburgh's annuity is £40,000 or $112,000 a year, and the Queen Mother's is £70,000 or $196,000.

These payments are only one of many sources of income. The House of Windsor is very rich, although its fortune is modest compared with the holdings of the House of Ford or the House of Rockefeller.

Queen Victoria died leaving the monarchy more firmly established than ever before and her family richer by millions of pounds. During her long reign the remarkable daughter of an unambitious Duke of Kent and an improvident German princess amassed a fortune of about £5,000,000 or, at the exchange rates of the day, about $25,000,000. The financial dealings of the royal house are secret. But both Albert, Victoria's Prince Consort, and his son Edward VII benefited from the advice of financiers. Reputedly the family owns large blocks of American railroad stock. The financial structure is complex, however. It is hard to say just how much Elizabeth owns as Queen and how much as an individual.

As one of the greatest landowners, the Queen derives an income of about £94,600 or $265,000 a year from the Duchy of Lancaster. The royal family also receives the revenues of the Duchy of Cornwall, which amount to about £90,000 or approximately $250,000 a year. This duchy, comprising about 133,000 acres spread throughout the west of England, includes farms, hotels, tin mines, even pubs. Seven palaces and eight royal houses also are the property of Elizabeth as Queen. One, Sandringham in Norfolk, an estate of 17,000 acres including fifteen well-kept farms, is a family holding. The Balmoral estate in Scotland comprises 80,000 acres.

The family holds more than seventy-five choice bits of London real estate. Both fortune and property are carefully managed. Nothing is wasted. The game birds that fall to the guns of shooting parties at Sandringham and Balmoral are sold on the commercial market after the household's requirements have been met.

The Crown is not only a prosperous and wealthy establishment. It is also the center of a unique complex of commercial interests. The manufacture of souvenirs connected with the royal family is big business. These souvenirs range from hideous, cheap glass ash trays and "silver" spoons stamped with a picture of Buckingham Palace or of the Queen and the Duke to "coronation" wineglasses and dinner services sold to wealthy tourists. A whole section of British publishing is devoted to postcards, picture books, and other records of royal lives and royal occasions.

The Queen's world tour in 1953–4 produced a bumper crop of pictorial and prose reports to fit every purse and the prevailing taste for flowery adulation. These books were bought and read, or at least looked at, after the British public already had been exposed to newspaper accounts, magazine reports, radio bulletins, and television newsreels. Once at a dinner party the wife of a famous writer remarked: "I'm sick of this damned tour." The other guests broke into a flurry of conversation that had nothing to do with the royal voyage. Yet I learned that three of them felt "exactly as dear Betty does, but, my dear, you don't say it."

Some thoughtful students of the institution believe that the newspapers, magazines, radio, and television have forgotten Bagehot's injunction about letting too much light fall on the monarchy. But I have seen no diminution of popular interest. The highbrows may be bored, but the lowbrows and middlebrows love it.

The extensive coverage given the royal family has propaganda uses. In the years since the war there has been a quiet but intensive effort to reinforce the position of the monarch as the titular head of the Commonwealth. The rulers of Britain, Labor or Conservative, recognizing how slender are the ties that bind the Commonwealth, have worked steadily to strengthen the chief spiritual tie, the Crown, as political and economic ties have become attenuated.

The Queen is the Queen of Canada and Australia as well as of the United Kingdom. Canada, in fact, is a monarchy. Royal tours of Commonwealth countries emphasize the common tie of monarchy and are also intended to reawaken interest in Britain and, as these are a commercial people, British manufactures.

The reports that have reached London show that, from the standpoint of strengthening identity with the Commonwealth, the visit to Australia and New Zealand during the world tour was an outstanding success. To the exuberant, vigorous Australians, for instance, the Queen symbolized their relationship with the island many of them still call home. Criticism of the "pommies," the slang term for the British, was drowned in the swell of cheers for the Queen of Australia.

Nor should the effect of such tours on the younger members of the Commonwealth be underestimated. The visit to Nigeria in 1956 flattered its people and gave new meaning to the honors and titles that successive governments have bestowed on worthy—which in this context means loyal—natives of the country. Those in government who value the Commonwealth and Empire see such visits as a method of impressing new members of the Commonwealth with the permanence of a symbol that binds all members. Perhaps only South Africa, in its present government's mood of Boer republicanism, is proof against the loan of the Crown.

Curiously, this extension of the monarchy is not generally appreciated in Britain. There the supporters of the Crown are gratified, of course, when the newspapers report an ovation for the Queen in Wellington. But they are slow to accept the idea of the Queen as Queen of New Zealand.

The process of identifying the Queen with various parts of the Commonwealth may go further than visits to its members. Some officials suggest that the Queen should live a part of each year in one or another of the Commonwealth countries. From the constitutional standpoint this is a revolutionary suggestion. And Britain prefers evolution to revolution. But it is an indication of the progressive viewpoint that some supporters of the Crown have adopted toward its political uses in the modern world.

No institution in Britain escapes attack, and so the institution of monarchy is attacked. But such criticism is rarely coherent, popular, or direct. On the whole, there is less criticism than there was a century ago. Republicanism died as a political force in the 1870's. The Chartists in their peak period, roughly between 1838 and 1849, included in their demands the establishment of a republic. When Victoria withdrew into her grief after the death of the Prince Consort, a republican movement of some importance developed. New impetus was given by the establishment of the Third Republic in France in 1871. Charles Bradlaugh and George Odger, men of some importance, spoke eloquently in support of a republic. But the last "Republican Conference" was held in 1873, and Sir Charles Dilke later ascribed his youthful republicanism to "political infancy."

The Labor Party, despite its strong infusion of Marxism, treats the issue as a dead letter. Not since the party conference of 1923 has there been a serious debate on the monarchy. At that conference a motion that republicanism should be the policy of the party was rejected by 3,694,000 votes to 386,000.

Criticism of the monarchy in contemporary Britain is most telling when it hits the cost of the institution. The great wealth of the royal family and the heavy expenses of the monarchial institution invite criticism in a period when Britain seems to live perennially on the rim of economic disaster.

Early in 1956 it was suggested that the Queen's Flight, her personal transport planes, be re-equipped with one, possibly more, of the big new Britannias, the nation's newest air liner. At the same time a new dining-car was ordered for royal travel, and it became known that the royal waiting-room at London airport was to be renovated at considerable expense. These matters received extraordinarily detailed coverage in the newspapers owned by Lord Beaverbrook. Letters criticizing the added expenses found their way into the letter columns of the *Daily Express,* the *Evening Standard,* and the *Sunday Express.* Columnists inquired the reason for such expenditures when the nation was being asked to tighten its belt, spend less, and defeat inflation.

Constant readers of these newspapers, which are among the most sprightly and technically expert in Britain, have long noted their oblique criticism of Duke of Edinburgh. Usually this deals with the Duke's "interference" in the field of industrial relations. It is believed to spring from Lord Beaverbrook's long-standing animus for the Duke's uncle, Earl Mountbatten. The criticism of the proposed expenditures for the Britannias, the dining-car, and the waiting-room gave the newspapers a chance to hint that the young man was getting a bit above himself.

The *Sunday Express* gave the widest possible publicity to its serialization of the autobiography of the Duchess of Windsor, an opus that, although interesting, cannot be considered an enthusiastic recommendation for the institution of monarchy.

The inevitable conclusion is that William Maxwell Aitken, first Baron Beaverbrook, New Brunswick, and Cherkley, nurses crypto-republican sentiments at heart. He has confessed to being a propagandist in his newspapers, and he is so unpredictable that he might sometime direct all his energies against the institution. I mentioned this to a cabinet minister, who replied that the monarchy would welcome it. "Nothing helps a politician more than the enmity of the Beaver," he commented.

Although republicanism is no longer an issue in the Labor Party, the party itself contains a strong element that is hostile to the monarchy. Yet neither the *Daily Mirror* nor the *Daily Herald,* the journalistic pillars of the left, snipe quite so often or so accurately as the Beaverbrook press.

The *New Statesman and Nation* does. Its indirect attacks on royalty are based on establishing a link between royalty and the wealthy, showy, and, of course, non-socialist world of London's fashionable West End. The *New Statesman*'s complaint, delivered in the tones of a touring schoolmarm who has been pinched by a lascivious Latin, is that the Queen should use her influence to halt ostentatious spending on debutante parties and the revels of the young. Its anonymous editorial-writer was severe with young people who drink too much (although abstinence has never been particularly popular on the left) and generally whoop it up. The editorial ended with a hint that the Queen would have to exercise some restraint when a Labor government came to power.

Despite such criticisms and warnings, the monarchy pursues its course virtually unchallenged. One reason for the lack of a serious political challenge may be that the monarchy is not now identified with a rich, powerful, and coherent aristocracy, as it was a century ago, but with the ordinary citizen. Then, too, there are many who look to the royal family as an example.

Long ago a compositor in a London newspaper, a good union man and a Socialist, explained this attitude. "I'd rather have my two daughters reading about the Queen and all that stuff than reading those magazines about the flicks. Who'd you want your daughter to follow, Lana Turner or the Queen?"

So we return again to the indefinable and powerful tie that binds people and Crown.

Perhaps it is a sense of historical identity experienced as the Queen rides past, carrying with her the atmosphere of other Englands. Here before the eyes of her people is a reassurance of survival, an example of continuity. This is one of those periods in history when the British need reassuring.

Perhaps as the monotony of life in a nation that is becoming one huge industrial suburb spreads over Britain, the ceremony and glitter of the Crown mean more than ever before. The great noblemen are prosaic characters in business suits showing the crowds through empty palaces and castles. But the Queen, amid the uniforms and palaces and castles, remains the Queen.

Perhaps as the storms buffet England in this second half of the century, the position of the Queen as a personification of goodness and justice becomes more important. Here is an enduring symbol, a token of the past and a promise for the future. As the world and its problems become more complex, the single, simple attraction of the representative of an institution that has survived so many complexities and problems will grow upon the confused and unhappy.

The Crown stands as it has for a thousand years. Its power is less and its influence is greater than many know. It is an integral part of a flexible and progressive society.

III. *How the British Govern Themselves*

Parliament can do anything but turn a boy into a girl.
ENGLISH PROVERB

Politics I conceive to be nothing more than the science of the ordered progress of society along the lines of greatest usefulness and convenience to itself.
WOODROW WILSON

THE BRITISH are pre-eminently a political people, as Americans are, and as Germans, Russians, and Italians are not. They regard politics and government as serious, honorable, and, above all, interesting occupations. To many Britons the techniques of government and politics in Nigeria or Louisiana or Iceland are as fascinating as the newest jet fighter is to an aviation enthusiast. They have been at it a long time, and yet politics and government remain eternally fascinating.

The comparative stability and prestige of government and politics result in part from tradition and experience. The British govern themselves by a system evolved over a thousand years from the times of the Saxon kings, and they have given much of what is best and some of what is worst in that system to nations and continents unknown when first a Parliament sat in Westminster. Although it was dominated by peers and bullied by the King, a Parliament met in Westminster when France seethed under the absolute rule of His Most Christian Majesty. Some of the greatest speeches made *against* the royal policy during the American War of Independence were made in Parliament.

The course of history has strengthened the position of parliamentary government. Parliament and Britain have survived and triumphed, but where is the Europe of Louis XIV, of Napoleon, of Wilhelm II, of Hitler? Even in times of great stress the business of government must go on. I remember my astonishment in June of 1940 when I returned from a stricken, hopeless France to learn from a Member of Parliament that a committee was considering plans for uniting the West Indian islands in a single Commonwealth unit after the war.

The idea that politics and government are essential to the well-being of the nation fortifies tolerance in British public life. The political and military disasters of 1940 were far more damaging and dangerous to Britain than Pearl Harbor was to the United States. They invited bitter recrimination. Yet Winston Churchill, himself bitterly attacked in the locust years for predicting these very disasters, took Neville Chamberlain into his cabinet and silenced recrimination with the salient reminder that if the nation dwelt too much on the past it might lose the future.

For a century the British have avoided the dangers of an important extremist political party comparable to the Communists in France and Italy or the Nazis in Germany. The Communist Party exists in Britain, of course, but only barely. Sir Oswald Mosley and his blackshirts made some impression just before and just after the last war, but their direct political influence is negligible.

The British don't think extremism is good practical politics. They went through their own period of extremism in the sixteenth, seventeenth, and early eighteenth centuries when for a variety of reasons, religious as well as political, they cut off one king's head, tried a dictatorship, brought back a king, and finally found comparative tranquillity in the development of a constitutional monarchy.

The memory of these troubled times is not dead. At the height of McCarthyism in the United States a British diplomat explained: "We've very fortunate; we went through the same sort of period under the Tudors and the Stuarts when treason and slander and libel were the common coin of politics."

With exceptions, the great political parties in the country have now identified themselves with the national interest rather than with a partisan one. Even the exceptions change. As the status of the working class has changed for the better, the Labor Party has moved perceptibly away from its early position as a one-class party. The heirs of Keir Hardy—the Attlees, Morrisons, and Gaitskells—understand that Labor must appeal now to the whole people.

The national interest is something the whole people has always understood and accepted in the past. For the British are guided politically not by an ideology but by interest. This interest is a free world, free from the economic as well as the political standpoint. One factor in the decision to withdraw from India was the conviction that, in the end, withdrawal would serve British commercial interests. I do not suggest that this was the only factor. There were others, including the belief of the leaders of the Labor government that India could not and should not be kept within the Empire by force.

Similarly, Britain is ready to give way on the independence of other parts of the Empire when she thinks these areas are ready for independence as democracies, and when she believes that their emergence as independent democracies will benefit her own commercial interests. This mixture of realism and idealism is difficult for outsiders to grasp, especially when the British cling to a territory such as Cyprus for reasons that are largely connected with their commercial interests in that part of the world.

Yet although the British have acquired, and are now in the process of losing, a world-wide empire, they never suffered from a desire to remake the world as did the French of 1789, or the Russians of 1917, or the Germans of 1939. As a commercial people their basic interest was, and is, peace. The British will go to almost any lengths to prevent a war, as they did in 1938 and 1939. Once at war, however, they fight with cold ruthlessness.

The allegiance of the great political parties to the national interest is one reason why British politics and politicians are flexible and tolerant. Another is that politics are still touched by the shadowy influence of the Crown. Here is a higher, if weaker, authority than Prime Minister or cabinet. Does the presence of the sovereign at the peak of government draw some of the exaggeration and extremism from politics?

Certainly no British Prime Minister, not even Churchill in 1940, has ever been bathed in the sycophancy that deluged President Eisenhower in his first term. Certainly no British Prime Minister, not even Chamberlain in 1938 and 1939, has been reviled so relentlessly by critics as were Presidents Roosevelt and Truman. Convictions are as deeply held in London as in Washington. But anyone moving between the two cities must be convinced that the political atmosphere in London is calmer, less subject to emotional cloudbursts.

The center of British politics is Parliament—the House of Commons and, to a lesser degree, the House of Lords.

Parliament represents all the countries of the United Kingdom. It can legislate for the whole kingdom or for Great Britain itself or, separately, for England and Wales. But, as this is Britain, the country of contradictions, the Parliament at Westminster is not the only parliament. Northern Ireland has its own. But it also sends MP's to Westminster. The Tynewald sits in the Isle of Man, and the States legislate for the Channel Islands.

Opposition to the power of the central government, which means Parliament, comes from the nationalist movements of Scotland and Wales. Supported by minorities fiercely antagonistic toward the Sassenach (as they call the English), these movements provide emotional stimuli for the very young and the very old. At best they are gallant protests against the accretion of power to a central government, a process that goes on in Britain as it does in the United States and elsewhere. At worst, considering the extent of Britain's real problems, the national movements are a nuisance.

But these are not rivals, and legally the Parliament in London can do anything it desires. During the five-year life of a Parliament the assembly can make or unmake any law, destroy the constitution, legalize past illegalities and thus reverse court decisions. Parliament also has the power to prolong its own life.

Is Parliament therefore supreme and absolute? Legally, yes. But legislative authority is delegated increasingly to ministers, and specific powers to local authorities and to public corporations. Such delegated powers can be withdrawn at any time, although the pressure of work on Parliament is so great that this is unlikely.

Finally, Britain has its own system of checks and balances. The two-party system forbids arbitrary action, for the abuse of parliamentary power by the party in power would invite repudiation by the electors.

Of the two houses, the House of Commons is infinitely the more powerful. In this popularly elected assembly there are 630 members. Of these, 511 sit for English constituencies, 36 for Welsh, 71 for Scotch, and 12 for Northern Irish. Each constituency elects one member. The composition of the present House of Commons, elected in May 1955, is: Conservatives and their supporters, 346; Labor, 277; Liberal, 6; and the Speaker, who does not vote, 1.

What does Parliament do? It regulates the life of the community through the laws it makes. It finances the needs of the people and appropriates the funds necessary for the services of the State by legislative action. It controls and criticizes the government.

One reason for the supremacy of the House of Commons is

that bills dealing with finance or representation are always introduced in that house. Moreover, the Lords avoids the introduction
of controversial bills.

Almost all bills are presented by the government in power.
They reflect policy decisions taken in the cabinet at the instigation
of government departments that will be responsible for the administration of the decisions when the bills become law. The principal
exceptions are Private Bills, which relate solely to some matter of
individual, corporate, or local interest, and Private Members' Bills,
which are introduced by individual MP's.

The manner in which Parliament—generally the House of Commons—controls the government in power emphasizes the difference
between the British system and our own. The ultimate control is
the power of the House of Commons to pass a resolution of "no
confidence" in the government or to reject a proposal which the
government considers so vital to its policy that it has made the
proposal's passage a "matter of confidence." If such a proposal is
rejected, the government is obliged to resign.

In addition, there is that very British institution, Question
Time. Between 2:30 and 3:30 each afternoon from Monday
through Thursday, MP's may question any minister on the work of
his department and the Prime Minister on general national policy.
The questions range from the trivial to the significant. A query
about the heating in a remote Army barracks may be followed by
one about progress on the hydrogen bomb. The growth of Question Time as an institution has put a special premium on those
ministers or junior ministers best able to parry and riposte. For the
opposition can press the minister, and if his original reply is unsatisfactory, the questioner will follow with a supplementary question designed to reveal the minister as incapable and ignorant.

The majority of questions are put by the opposition in the
hope of focusing public attention on the government's weaknesses.
But government Members also put questions dealing with affairs
in their constituencies. A number of them also can be counted
upon to offer ministers congratulatory queries along the lines "Is

the Right Honorable Gentleman aware that his reply will be welcomed by all those . . . ?"

Questions and answers are couched in the glistening phrases of polite debate, but occasionally tempers rise and the Speaker intervenes. Because of the variety of subject matter and the importance of some of the questions, Question Time is an exciting period. It was never more so than in the last administration of Sir Winston Churchill.

That Prime Minister, armed with the political experience of fifty years, was a joy to watch in action. One of his last memorable sallies was at the expense of Woodrow Wyatt, an earnest young Labor MP.

What plans had the government, Wyatt asked, for evacuating itself from London in the event of atomic attack?

Sir Winston regarded him owlishly. "Surely the Honorable Member does not wish me to take the bread out of the mouths of the Soviet secret service," he said.

Even without these moments, Question Time would be useful as a sort of national catharsis and as an example of democracy in action. The spectacle of the House of Commons, representing a Britain beset by a multitude of problems, pausing to discuss the affairs of a crippled veteran in a remote Welsh village is a moving one.

There is a slight similarity between Question Time and the Presidential press conference as it has developed in Washington. Both give the executive a chance to explain the workings of policy and government. But in Britain the penalties for failure to answer are much greater than in Washington. The President is answering reporters, and he is under no compulsion to answer the questions put to him. The Prime Minister, on the other hand, is confronted directly by his political foes. If he fails to answer a question or offers an unsatisfactory reply, he may provoke debate later on the matter at issue.

Certainly the President is often roughly handled, but most of the press-conference questions seem to lack the bite and sting of those posed in the House of Commons. Perhaps this is inevitable under present circumstances. President Eisenhower has answered the questions of representatives of newspapers, magazines, and radio and television systems that are overwhelmingly Republican. A British Prime Minister and his ministers, on the other hand, must battle all the way.

Finally, all the government departments are represented in the House of Commons, and their representatives, as well as the Prime Minister, can be subjected to prolonged and, at times, merciless questioning. A comparison of Hansard's Parliamentary reports and the reports of Presidential press conferences since 1952 will show, I think, that there is greater pressure and a good deal more precise information in Question Time than in a Presidential press conference.

But Question Time is only one means by which the House of Commons can criticize and control the government. The opposition can move the adjournment of the House on a matter that the Speaker considers definite, urgent, and the responsibility of the government. Or it can use one of the days formerly devoted to consideration of the Estimates in Committee of Supply for a debate on some part of government policy.

The big debates on such issues as foreign affairs and economic policy are the summit of parliamentary effort. Government and opposition put forward their leading spokesmen on the issue under debate. But debates also provide an opportunity for the back benchers of all parties. The back benchers—Members who are not in the government or in the opposition's shadow cabinet—rise to make their points on the issue, and often remarkably good speeches, as well as bad ones, are delivered.

But parliamentary business is concerned with much more than questions and debates. Bills must be passed. This procedure is involved and lengthy, paying due attention to the rights of the House and the people it represents.

The bill receives a formal First Reading on its introduction and is then printed. After a period varying from one to several weeks, depending on the bill's nature, it may be given a Second Reading as the result of a debate on its general merits. Then the bill is referred to one of the standing committees.

During the committee stage, Members can amend the bill if a majority of the House agrees. When this stage is finished, the bill is reported to the House and a further debate takes place during which the Committee's amendments may be altered, additional amendments may be suggested and incorporated, and, if necessary, the bill may be recommitted to committee. Finally, the bill is submitted for a Third Reading, and if passed, it is sent on from the Commons to the House of Lords. There it enters upon the same course.

There, also, it may awaken the interest of Lord Cholmondeley, my favorite peer. Lord Cholmondeley spoke in the House of Lords recently for the first time in thirty-two years. What he had to say— about rabbits and other small game—was brief and to the point. To many, Lord Cholmondeley must symbolize the vague absurdities of the House of Lords.

Yet this peculiar institution has its defenders, and these are not all peers. There is something to be said, it is contended, for an upper chamber that debates on terms other than partisan politics the great issues of the day. The House of Lords, like the Crown, has influence but, as money bills must be introduced in the House of Commons, little direct power. From the standpoint of active politics its limited power is of a negative nature. It can, for instance, delay the passage of legislation by rejecting a bill previously passed by the House of Commons.

This occurred when the Lords rejected the bill to nationalize the steel industry and the bill to abolish capital punishment. These delaying actions demonstrated that, although the powers of the House of Lords have been drastically curtailed, they can still have considerable political importance. Inevitably, such action evokes dark mutterings from the Labor Party about the ability of hereditary peers to flout the will of the people. The Lords retort that the bill in question is not the will of the people at all, but the will of some of the people's representatives.

Theoretically, the House of Lords is a good deal larger than the House of Commons, consisting of 878 peers. Only about one tenth of them, however, take an active part in the work of the House of Lords. The peers include princes of the royal blood, who by custom take no part in proceedings; 26 spiritual peers, the archbishops and senior bishops of the Church of England; all hereditary peers of England, Great Britain, and the United Kingdom; 16 hereditary peers of Scotland elected from their own number for each Parliament; 5 representative peers of Ireland elected for life; and the Lords of Appeal in Ordinary appointed to perform the judicial duties of the House and holding their seats for life.

Such are the bare bones of the parliamentary system of Britain. Like many other British institutions, it conceals beneath a façade of ceremonial and tradition an efficient, flexible machine. The debates, the great speeches, and the days of pomp when the Queen rides amid the Household Cavalry to open Parliament are in spectacular contrast to the long grind of unremitting and, by modern standards, financially unrewarding work by Members of both Lords and Commons.

When the visitor sits in the gallery high above the well of the Commons and hears a minister patiently explaining some point connected with an obscure aspect of British life, it is well to remember that this system is one for which men fought and suffered, that this House is the cradle of liberties and freedoms.

The members of the government—"Her Majesty's Government in the United Kingdom," as it is formally titled in Britain—are all Members of the House of Commons or the House of Lords. The government and the cabinet are separate entities, for the government includes the following ministerial offices: the Prime Minister, who is the recognized head of the government but who has no department; the Departmental Ministers, seven of whom are Secretaries of State for Foreign Affairs, the Home Department, Scotland, Commonwealth Relations, Colonies, War, and Air; the Ministries, of which there are twelve, each headed by a Minister; and some of the older posts with special titles such as the Chancellor of the Exchequer, who is responsible for the Treasury, and the First Lord of the Admiralty.

The government also includes non-departmental ministers who hold traditional offices, such as the Lord President of the Council, the Lord Privy Seal, the Chancellor of the Duchy of Lancaster. With the flexibility that is so conspicuous a part of the British system, successive governments have found major responsibilities for these posts.

The present Lord President of the Council, the Marquess of Salisbury, is responsible to Parliament for two immensely important organizations: the Atomic Energy Authority and the Department of Scientific and Industrial Research. Yet Lord Salisbury, one of the most important members of the present government, is not an elected representative of the people but sits in the House of Lords as a peer.

The Lord Chancellor and the Law Officers are also members of the government. The Lord Chancellor is in fact a Minister of the Crown who is also head of the judiciary in England and Wales. The four Law Officers of the Crown are the Attorney General and the Solicitor General for England and Wales and the Lord Advocate and the Solicitor General for Scotland.

Finally, there are Ministers of State—who are deputy ministers in departments where there is a heavy load of work or where, as in the case of the Foreign Office, the duties involve frequent overseas travel—and junior Ministers, Parliamentary Secretaries, or Parliamentary Under Secretaries of State.

The cabinet system, like so much else in British government, was not the result of Olympian planning. It "just growed." The Tudors began to appoint *ad hoc* committees of the Privy Council. By the time of Charles II the Privy Council numbered forty-seven. There then developed an occasional arrangement in which a council of people in high office was constituted to debate questions of domestic and foreign affairs.

Such committees or cabinets persisted until the reign of Queen Anne. Usually, but not always, they met in the presence of the sovereign. In 1717, George I, the first Hanoverian King, ceased to attend cabinet meetings. Until recently the accepted historical reason for this was the King's ignorance of English—a circumstance that might, one would think, enable him to bear long debates with fortitude. However, J. H. Plumb in his recent life of Sir Robert Walpole has suggested that the King's absence from the cabinet was due to a quarrel between the monarch and the Prince of Wales.

At any rate, the cabinet system continued to flourish. Its members consistently ignored the provision in the Act of Settlements (1725) which forbade office-holders to sit in the Commons. The direct influence of the sovereign was reduced, although his indirect influence, as Lord North and "the King's Friends" demonstrated, was great.

Nowadays the members of the cabinet are selected from the government by the Prime Minister. Usually it has fewer than twenty members.

The cabinet determines the policy the government will submit to Parliament, it controls the national executive in accordance with policy approved by Parliament, and it co-ordinates and limits the authority of the departments of the government. In its operations the cabinet makes great use of the committee system, referring problems to one of the standing committees or to a temporary committee composed of the ministers chiefly concerned.

A British cabinet operates under the rule of collective responsibility and of individual responsibility. That is, ministers share collective responsibility for the policy and actions of the government and individual responsibility to Parliament for the functioning of their departments. A cabinet minister in Britain must appear before the legislature, of which he is a member, and submit to a lengthy questioning upon the work of his department. He must defend his department in debate. No such procedure affects American cabinet members, although they can, of course, be questioned by Congressional committees.

The members of the cabinet in Britain are a good deal more than advisers to the Prime Minister. Their relationship to ultimate policy is closer and their responsibility greater. Hence it is unusual, almost impossible, in Britain to find the Secretary of State for Foreign Affairs saying one thing about foreign policy and the Prime Minister another. Lord Melbourne said it did not matter what the members of his government said as long as they all said the same thing. This principle has been hallowed by time.

Although members of the cabinet often disagree furiously in private, there is an absence of open bickering. Moreover, the authority of the cabinet and the House of Commons is supreme. There have been no British General MacArthurs. Field Marshal Lord Montgomery is a wise, cogent, and talkative man. Occasionally he has offered the country his views on non-military matters. Invariably he has been told to leave government matters to the elected representatives of the people. When the cabinet requires the advice of the Chief of the Imperial General Staff or the First Sea Lord (not to be confused with the First Lord of the Admiralty) on military matters, the cabinet asks for it.

The cabinet minister is bound to secrecy. If he resigns from the cabinet because of a disputed issue, he must obtain through the Prime Minister the permission of the sovereign before he can make any statement involving a disclosure of cabinet discussions.

Nor may a cabinet minister repudiate either in Parliament or in his constituency policies that have been approved by the cabinet or propose policies that have not been agreed on with other ministers. He must be prepared to vote with the government on all issues and to speak in support or defense of its policy. Inability to agree or compromise with the view of the majority in the cabinet usually results in the minister's resignation from the government. A minister who remained in the cabinet under such circumstances would be held responsible for the policy he opposed.

Political conflict flourishes in Britain. Yet for many reasons the government of the day and the opposition practice a basic bipartisanship on basic issues. To a considerable degree this is the result of the change in Britain's position over the last two decades. There is an unspoken recognition by the leaders of the two great parties that the present situation of the United Kingdom is too precarious for prolonged and violent differences on essentials. There are, of course, exceptions. Violent controversy does break out on essentials between party and party and within a party.

Consider two essentials of British policy: the Anglo-American alliance and the decision to make the hydrogen bomb.

The relations between the United States and Britain developed their contemporary form in World War II. Since 1945 they have been strengthened by the rise of an aggressive Soviet Union. There are other contributing factors, some of which are not particularly attractive to political or economic groups within each partner to the alliance. Moreover, there has never been a time when there were not powerful critics of various aspects of the alliance in both countries.

Aneurin Bevan and his friends on the radical left of the Labor Party have often lambasted the United States and Britain's dependence on her. Similar criticisms could be heard in private from Tories. When the United States voted with the Soviet Union against Britain in the United Nations after the British and French had invaded Suez, the Conservatives were moved to put their protest into the form of a motion in the House of Commons. This was accompanied by much sharp criticism, which had a therapeutic effect in encouraging some realistic thinking about the alliance.

A great deal of the anxiety about United States policy, of the jealousy of United States power, of the anger at Mr. Dulles's self-righteous sermons about colonialism was vented during this period. It did some harm, certainly. But from the standpoint of the honest expression of Conservative Party opinion and of American realism about the British attitude, it also did some good.

The alliance is an essential. Even when indignant Conservatives—and a number of Socialists, too—were thinking up pet names for Mr. Dulles, the leaders of the party were doing their best to mollify their followers. They were themselves anxious and angry, but they never suggested defection from the alliance.

It may be suggested that the British had nowhere else to go. This may be true, but even so it would be no bar to their departure. They are happy when they are on their own, and many on this little island would count the alliance well lost in exchange for a vigorous reassertion of independence.

In 1940 the cockney, the inevitable cockney, used to remark, for the edification of American correspondents: "Cor, we're alone. What of it, guv?" Now, I have always regarded this not as a piece of patriotic rhetoric but as a natural response to events by a brave people. Shakespeare, of course, said it better.

> Come the three corners of the world in arms,
> And we shall shock them. Nought shall make us rue,
> If England to itself do rest but true.

The important word is "itself." If there comes a time of great outside pressure when alliances and confederations are in danger, Americans will be well advised to remember that word.

The decision to make the hydrogen bomb, a project involving the expenditure of great sums that Britain could ill afford, again was a bipartisan matter. The Conservative government proposed it. The Labor opposition (with Mr. Bevan dissenting in a burst of Welsh oratory) agreed. There have been recurrent criticisms of how the work was being done, of the cost, of the necessity for testing the weapon, and of the arrangements for the tests. But there has been very little criticism of the bomb's manufacture from the leaders of the Labor Party—excepting always Mr. Bevan.

Bipartisanship is assisted by consultation on issues of major national importance between the Prime Minister and the Leader of the Opposition. But the achievement of bipartisan policies owes much more to a general understanding in both parties in the House of Commons of the country's present position.

Socialist reform and experimentation in the years between 1945 and 1951 aroused Conservative fears as fierce as Labor Party hopes. The enmity aroused in the largely Conservative middle class by the Labor governments of those years certainly has not disappeared. But much of it has been re-directed against the moderate policies of the Conservative government, which has long claimed the allegiance of the middle class.

The leaders of the two great parties—Harold Macmillan, Lord Salisbury, and R. A. Butler for the Conservatives, and Hugh Gaitskell, Harold Wilson, Jim Griffiths for Labor—are moderates. On the periphery of each party stand the radicals advocating extreme measures at home and abroad. Should Britain's economic and international troubles persist, the moderate approach to their solution may not satisfy either the Conservative or Socialist voters.

British politics in May of 1955 continued one of those rhythmic changes of direction which feature political life in every democratic nation. The Conservatives won a smashing victory in the general election and became the first party in ninety years to be returned to office with an increased majority.

The victory gave the Tory government a majority of 61 in the House of Commons. But this majority is not an exact reflection of the way the electorate voted. The Conservatives and their supporters got 13,311,938 votes and Labor won 12,405,146. The Liberals got 722,395 and the Communists 33,144.

This almost even division of the British electorate between the two major parties must be kept in mind when we examine the right and the left in British politics. Not since 1945, when the Labor Party swept into office, has there been a difference of a million votes between the two in general elections.

Labor's sun was sinking in the election of 1950, which the party won by a narrow margin. The Conservatives took over in 1951 and boosted their majority in 1955. Has the pendulum's swing to the right ended? The answer may lie in the policies and personalities of the two great parties today.

IV.   *The Conservatives*

A PARTY AND A WAY OF LIFE

The Conservative party have always said that, on the whole, their policy meant that people had to fill up fewer forms than under the policies of other parties.

SIR ALAN HERBERT

The man for whom the law exists—the man of forms, the Conservative, is a tame man.

HENRY THOREAU

ALTHOUGH they have little in common otherwise, the Great American Public and the radical wing of the British Labor Party share a strange mental image of the British Conservative. They see him as a red-faced stout old gentleman given to saying "Gad, sir," waving the Union Jack, and kicking passing Irishmen, Indians, and Egyptians. He is choleric about labor unions, and he stands for "no damned nonsense" from foreigners.

The picture was a false one even before World War II. No party could have existed for a century, holding power for considerable periods, without a basis of support in the British working class.

Such support would not be granted to the caricature of a Conservative described above. Certainly the Conservative Party has now, and has had in the past, its full share of reactionaries opposed to change. The inquiring reporter will encounter more than a smattering of similar opposition to change among the leaders of Britain's great unions.

Britain's altered position in the world and the smashing Labor victory of 1945 combined to whittle away the authority of the reactionaries in the Conservative Party in the years between 1945 and 1951 when it was out of office. Since then other influences, including the rise within the party of young politicians whose education and experience have little in common with those of the recognized Tory leadership, has further altered the character of the party. It has come a long way since 1945.

A young Conservative minister recalls with horror the annual Conservative conference of that year. The chairwoman, a billowy dowager wielding a lorgnette, announced with simpering pride that she had a surprise for the conference. It was, she said, "a real Conservative trade-unionist." Had the Archbishop of Canterbury appeared on the platform and danced the can-can, the surprise could not have been greater. When a Negro student went to the platform a decade later to discuss colonial affairs, no one turned a hair.

In retrospect, the election of 1945 was one the Tories could not win. Almost everything was against them: the pre-war Tory government's appeasement of Germany, the military disasters of 1940, the distrust of Churchill in time of peace, his own exaggerated campaign attacks on Labor, the superb organization of the Labor Party machinery by Herbert Morrison. Ten years later the Conservatives faced an election they could not lose. Even when all other conditions are taken into account, this was a singular example of the adaptability and mobility of the Tories.

The Tories saw that the nation had changed, and they changed with it. Both the political philosophy of the party and the organization of the party were altered—the latter change being more drastic, more complete, and more rapid than the former.

In the organizational change the reports of the Committee on Party Organization in 1948 and 1949 were of paramount importance. The committee was headed by Sir David Maxwell Fyfe, later Viscount Kilmuir and Lord Chancellor.

Before the party could win an election on its altered policy, a reconstruction of its machinery was necessary. To reconstruct along the lines advised by the experts, the Tories first brought in Lord Woolton, who had been a successful Minister of Food during the war. It was a sagacious appointment. As Chairman of the Party Organization, Woolton created a young, enthusiastic body of workers whose propaganda on behalf of the party began to impress the electorate—largely, I suspect, because these workers were so unlike the popular idea of Tories.

While Winston Churchill, Anthony Eden, Harold Macmillan, R. A. Butler led the parliamentary fight against the Labor government, a group of young Tories built the party case for the leaders. Techniques of research and propaganda were developed. Promising young men and women from all classes were encouraged.

These younger Conservative tacticians included many who are now ministers. Iain MacLeod, who has been Minister of Health and Minister of Labor, Reginald Maulding, who has been Minister of Supply and Paymaster General, Selwyn Lloyd, the present Foreign Secretary, are representative of the nucleus of talent which was built during those years. They and a score of junior ministers are young, vigorous, and ambitious. They know their own party, and, what is equally important, they know the Labor Party and its leaders.

Talking with the leaders of both the major parties, one is struck by the breadth of the Tories' knowledge of the Labor leaders' personalities, views on national issues, and aspirations. "Know your enemy" is an axiom as wise in politics as in war.

Yet I doubt that all the political intelligence and administrative ability in the Tory ranks would have sufficed without Woolton.

Frederick William Marquis, the first Viscount Woolton, is not, as one might suppose from his imposing name and title, the son of a hundred earls. He is very much a self-made man who fought his way to success in commerce and finance. He is a Jim Farley, rather than a Mark Hanna.

When Woolton took over the chairmanship of the Party Organization, the party was defeated and discredited. He left it after the triumph of May 1955 with Conservative fortunes at their postwar zenith. I have mentioned Woolton's reorganization of the Central and Area offices, but his influence on the party went beyond this. In the years when the Socialists ruled in Whitehall, Woolton transferred to the beaten Conservatives some of his own warmth and vigor. He is an urbane, friendly man; the young Conservatives then emerging from the middle class felt that they were directed not by an aristocratic genius but by a fatherly, knowledgeable elder. Indeed, his nickname was "Uncle Fred." The revived party began to talk like a democratic party and even, occasionally, to act like one. Under Woolton the Central Office in London changed from a remote, austere group controlling the party into a Universal Aunt or Uncle, ready to help constituency parties solve their problems. Yet the leader of the party and the chairman of the Party Organization continued to direct and control.

Conservative Party policy, as it has evolved in the past decade, has moved to the left. This is not solely because, as the Labor Party often charges, it wanted to steal or adopt parts of the Socialist platform. A great many of the young men in the Tory party in 1945 sympathized with many of the Socialists' policies. "I'd have voted Labor myself if I hadn't been a Tory candidate," one of them reflected a decade later. What offended the Tories' self-esteem was that great, revolutionary changes were being made in British life by the Labor government and they, who had always assumed a special right to rule Britain, were not making the changes.

A large part of Conservative political tactics in the late forties consisted of negative criticism. The parlous state of the British economy, the withdrawals from India and Burma, the decline of British influence and power in the world offered great opportunities to a party that traditionally combines business interests and experience with an assumption of omniscience in the direction of international affairs. At the same time, the work of the back-room boys in the Central Office on the solution of Britain's economic difficulties, expressed in speeches of party leaders, gave the impression that the Conservatives, whatever their past faults, were moving to the left in their approach to the economic problem.

The present leadership of the Conservative Party—Harold Macmillan, Lord Salisbury, R. A. Butler, and a number of the younger ministers—is well to the left of the economic position assumed by the party in the 1945 election. Indeed, the complaint of the party's middle-class rank and file that the Conservatives are carrying out a pseudo-socialist program rather than a truly Tory one is an important factor in estimating the party's ability to retain power.

A word is needed here about "left" and "right" as applied to British parties. Although the Conservative Party is frequently compared with the Republican Party in the United States and has many similarities of outlook, the Conservatives are, on the whole, well to the left of the Republicans. Thinking in the Labor Party, moreover, is well to the left of both Democratic and Republican parties in the United States.

After the Conservative victory in the election of 1955 it was generally expected that the party would move toward the right. Critics will seize upon British intervention in Egypt as evidence of such a movement. But it can be asked whether a policy designed to bring down a dictator—in this case President Nasser of Egypt—when it was evident that the United Nations was unable or unwilling to do so can be classified as a right-wing, reactionary policy. Similarly, the movement of the British government under the leadership of Sir Anthony Eden and Harold Macmillan toward entry into the European common market can scarcely be considered an example of right-wing extremism. The attacks on this policy by the newspapers controlled by Lord Beaverbrook, the most imperialist of the press lords, testify to the anger aroused by the progressive internationalism of the Conservatives.

No one can gainsay the existence of a strong nationalistic element within the Conservative Party in the House of Commons and in the country. This element rebelled against the Anglo-Egyptian treaty by which Britain agreed to quit Egypt. It supported the decision to intervene in Egypt. Parenthetically it should be noted that the moving spirits in this decision were Sir Anthony Eden and Harold Macmillan, men who, by conviction, belonged to the progressive wing of the party. Finally, when the government agreed first to a cease-fire and then to a withdrawal from Egypt, this group censured both the United Nations and the United States for their part in bringing this about.

Given the character of the Conservative Party's support in the country, the presence of such a group within the party in Parliament is natural. But do not discount the adaptability of the party. When Harold Macmillan formed his government in January 1957 he found it possible, with the approval of the party, to include in it both Sir Edward Boyle, who had resigned from the government over the Egyptian invasion, and Julian Amery, who had rebelled against the government because it listened to the United States and the United Nations and halted the invasion.

The Conservatives' approach to Britain's economic and financial problems is well to the left of the policies followed by their pre-war predecessors. Britain's is a managed economy to an extent that would shake the late Stanley Baldwin and the present Secretary of the Treasury in Washington. Mr. Macmillan and his ministers are not secret readers of *Pravda*. They are political realists who understand the changes in power which have taken place in Britain, who understand that the Council of the Trades Union Congress is as important today as the Federation of British Industries.

The Labor Party, it often seems, suffers from an inability to understand the changes that have taken place in their opponents. It may be, as Socialists contend, that the changes are only a façade hiding the greedy, imperious capitalists beneath. But to an outsider it seems that the Labor Party pays too much attention to the surviving extremists of the Tory party and not enough to the venturesome, progressive younger men who will inherit the party. Surely the appeal of the Conservative Party to the electorate is based more upon the personalities and policies of these rising stars than upon the reactionaries of the right wing.

The Conservative Party arouses and holds some strange allegiances. I remember Michael Foot, the editor of the left-wing weekly *Tribune,* saying that in his old constituency of Devonport there were solid blocks of Conservative votes in the poorest areas. Foot could not understand it. The rather contemptuous explanation offered by a Conservative Party organizer was: "Why not? People who are poor aren't necessarily foolish enough to buy this socialist clap-trap."

The Conservatives have been making inroads into the new middle class created by the boom of 1953–5. This group emerging from the industrial working class was formerly strongly pro-Labor. There are indications that the more prosperous are changing their political attitudes as their incomes and social standing improve.

The Conservatives concentrate on a national appeal. Labor by its origins is a class party. In a country as homogeneous as Britain, the Conservative boast that they stand for all the people rather than for merely one class or one geographical area is effective. To this the Tories add the claim that they are the party most suited by training and experience to deal with the international problems faced by the nation.

This assumption of the right to rule is not so offensive to Britons as it might be to Americans. There is little historical basis for it. If an aristocrat, Winston Churchill, led Britain to victory in World War II, a small-town Welsh lawyer, David Lloyd George, was the leader in World War I. Nevertheless, there is a tendency—perhaps a survival of feudalism—among some Britons to believe that their affairs are better handled by a party with upper-class education and accents. And of course the Conservatives look the part. Mr. Macmillan, the Prime Minister, is a far more impressive figure than Hugh Gaitskell, who probably would be Prime Minister in a Labor government. The accents, the clothes, the backgrounds of the Tory leaders give the impression of men born to conduct government. Brilliant journalists have argued that the class they represent is unrepresentative, and that the Suez crisis proved its inability to understand the modern world. Surely the present Conservative leaders and their predecessors have been guilty of quite as many errors as the Socialists and Liberals of the past. However, they give the impression of competence. As any politician knows, even in the most enlightened of democracies such impressions are as important as the most brilliant intellects or the wisest programs.

The Conservatives enjoy another important political advantage. Until the present the leaders of the party generally have been drawn from one class, the old upper middle class. They went to the same schools, served in the same regiments. Families like the Cecils, the Churchills, the Edens, the Macmillans intermarry. The closeness of the relationship breeds coherence. Basically there is an instinctive co-operation when a crisis arises. The manner in which the Tories closed ranks after Sir Anthony Eden's resignation was an example.

The upper ranks of the civil service, of the Church of England, and of the armed services are drawn largely from the same class. Usually this facilitates the work of government when the Tories are in power. But recently there has been a change. In their drive to broaden the base of the party, the Conservatives have introduced to the House of Commons a number of young politicians who do not share the Eton-Oxford-Guards background of their leaders.

The environment and education of this group and their supporters in the constituencies is much different. For Eton or Harrow, substitute state schools or small, obscure public schools. Some did go to Oxford and Cambridge, but they moved in less exalted circles than the Edens or Cecils. They are usually businessmen who have made their way in the world without the advantages of the traditional Tory background, and they are highly critical of the tendency to reserve the party plums for representatives of its more aristocratic wing.

They seem to be further to the right in politics than such "aristocrats" as Macmillan, Butler, Eden, or Lord Salisbury. They have risen the hard way, and they are more interested in promoting the interests of the business groups for which they speak than in the traditional Tory concept of speaking for the whole nation. This national responsibility on the part of the "aristocrats" was in many ways a liberal attitude. Macmillan and Butler, for instance, appear much more responsive and tolerant on the subject of trade unions than most members of the new group.

As the power of this group increases—and it will increase as the Conservative Party continues to change—sharper disputes on policy, especially economic policy, can be expected. This encourages some Socialists, naturally sensitive on the point, to believe that their opponents are headed for a period of fierce feuding within the party. Their optimism may be misplaced.

The Tories are adept at meeting rebellion and absorbing rebels. The indignant "red brick" rebel of today may be the junior minister of tomorrow whose boy is headed for Eton. Despite the advent of these newcomers, the party does not appear so vulnerable to schism as does the Labor Party with its assortment of extreme-left-wing intellectuals, honest hearts and willing hands from the unions, and conscientious and intelligent mavericks from the middle class.

Finally, the power of what has been called the "Establishment" is primarily a conservative power that wishes to conserve the governmental and social structure of Britain against the majority of reformers. On great national issues this usually places it upon the side of the Conservative Party. If it can be defined, the Establishment represents the upper levels of the Church of England, of Oxford and Cambridge, *The Times* of London, the chiefs of the civil service. The direct power of this group may be less than has been described, but few would deny its influence.

The common background has served the Conservatives well in the past. Open political quarrels within the party are rare. (The conflict over the Suez policy was an exception.) "The Tories settle their differences in the Carlton Club," Earl Attlee once said. "We fight ours out in public. We're a democratic party that thrives on contention." Perhaps, but the contention nearly wrecked the Labor Party between 1953 and 1955 and had much to do with its defeat in 1955.

Much of the comparative tranquillity of the Conservative Party is due to the power of the party leader. Nominally, he is elected by the Conservative Members of the House of Commons and the House of Lords, all prospective Tory candidates for Commons, and the executive Committee of the National Union. But, as Robert T. McKenzie has pointed out in his *British Political Parties,* the leader is often selected by the preceding leader of the party when it is in power. Thus, Sir Winston Churchill made it clear that Sir Anthony Eden was his heir as leader, and Sir Anthony was duly elected.

A different situation arose when Sir Anthony resigned as Prime Minister because of illness. In that instance the Prime Minister was selected before he became leader of the party. It was widely believed outside the inner circles of the party that there was a choice between Harold Macmillan and R. A. Butler. Actually the leaders of the party, including Sir Anthony, Sir Winston, and Lord Salisbury, and a substantial number of ministers, junior ministers, and back-bench Members had made it clear that their preference lay with Macmillan.

The structure of the British government and of the Conservative Party give the leader a good deal more authority over his party than is enjoyed by a President of the United States as the head of the Republican or Democratic Party. In power or in opposition the leader has the sole ultimate responsibility for the formulation of policy and the election program of his party.

The annual party conference proposes, the leader disposes. Resolutions passed at the conference do not bind him. The party secretariat (the Central Office) is in many ways the personal machine of the leader. He appoints its principal officers and controls its main organizations for propaganda, finance, and research. Consequently, it is unlikely that a Conservative politician would chal-

lenge the authority of the leader as sharply and directly as Senator
McCarthy challenged the authority of President Eisenhower in the
latter's first administration. The conclusion is that, although Tory
democracy is an attractive political slogan, it has little connection
with the almost autocratic authority of the party leader.

In the field of political tactics moderation is the guiding principle
of the new Conservatism. This became evident in the election of
1955, which the Tories fought soberly and efficiently. Pointing to
Britain's evident prosperity—the stormclouds were already piling
on the horizon, but campaign orators seldom see that far—the Conservatives asked the people if this combination of good times at
home and easier relations abroad (the summit conference at Geneva
was in the offing) was not better for the nation than revolutionary
policies and hysterical oratory.

The party's appeal for votes seemed to reflect a surer grasp of
popular attitudes than the Labor Party's. In retrospect the Conservative message was a consoling one. Everyone had work. Almost
everyone had more money than he had had three or four years
before, although the established middle class already was feeling the
effect of rising prices and continued heavy taxation on real income.
The roads were filling up with cars that should have been sold for
export, running on gasoline that was imported with an adverse
effect on the balance of trade.

During six years of Socialist control the Labor politicians had
informed the British that a return to Conservative rule would mean
a revival of the bad old days of unemployment, dole and hunger
marches, strikes and lockouts. Yet here were Sir Anthony Eden pat-
ting the unions on the head and Harold Macmillan talking warmly
of the chances of a successful conference with the Russians at
Geneva. It was all a little confusing and, from the Conservative
standpoint, very successful.

Traveling around Britain during the weeks prior to the 1955
election, I was struck by the number of people of both parties prepared to accept the Conservatives' contention that their party was,

by some mysterious dispensation, uniquely suited to the business of conducting the nation's foreign policy. In some areas, notably in the North and the Midlands, this seemed to spring from Eden's long and, on the whole, successful record in international affairs. In others I encountered a feeling that the withdrawals from India and Egypt and such blunders as the loss of the Abadan oil refinery had lowered the prestige of the country. Certainly the Tories were not guiltless. Nonetheless, there was a persistent conviction that the Tories handled foreign affairs best. Occasionally—this was at the nadir of Socialist fortunes—I met Labor supporters who subscribed to this view.

The first public reaction to British intervention in Egypt in 1956 was a triumph for organized public opinion as directed by the Labor Party. From the resolutions that flooded into London from factory and local unions, one would have concluded that the whole of the British working class was violently opposed to governmental policy. Actually, a number of public-opinion polls showed that the country was pretty evenly divided. My own experience, traveling around Britain in January and February of 1957, convinced me that, on the whole, the working-class support for the Suez adventure was slightly stronger than that of the professional classes. Of course, as in most situations of this kind, the supporters did not bother to send telegrams of support.

The Labor Party in the House of Commons made a great offensive against the Conservative position on Egypt. This played a part, but not the dominant part, in the cabinet's decision to accept a cease-fire. The paramount factor was the indication from Washington that unless Britain agreed to a cease-fire, the administration would not help Britain with oil supplies and would not act to support the pound sterling, whose good health is the basis of Britain's position as an international banker.

The Socialists' attack did result in the emergence of Aneurin Bevan as the party's principal spokesman, and a most effective one, on foreign affairs. This is an area where the Labor Party has been weak in recent years. Death removed Ernest Bevin, a great Foreign Secretary, and Hector McNeil, the brightest of the party's younger experts on foreign affairs.

Moderation, a national rather than a class approach, the middle way—all these sufficed for the Tories in 1955. Two years later there are abundant signs that a sharper policy will be necessary to meet international and internal situations vastly more difficult. Drastic policies invite harsh argument in their formulation. Can the Conservatives continue to settle their differences in the Carlton Club or will these spill out onto the front pages of the newspapers?

The primary political problem the Conservative government faced before Suez was whether it could continue its policies, especially where they related to defense and taxation, and retain the support of a large and influential group of Conservative voters. This group is offended and rebellious because, although the Conservatives have now been in office for over five years, it still finds its real income shrinking, its social standards reduced, and its future uncertain. It regards the moderate Conservatives' economic policy and attitude toward social changes as akin to those of the Labor Party. By the middle of 1956 its resentment was being reflected by the reduction of the Conservative vote in the elections.

The group can be defined as the old middle class. During the last century it has been one of the most important and often the most dominant of classes in Britain. Its fight to maintain its position against the challenge of the new middle class and the inexorable march of social and economic changes is one of the most interesting and most pathetic parts of Britain's modern revolution.

The leaders of the old middle class represented a combination of influence and wealth in the professions, medicine, the church, the law, education, and the armed forces. The members of these professions and their immediate lieutenants administered the great institutions that had established Britain in the Victorian twilight as the world's greatest power. They were responsible for the great public schools, the Church of England, the Royal Navy, the banks, the largest industries, the shipping lines, the universities.

They were not the aristocracy. The decline of the aristocracy, with its ancient titles, its huge estates, and its huge debts, began over a century ago. The old middle class began life as the aristocracy's executors and ended as its heirs.

The pattern of life in the old middle class was shaken by World War I, but it existed relatively unchanged in 1939. The class was the butt of the bright young playwrights of the twenties and has received the acid attentions of Mr. Somerset Maugham. It supported Munich and Chamberlain, and it sent its sons away to die in 1939.

As a group, the class was well educated. The majority of the men had been to a public school and a university. Both men and women bought and read books and responsible newspapers. They traveled abroad, they knew something about the world. Some had inherited wealth. Others invested their savings.

Beneath this upper stratum of the old middle class was a lower middle class that sought to rise into it. This was made up of shopkeepers, small manufacturers, the more prosperous farmers, the black-coat workers in business, and the industrial technicians.

The future welfare of these two groups is the political problem that the Conservative Party must face. Since the decline of the Liberal Party, the Tories have counted upon the support of this class. There were many defections in the election of 1945, but it is probable that a more important reason for the Tory defeat that year was the party's failure to win the support of a new middle class that was then arising as a factor in British politics.

The chief reason why the old middle class is defecting from the Tory standard is that it believes that the Conservative governments since 1945 have not done enough to halt the drain on its incomes. Prices have risen sharply in the years since Chamberlain went to Munich. One estimate is that the 1938 income of £1,000 a year for a married man with two children would have to be raised to £4,000 to provide the same net income today. But in this class the number of men whose incomes have quadrupled or even doubled since 1938 is small.

What do the figures mean in terms of a family's life? They

mean that to send the children to a public school, which the majority of this class regards as indispensable from a social and even occasionally from an educational standpoint, the father and mother must do without new clothes, books, the occasional visit to the theater. Instead of two regular servants, the family must "make do" with a daily cleaning woman. The family vacations in some quiet French or Italian seaside resort must be abandoned. The father and mother are unable to save and are increasingly worried about their future. They see a future decline in the family's social standards and economic health.

All this is aggravated in their minds by the appearance of a new middle class arising from a different background and doing new and different jobs. Its income, its expense accounts, its occasional lack of taste stir the envy and anger of the old middle class.

What the old middle class asks from the government—and, through the government, from the big trade unions and the big industrialists—is an end to the rise in the cost of living which it, subsisting chiefly on incomes that have not risen sharply, cannot meet. Directly it asks the government for an end to punishing taxation and to "coddling" of both the unions and the manufacturers.

The dilemma of the Conservative Party and its government is a serious one. To lose the support of the old middle class will be dangerous, even disastrous. For although the Tories have attracted thousands of former Socialist votes in the last two elections, these do not represent the solid electoral support that the old middle class has offered.

Perhaps in time the government may be able to reduce taxation. Before this can be done, it must halt inflation, expand constructive investment in industry, and increase the gold and dollar reserves. Each of these depends to a great degree on economic factors with world-wide ramifications. The old middle class understands this and is justifiably suspicious of "pie in the sky" promises.

Such suspicion is increased by the understanding of the other serious long-term problems that British society faces. We need mention only one in this context: how is Britain to maintain its present standards of life and the present levels of government expenditure when it is faced with the coming change in the age distribution of the population?

The steady fall in death rates and the low birth rates of the years between the two world wars are beginning to increase the proportion of elderly people, and thus to reduce the proportion of the working population to the total population. The size of the age groups reaching retirement age increases yearly. It is predicted, on the basis of present population trends, that over the next fifteen years the population of the working-age group will remain about the same but that the number of old people, persons over sixty-five, will rise over the next thirty years by about three million. At the same time the number of children of school age is expected to increase.

Britain thus is faced with a steady increase in the number of the aged who need pensions and medical care and the young who need medical care and education. This charge will be added to the burdens already borne by the working-age group.

The country needs more hospitals and more schools. It needs new highways. It has to continue slum-clearance and the building of homes. Yet Britain has been spending $7,000,000,000 a year on social services and $4,200,000,000 on defense. Under existing circumstances, and in view of present Conservative policies, can the old middle class look forward to an important reduction in taxation under any government?

Reduction of taxation was one of the goals sought by Conservative government when it planned a revision of Britain's defense program. This revision, first planned by the ministry of Sir Anthony Eden and given new impetus by the Macmillan government, has other objectives, including the diversion of young men, capital, and productive capacity from defense to industrial production for export. But an easing of the defense burden would create conditions for tax relief in the Conservative circles that need it most.

The reduction of defense expenditures places any Conservative government in a dilemma. The party expects the government to maintain Britain's position as a nuclear power—that is, as a major power. The political repercussions of the Suez crisis showed the depth of nationalism within the party, and, indeed, within the country. Yet it seems plainly impossible for the Tories to reduce taxation of the middle class drastically without cutting the defense expenditure that has maintained Britain, somewhat precariously, in the front rank of world powers.

Of course, tax relief will not fully answer the difficulties of the old middle class. Its incomes, ranging from the pensions of ex-officers to the profits of small businessmen, have lagged behind prices. Stabilization of prices is essential if this class is to maintain its standards.

The rebellion of the old middle class against Tory policy and leadership, if carried to the limit, might result in the creation of an extreme right-wing party. Such a party would be brought into being more easily if the sort of inflation which helped wreck the German democracy after World War I were to appear in Britain. Would the political good sense of the British enable them to reject the vendors of extreme political panaceas who would appear at such a juncture?

The old middle class contains today, as it has since 1945, persons and organizations fanatically opposed to the unions and to labor in general. Extremist organizations, some of them modeled on the Poujadist movement in France, have appeared. In many cases the opposition to labor policies and personalities has been expanded in these groups to include the "traitors" at the head of the present Tory government, who are considered betrayers of their party and their class.

There is a reasonable expectation that Britain will continue to encounter economic problems whose solution will involve economic sacrifices by all classes in the future. The old middle class feels that it has sacrificed more than any other group. There is thus a potential of serious trouble within the Conservative party. The most probable development, it seems to me, is an attempt by the right wing of the party to win and hold power. But a rapid deterioration of the economic situation under a moderate Tory government followed by the return to power of a Labor government might well encourage the transformation of the Tories into a radical right-wing party.

At the moment the right wing of the Conservative Party wants too much. It asks for an uncontrolled economy and is restless under the measures imposed to defeat inflation. But it also wants a stabilization of prices. It wants a "tough" foreign policy, but it opposes the taxation necessary to make the arms on which such a policy must rest. It has an almost reckless desire to curb the trade unions without reckoning the effect on industrial relations.

The moderates who fashioned the present Conservative Party and who now lead its government appear to understand their country and its position better than their critics on the right wing. In addition, their programs have attracted the attention and support of young people to a degree unknown on the right wing.

In the late thirties, when I first was indoctrinated in British politics, it was smart to be on the left. The young people before the war were very certain of the stupidity of the Conservative government policies, at home as well as abroad, and their political convictions ranged from communism to the socialism of the Labor Party. "All the young people are Bolshies," a manufacturer told me in 1939. "If we do have a war, this country will go communist."

A good proportion of young people still are on the left. But they do not seem to hold their convictions as strongly as those I knew in the pre-war years. On the other side of the fence there has been a movement toward an intellectual adoption of conservative principles. In some cases this verges on radicalism, in a few almost to nihilism: the "nothing's any good in either party, let's get rid of them both" idea.

There is always a danger to democracy in such attitudes. They are encouraged in Britain by a tendency in some circles to adopt an arrogant, patrician distaste for all democratic politics. This is under-

standable. The revolution that began with the war has weakened
the economic and political power of a once dominant class. But that
does not excuse those who seek to destroy faith in democratic
processes.

The position of the Conservative Party is both stronger and
weaker than it appears. There are reasons for believing that by the
next general election, probably in 1959 or 1960, the policies of the
government will have relieved the more immediate problems such
as inflation and the need for increased exports. This success will not
change Britain's position as a comparatively small power competing militarily, politically, and economically with the larger established powers, such as the Soviet Union and the United States, and
the reviving powers, Germany and Japan.

The dominant group in the Conservative Party and government has, however, a considerable degree of competence and experience in government. It has an effective parliamentary majority
during the present administration. Against these positive factors we
must place the probability that some of its policies will continue to
alienate an important group of its supporters; the result may be a
rebellion within the party or worse.

The Tories are not politically dogmatic. Like the people, the
whole people, they claim to represent, they are flexible in their
approach to policies and programs. They change to suit economic
conditions and political attitudes. In Britain's present position, the
appeal of a party that contends it is working for the nation rather
than a class or a section should not be minimized.

But it is precisely Britain's position in the modern world that
forces upon the Conservatives today, and would force upon Labor
if it came to power tomorrow, certain policies that are at odds with
the principles of each faction. The Tories, for instance, must manip-
ulate the economy. The idea of "getting government out of business" may be attractive to some industrialists, but in the nation's
situation it is impractical and dangerous. Similarly, the Labor Party,
despite its anti-colonialism, must follow policies that will enable

Britain to keep her investments in Malaya's tin and rubber and in the oil of the Middle East.

We see the two great parties meeting on such common ground. Perhaps because they are less restricted by dogma and can boast greater talents at the moment, the Tories appear slightly more confident of their ability to meet the challenges of Britain's position.

V.   *The Labor Party*

POLITICAL MACHINE OR
MORAL CRUSADE?

*The idea of Socialism is grand and noble; and it is, I am
convinced, possible of realization; but such a state of
society cannot be manufactured—it must grow. Society is
an organism, not a machine.*

HENRY GEORGE

We are all Socialists nowadays.

EDWARD VII WHEN PRINCE OF WALES

"'THE TORIES won the election because they understood the
changes that had taken place since 1945," said a Labor politician
in 1955. "We misunderstood them and we lost. Yet we call ourselves 'the party of the people.' "

This assessment, made on the morning of defeat, explains to
some degree the Labor Party's defeat in the general election of
1955. It raises the question of whether the party, as now constituted, is in fact a working-class party. The growth of the Labor
Party, the emergence of its saints and sinners, the triumph of 1945,

the disaster of 1955 make up one of the truly significant political stories of the century.

For Americans it is especially important. The British Labor Party is the strongest non-communist left-wing party in any of the great democracies of the West. Granted the normal shifts in political support, it will be back in power sometime within the next ten years. The government and people of the United States must regard it as a permanent part of British political life, and they will have to understand it better than they have in the past if the alliance between the United States and the United Kingdom is to prosper.

The British Labor Party is the political arm of what the old-timers like to call "the movement." And it is as well to remember that not so very long ago—Winston Churchill was a young politician then and Anthony Eden was at Eton—it was a "movement" with all the emotional fervor the word implies. The men who made the Labor Party a power in the land were not cool, reasoning intellectuals (although, inevitably, these assisted) but hot-eyed radicals who combined a fierce intolerance with a willingness to suffer for their beliefs.

The movement includes the Labor Party itself; the Trades Union Congress, known universally in Britain as the TUC; the Co-Operative Societies; and some minor socialist groups.

The Trades Union Congress is one of the centers of power in modern Britain. We will encounter it often in this book. Here we are concerned with its old position as the starting-point for British working-class power. The first Labor Party representatives who went to the House of Commons in 1906 were supported almost entirely by members of unions. The Parliamentary Labor Party came into being as an association of the Labor members of the House of Commons. Today it includes members of the House of Lords. There was originally a much closer co-ordination between the unions and the Labor MP's than exists now.

Today the TUC, although it exerts great political power both directly and indirectly, is important principally as the national focus of the trade-union movement. All the unions of any size or importance except the National Union of Teachers, the National Association of Local Government Officers, and some civil-service staff associations, are affiliated with it.

Its membership is impressive. The unions have a total membership of 9,461,000, of which 8,088,000 are affiliated with the TUC—this in a population of just over 50,000,000. The TUC's power is equally impressive. It is recognized by the government as the principal channel for consultation between the ministries and organized labor on matters affecting the interests of employees generally.

This power is not unchallenged. One of the disruptive situations in the Labor movement today is the restlessness of a number of constituency labor parties under the authority of the TUC. The constituency labor parties are the local organizations in the parliamentary constituencies or divisions. A number of them are and have been well to the left of the official leadership of the party. In them Aneurin Bevan finds his chief support for the rebellion he has waged intermittently against the leadership during the last five years.

Another source of anxiety to the TUC is the unwillingness of some unions—mostly those infiltrated by the Communists—to follow its instructions in industrial disputes. The TUC leaders with whom I have talked regard the strike weapon as the hydrogen bomb in labor's armory. They oppose its indiscriminate use. But in a large number of cases they have been unable to prevent its use.

The labor movement represents generally the industrial urban working class in Britain. But it is no longer an industrial urban working-class party. The modern movement relies on other sections of the population for both leaders and votes. Just as there are working-class districts that vote Tory in election after election, so are there middle-class groups who vote Labor.

Horny-handed sons of toil still rank among the party's leading politicians, but the post-war years have seen a steady increase in two other types. One is the union officer, whose acquaintance with physical labor is often somewhat limited. The other is the product of a middle-class home, a public-school education, and an important job in the wartime civil service. Hugh Gaitskell, the present leader of the Parliamentary Labor Party, is a notable example of this second group.

The party still includes intellectuals treading circumspectly in the footprints left by the sainted Sydney and Beatrice Webb. The intellectuals, perhaps in search of protective coloring, often assume a manner more rough-hewn than the latest recruit from the coal face. Incidentally, it was my impression that the defeat of 1955 shook the intellectuals a good deal more than the practical politicians. They departed, as is their custom, into long, gloomy analyses of the reasons for the defeat. They, too, may have been out of touch with the people.

Of course the defeat of 1955 did not finish the Labor movement in Britain any more than its victory in 1945 doomed the Conservative Party. True, the Labor vote dropped from 13,949,000 in 1951 to 13,405,000 in 1955 and the party's strength in the House of Commons fell from 295 to 277 seats. But the prophets of gloom overlooked the movement's immense vitality, which comes in part from its connection with certain emotions and ideals well established in modern Britain.

Within the movement the accepted reason for the defeat was the interparty feud among the Bevanites on the left and the moderate and right-wing groups. The moderates, representing the TUC and the moderate elements of the Parliamentary Labor Party, provided most of the party leaders in the election campaign. But in the year before the election the squabbling within the party in the House of Commons and on the hustings created a poor impression. One leader went into the campaign certain that the party had not convinced the electorate that, if elected, it could provide a competent, united government. These bickerings thus were a serious factor in the Socialist catastrophe.

They were related to what seems to me to have been a much more important element in the defeat. This was the party's lack of understanding of the people, a defeat emphasized by the politician quoted at the start of this chapter. There were times during the campaign when Socialist speakers seemed to confuse their audiences with those of 1945, 1935, or even 1925. This was understandable, for the Labor Party owes much of its present importance to its position in the twenties and thirties as the party of protest. There was plenty to protest about. There was poverty—black, stinking poverty, which wears a hideous mask in the bleak British climate. There was unemployment—the miners stood dull-eyed and shivering in the streets of the tidy towns of South Wales. There was the dole. There was, in London and other big cities, startling inequality between rich and poor, such inequality as the traveler of today associates with Italy or France or West Germany's Ruhr.

Memories of those times scarred a generation. The bitterness spilled out of the areas worst hit and infected almost the entire working class. During the 1955 election I talked with a group in Merther Tydfil in Wales. They were working, and had been working for ten years at increasingly higher wages. They were well dressed, they had money to buy beer and to go to see the Rugby Football International. The majority—young fellows—seemed satisfied with their lot. But one elderly man kept reminding them: "Don't think it's all that good, mun. Bad it's been in this valley, and it may be again."

Just as the Democrats in 1952 harked back to the days of Hoover and Coolidge, so the Labor orators in 1955 revived the iniquities of Baldwin and Chamberlain. They saw behind the amiable features of R. A. Butler and the imposing presence of Anthony Eden the cloven hoofs of the Tory devils. They warned, with much prescience, that the economic situation would deteriorate. They cajoled and pleaded. They waved and sang "The Red Flag." It didn't work.

One statistic is important in this connection: since 1945, millions who had voted for Labor in that election had died. It is reasonable to assume that a high proportion of them were people with memories of the twenties and thirties who would have voted Labor under any circumstances.

Some died. Others changed. The spring of 1955 marked the

zenith of Britain's first post-war boom. A very high proportion of the population felt that they had left the hard road they had traveled since 1940, and had emerged from war and austerity into the sunny uplands of peace and prosperity. They felt that to a great degree this change had been due to their own efforts, which was true. They believed they had earned the right to relax. It may be that a decade hence Britons will look back on that period as a golden echo of the great days of the Empire. Perhaps never again will Britain know a comparable period of prosperity and peace.

Given this primary circumstance, it was almost impossible for a party of protest to win an election. The industrial urban working class to whom the Socialists chiefly appealed were doing nicely. The workers had houses and television sets (known in Britain as "the telly"); bicycles and motorcycles were giving way to small family cars. There had been a steady rise in the supply of food, household appliances, and other items for mass consumption.

A large group of Labor voters were consequently not so interested in the election as they had been in the past. They voted, but in smaller numbers. Some votes switched to the Conservatives, but I do not regard this as a substantial element in the Tory victory. What did hurt Labor and help the Tories was the apathy of many Labor voters. Repeatedly I visited Labor election centers where a few elderly and tired people were going through the motions. The Tory centers, on the other hand, were organized, lively, and efficient.

For decades the Labor Party had promised the industrial workers full employment, higher wages, social security. Now there was full employment, wages were higher, present medical needs and future pensions were assured by national legislation. To a great degree these things had been achieved by the Labor governments of 1945 and 1950. But monarchies can be as ungrateful as republics, and the Tory boast that its government had ended rationing and produced prosperity probably counted as much as the benefits given the industrial working class by the socialist revolution carried out in six years of Labor government.

Another factor operated against the Labor campaign. There was then and still is a perceptible drift from the industrial working class into a new middle class. Later this drift must be examined in detail. It is part of the pattern of constant change in British history, a change that provides much of British society's strength. It is a change in which new blood constantly flows upward into other classes, a change in which the proletarian becomes lower middle class and the lower middle class becomes upper middle class in respect to income and social standing.

Here we are concerned with the political change. In many cases the industrial worker who becomes a foreman and then a production chief moves politically as well. He may still vote Labor, but it is increasingly difficult for him to identify himself with the proletariat or with Marxist doctrines. He lives in a better home, away from his old associates. His new friends may spring from the same class, but they are no longer preoccupied with the political struggle; often they are enjoying the fruits of its victories.

Nor is he worried, politically. For the Tories' return to power in Britain in 1951 did not produce a reactionary government. Sir Winston Churchill, once regarded by the workers as a powerful and unrelenting enemy, appeared in his last administration as a kindly old gentleman under whose sunny smile and oratorical showers the nation prospered. Why, he was even trying to arrange a talk with the Russian leaders! The absence of openly reactionary elements in the Conservative government, despite the presence of such elements in the party, and the promotion of moderation by Conservative speakers encouraged a gradual movement of the industrial working class away from the standards of pre-war socialism.

The changes in British society between 1945 and 1955, the people's refusal to respond to the old slogans in their new prosperity, the damaging split within the Parliamentary Labor Party all are contributing to the evolution of a new Labor Party that seems to be a better reflection of its electoral support than the one which went down to defeat in 1955. This does not mean, of course, that it is better fitted to rule Britain.

Almost all the leaders of the Labor governments of the post-war years have gone. Ernest Bevin and Sir Stafford Cripps are dead. Clement Attlee has passed from the House of Commons into the Lords. Herbert Morrison and Emanuel Shinwell are back benchers in the Commons, exchanging grins with their political enemy and personal friend Sir Winston Churchill.

These men represented the old Labor Party. Bevin, Morrison, and Shinwell were hard, shrewd politicians, products of the working class they served. Cripps and Attlee were strays from the old upper middle class who had been moved to adopt socialism by the spectacle of appalling poverty among Britain's masses and what seemed to them the startling incompetence of capitalist society to solve the nation's economic and social problems.

This group and its chief lieutenants were bound, however, by a common fight. They could remember the days when there was no massive organization, when they had stood on windy street corners and shouted for social justice. They remembered the days when "decent people" looked down their noses at Labor politicians as unnecessary and possibly treasonable troublemakers.

It was inevitable, I think, that this group would pass from the leadership of the Labor party. When they did, however, the party lost more than the force of their personalities. It lost an emotional drive, a depth of feeling, that will be hard to replace.

Fittingly, the new leader of the Parliamentary Labor Party, Hugh Gaitskell, is an exemplary symbol of the new party. He is a man of courage and compassion, intellectual power and that cold objectivity which is so often found in successful politicians. He represents the modern middle-class socialists just as Attlee two decades ago represented the much smaller number of socialists from that class.

Attlee, however, led a party in which the working-class politician was dominant. Gaitskell is chief of a party in which the middle-class intellectual element and the managerial group from the unions and the Party Organization have become powerful if not dominant.

Clement Attlee was leader of the party for more than twenty years. Gaitskell has the opportunity to duplicate this feat. But he must first heal the great schism that has opened in the movement in the last five years, and to do so he must defeat or placate the left wing and its leader, Aneurin Bevan.

Although the split within the Labor movement distresses all good socialists, it has added notably to the vigor and, indeed, to the gaiety of British politics. Aneurin Bevan was moved to flights of oratorical frenzy and waspish wit. Nor is it every day that one sees Clement Attlee temporarily discard his air of detachment and descend into the arena to entangle his party foes in the streamers of their own verbosity. It was a great fight, and, fortunately for those who like their politics well seasoned, it is not over yet.

For the quarrel within the movement represents forces and emotions of great depth and significance. In moments of excitement men and women on both sides have described it as a battle for the soul of the party. It may be more accurately described, I think, as a battle to determine what type of political party is to represent the labor movement in Britain.

Since the center and the right wing of the movement today dominate the making of policy and fill most, but not all, of the important party posts, it is the left that is on the offensive. But the left itself is not a united band of brothers. It has its backsliders and its apostates who sometimes temper their criticisms when they think of minor government posts under a Labor government headed by Hugh Gaitskell. But, personalities aside, convictions are so strongly held that there seems to be little likelihood of an end to the offensive.

What, then, does the left represent? One definition is that it represents those elements in the party who seek to complete the revolution of 1945–51. They want the extension of nationalization to all major industries and some minor ones. Aneurin Bevan, who enjoys making flesh creep, once told a group of Americans that he wanted to nationalize everything "including the barber shops." Extreme, of course, and said in jest; but "Nye" Bevan is an extremist, and many a true word is spoken in jest.

The left wing would move, too, against the surviving citadels of pre-war England such as public schools and other types of private education, and the power of the Church of England. It would impose upon Britain an egalitarianism unknown among the great powers of the West. It would limit Britain's defense efforts—this was the issue on which Bevan broke with the party leadership—to forces barely sufficient for police operations. It would liquidate as quickly as possible the remains of the Empire. Finally, it would turn Britain from what the radicals consider her present slavish acceptance of United States policy to a more independent foreign policy. This would mean that Britain would quit her position at the right hand of the United States in the long economic and political struggle with the great Communist powers and adopt a more friendly attitude toward Russia and Communist China. Bevan has descried, along with a great many other people, important economic and political changes within those countries, and he pleads with the Labor movement for a more sensible approach to them.

Naturally many members of the movement's center and right subscribe to some of these ideas. The admission of Communist China to the United Nations is an agreed objective of the Labor movement. It is even favored "in due course" by plenty of Conservative politicians. The explanation is a simple illustration of British bipartisanship. China means trade, and Britain needs trade. There are other considerations involving long-term strategic and political planning, including the possibility of luring China away from the Russian alliance. But trade is the starting-point.

The left wing boasts that it speaks for the fundamentalists of socialism, that it echoes the great dream of the founders of the party who saw the future transformation of traditional Britain with its economic and social inequalities into a greener, sweeter land. There is and always has been a radical element in British politics, and, on the left, the Bevanites represent it today.

The term "Bevanites" is inexact. The left-wing Socialists include many voters and politicians who dislike Aneurin Bevan and some of his ideas. But the use of his name to describe the group is a tribute to one of the most remarkable figures in world politics today. Aneurin Bevan has been out of office since 1951. He has bitterly attacked all the official leaders of his party, and he has come perilously close to exile from the party. His following, as I have noted, is subject to change. He often says preposterous things in public and rude things in private. He has made and continues to make powerful enemies.

"After all, Nye's his own worst enemy," someone once remarked to Ernie Bevin.

"Not while I'm alive, 'e ain't," said Ernie.

Bevan is a man of intelligence, self-education, and charm. At ease he is one of the best talkers I have ever met. He has read omnivorously and indiscriminately. He will quote Mahan to an admiral and Keynes to an economist. He has wit, and he knows the world. He likes to eat well and drink well.

Bevan, in his eager, questing examination of the world and its affairs, sometimes reminds his listeners of Winston Churchill. Each man has a sense of history, although the interpretation of a miner's son naturally differs from that of the aristocratic grandson of a duke. There is another similarity: each in his own way is a great orator.

To watch Bevan address a meeting is to experience political oratory at its fullest flower. He begins softly in his soft Welsh voice. There are a few joking references to his differences with the leader of the party, followed by a solemn reminder that such differences are inescapable and, indeed, necessary in a democratic party. At this point moderate Socialists are apt to groan. As Bevan moves on to his criticisms of the official leadership of the movement and of the Conservatives, it is clear that this is one orator who can use both a rapier and a bludgeon. He is no respecter of personalities, and at the top of his form he will snipe at Eisenhower, jeer at Churchill, and scoff at Gaitskell. He is a master of the long, loaded rhetorical question that brings a volley of "no, no" or "yes, yes" from the audience.

Much of the preaching of left-wing Socialism is outdated, in view of the changes in the urban working class. But Bevan is the only radical who is capable on the platform of exciting both the elderly party stalwarts who hear in him the echoes of the great days and the younger voters who, until they entered the hall, were reasonably satisfied with their lot. This is a man of imagination and power, one of the most forceful politicians in Britain. One secret is that he, and precious few others, can re-create in Labor voters, if only momentarily, the spell of the old crusading days when it was a movement and not a party.

As Bevan typifies to many anti-Americanism in Britain, it should in justice be said that he is not anti-American in the sense that he dislikes the United States or its people. Nor could he be considered an enemy of the United States in the sense that Joseph Stalin was an enemy. Bevan believes as firmly as any Midwestern farmer in the democratic traditions of freedom and justice under law.

But in considering the outlook on international affairs of Aneurin Bevan and others on the extreme left of British politics there are several circumstances to keep in mind. The first is that, due to early environment, study, or experience, they are bitterly anti-capitalist. The United States, as the leading and most successful capitalist nation in the world, is a refutation of their convictions. They may have a high regard for individual Americans and for many aspects of American life. But as people who are Marxists or strongly influenced by Marxism they do not believe that a capitalist system is the best system for a modern, industrial state—certainly not for one in Britain's continually parlous economic condition. In power they would alter the economic basis of British society, and possibly they would change the government's outlook on trade with the Communist nations. This means a friendlier approach to the Russian and Chinese Communist colossi and a more independent policy toward the capitalist United States. The attractions of such a position are not confined to Aneurin Bevan; one will hear them voiced by members of ultra-conservative factions of the Tory party.

For a man who vigorously opposes all kinds of tyranny, Bevan has been rather slow to criticize the tyranny of the secret police in the Soviet Union or the ruthless methods of those Communists who have won control of some British unions. There is in Bevan, as in all successful politicians—Roosevelt and Churchill are the best-known examples in our day—a streak of toughness verging on cruelty. This may explain his apparent tolerance of some of the excesses of totalitarian nations. Again, as some of his followers explain, Nye expects everyone to realize that such tyrannies are culpable and to understand him well enough to know that he would never give them the slightest support. Or, they suggest, Bevan takes such a comprehensive view of world affairs and has such a glittering vision of man's goals that he has no time to concentrate on minor atrocities. Perhaps, but the excuse is not good enough. The great leaders of Western democracy have been those who never lost the capacity for anger and action against tyranny whether it was exercised by a police sergeant or by a dictator.

Bevan has made a career of leading the extreme left wing in British politics since 1945. He is sixty this year. If he is to attain power, he must do so soon. How great is his following? What forces does he represent?

The most vocal of the Bevanites are those in the constituency labor parties. If you wish to taste the old evangelical flavor of socialism, you will find it among them. Here are the angry young men in flannel shirts, red ties, and tweed jackets, the stoutish young women whose hair is never quite right and who wear heavy glasses. They are eternally upset about something; they don't think any government, Labor or Conservative, moves fast enough. They pronounce the word "comrades," with which laborites start all their speeches to their own associates, as though they meant it.

The majority are strongly impressed by what has happened—or, rather, by what they have been told has happened—in Russia. You can get more misinformation about the Soviet Union in a half-hour of their conversation than from a dozen Soviet propaganda publications. For in their case the Russian propaganda has been adulterated with their own wishes and dreams.

Some of them have been members of the Communist Party in Britain. Others have flirted with it. My own impression is that most of them rejected the discipline of the Communists and that, although they do not want to be Communists, they have no objection to working with the Communist Party to attain their ends. They know very little about the history of the Social Democrats in Eastern Europe who thought in 1945 that they too could work with the Communists.

The left-wing radicals are not confined to the constituency labor parties, but these parties are their most successful vehicles for propaganda. For the CLP's present resolutions to the annual conference of the movement, and these resolutions are usually spectacular, combining extreme demands with hot criticism of the dominant forces within the movement. The resolutions endorsing the official policies of the party leadership attract far less attention.

The radicals of the CLP's are supported on the left by other dissident elements within the movement. Some of these are union members who oppose the authority of the Trades Union Congress within the movement, considering it a reactionary brake on progressive or revolutionary policies.

There is also a considerable group of union members who make common cause with the political opponents of the TUC but oppose it principally on its position in the industrial world. They see it as too temperate in its objectives for wages and hours, too timid in its use of the strike weapon, too unwieldy in organization, and too old-fashioned in its approach to modern developments in industry such as automation.

In this opposition they are encouraged by the Communists. The Communist Party is without direct political power in Britain. In the 1955 election it polled only 33,144 votes and failed to elect a single candidate. But it has attained considerable indirect power in some key unions in the British economy, and as the present leadership of the TUC is moderate and fairly democratic, the party wages unceasing war against it.

One method is to win control of unions. Where this is impossible the Communists encourage opposition to the TUC—opposition that often needs little encouragement. On both the political and the industrial fronts the Communists support Bevanism and the extreme left wing because these elements weaken the Labor movement, which up to now has combatted Communist infiltration and sternly rejected invitations to form a common front. Basically, the Communist Party in Britain is just as strongly opposed to the Labor movement as it is to the Conservative Party. This is true of the Communists all over Europe in their relations with social democracy and conservatism. The difference is that because of the common roots in Marxism, it is easier for the Communists to infiltrate the unions and the socialist political parties.

Bevan is not the only spokesman for the radical left wing. R. H. S. Crossman, a highly intelligent but somewhat erratic backbench MP is another. Crossman's political views are often somewhat difficult to follow, but in the House of Commons he is capable of cutting through the verbosity of a government speaker and exposing the point. Mrs. Barbara Castle, a lively redhead, is a brisk, incisive speaker. Konni Zilliacus, elected in the Conservative landslide of 1955, was once ousted from the Labor Party because he was too friendly toward the Soviet Union. Zilliacus is often immoderate, especially when dealing with the ogres in Washington, but he has a considerable knowledge of international affairs.

One of the most effective of the Bevanites in Commons until 1955 was Michael Foot, next to Bevan the best speaker on the Labor left wing. Defeated in 1955 by a narrow margin, he provides the left with ideological leadership through the pages of *Tribune,* a weekly newspaper.

Tribune is the only real Bevanite organ. The *New Statesman and Nation* is a forum for extreme left-wing views, but is more temperate and stately. *Tribune* is a battle cry flaying the Tories and the official Labor leadership indiscriminately. Foot edits the paper and writes in it under the name of John Marullus. Like Bevan, he was once employed by Lord Beaverbrook.

Tribune does not confine its activities to news and editorial comments. Each year at the annual Labor Party conference the newspaper stages what is usually the liveliest meeting of the week. During the rest of the year it sponsors "brain trust" meetings throughout the country at which the Bevanite ideology is expounded and defended.

The tabloid *Tribune* is a good example of the old "hit him again, he's still breathing" type of journalism. It does a wonderful job of dissecting and deflating the stuffed shirts of the right and left. But it is monotonously strident. The *New Statesman and Nation,* although not so avowedly Bevanite as *Tribune,* may carry more weight with the radical left. It is a weekly of great influence.

This influence is exerted principally upon an important group of intellectual orphans—the young men and women whose education surpassed their capacities and who now find themselves in dull, poorly paid jobs, living on a scale of comfort much lower than that of the more prosperous members of the urban working class. They are dissatisfied with the system and the government that has condemned them to dreary days of teaching runny-nosed little boys or to routine civil-service jobs. Not unnaturally, they welcome political plans and projects which promise to install them in posts worthy of their abilities as they see them.

Politically they are on the extreme left. The *New Statesman* encourages their political beliefs and assures them that their present lowly estate is due to the system and not to their own failings. The members of this group are poor. They are occasionally futile and often ridiculous. But they are not negligible.

That wise man Sir Oliver Franks said once that the political outlook of this group would have an important effect on Britain's political situation ten or twenty years hence. My own conclusion is that this group, like the Bevanites in the constituency labor parties, and the dissidents in the unions, wants to remake the Labor Party in its own image and then, when the party has come to power, remake Britain.

The left-wing radicalism of Britain—what we call Bevanism—is thus a good deal more important than the occasional rebellions of a few MP's on the Labor side of the House of Commons. It represents in an acute form the evangelism that is so strong a part of the nonconformist tradition in Britain. It rebels against the present direction of the Labor movement and the Parliamentary Labor Party. It wants, not a Britain governed by the Labor Party, but a socialist Britain.

Can it come to power? Movements of this kind usually win power during or after some great national convulsion. A war or an economic depression comparable to that of 1929–36 would give left-wing radicalism its chance. But either might give right-wing radicalism and nationalism a chance, too. To win, the Bevanites would have to defeat the mature power of the great unions and the undoubted abilities of the present leaders of the party.

The great unions are the result of one hundred and fifty years of crusading agitation. The labor movement began with them. They have money and they have power. The "branch" or "lodge" is the basic unit of organization within the union. Every union member must belong to it. In an individual plant or factory, the workers of the various unions are represented by a shop steward, who recruits new members, handles grievances, and, as the intelligence officer for the workers, keeps in touch with the management and its plans.

There are regional, district, or area organizations on a higher level for the larger unions. Finally, there is a national executive council of elected officials which deals with the national needs of the unions. At the top is the Trades Union Congress, a confederation of nearly all the great unions.

The unions have grown so large—the Amalgamated Engineering Union, for instance, includes thirty-nine separate unions in its organization—that it is sometimes difficult for the TUC or the national executive of an individual union to control its members. But the moderate political outlook—moderate, that is, by Bevanite standards—still prevails at the top, and the system of card voting, under which all the votes of a union are cast at the annual conference according to the decision of its national executive, insures that the moderate policies of the union leaders will be approved at the conference.

The imposing voting strength of the unions has been employed at successive conferences to maintain the policies and leadership of men like Attlee, Morrison, and Gaitskell. The steamroller in action is an impressive and, to the Bevanites, an undemocratic sight. But it does represent millions who advocate a conservative policy for the labor movement and who, at the moment, are satisfied with evolutionary rather than revolutionary progress.

The left-wing constituency labor parties create a great deal of noise. Those which support the moderate leadership are less enterprising in their propaganda, and, because criticism is often more interesting than support, they make fewer headlines. But, despite the agonized pleas of the left wing, hundreds of CLP's are satisfied with the general ideological policy of the movement and its leaders. This is a manifestation of the innate conservatism of the British worker. Just as the Conservatives of twenty years ago distrusted the brilliant Churchill largely because he was brilliant, so thousands of Labor voters today distrust the brilliant Bevan.

This group puts its faith in the ebb and flow of the tides of political opinion in a democracy. It was downcast after the 1955 election, but it did not despair. "Give the Tories their chance, they'll make a muck of it," said a union official. "We'll come back at the next election and pick up where we left off in 1951."

The moderate section of the labor movement enjoys the support of the only two national newspapers that are unreservedly Labor: the tabloid *Daily Mirror* and the *Daily Herald*. The *Mirror,* with an enormous circulation of 4,725,000, consistently supported Hugh Gaitskell for leadership of the party. So did the *Herald,* but it is a quieter paper than the brash tabloid, and its influence in trade-union circles, once great, seems to be declining, although the TUC remains a large shareholder.

The election of Gaitskell as leader of the Parliamentary Labor Party on Attlee's retirement was a severe blow to the Bevanites. But the tactics employed by Gaitskell in his first months as Leader of the Opposition were probably even more damaging to Bevan's hopes.

Bevan came out of his parliamentary corner swinging at the new leader. In the past this had provoked Herbert Morrison, then deputy leader, and even Attlee to retaliatory measures. Gaitskell paid no attention to Bevan, but went about his work of presiding over the reorganization of the party machine and of leading the party in the House of Commons. Bevan huffed and puffed about the country making speeches on Saturdays and Sundays. But as his targets said little in reply, the speeches became surprisingly repetitious. Moreover, with the establishment of the new Labor front bench in the Commons, Bevan took one of the seats and became the party's chief spokesman, first on colonial affairs and then on foreign affairs. It is difficult to make criticisms of the party leader stick at Saturday meetings if, from Monday through Friday, the critic sits cheek by jowl in the House of Commons with the target in an atmosphere of polite amiability.

Bevan's bearing in the debate over the Suez policy increased his stature in the party and in the country. Indeed, his approach to the crisis impressed even his enemies as more statesmanlike and more "national" than that of Gaitskell. Gaitskell, of course, labors under the difficulty of being a member of the middle class from which so many Conservative politicians spring. They naturally regard him as a traitor, and criticisms by Gaitskell of Conservative foreign policy are much more bitterly denounced than those of Bevan. To the Tories, Bevan was speaking for the country, Gaitskell for the party.

The schism in the party is not healed. Too much has been said, the convictions are too firmly held for that. But Gaitskell has been successful in creating a façade of co-operation which thus far has been proof against Bevan's outbursts on the platform or in *Tribune*. However, the reaction of the two leaders to the Eisenhower doctrine for the Middle East demonstrated the width of their differences on a fundamental problem. The future of this struggle has a direct and decisive bearing on the future of the labor movement. If Labor is to return to power in an election that is unaffected by a national crisis, foreign or domestic, the schism must be healed.

As a major political party, the labor movement has been molded by many influences. Before the First World War, German Social Democracy and the Fabians affected it. The party then acquired the tenets of national ownership and ultimate egalitarianism in the most class-conscious of nations which give it its socialist tone. But a party so large covers a wide range of political belief. It is a socialist party to some. It is a labor party to others. Above all, it is a means, like the Republican and Democratic parties, of advancing the interests of a large number of practical politicans whose interests in socialism are modified by their interest in what will win votes.

The moderate center of the Labor Party now dominates the movement just as the moderate center of the Conservative Party dominates the Tory organization. In each the leader represents the mood of the majority within the parliamentary party. Macmillan is a little to the left of center among Conservatives. Gaitskell is a little to the right of center in the Labor Party. The identity of interest among the two dominant groups is greater than might appear from the robust exchanges in the House of Commons.

The radical wings in both parties are handicapped at this point by a seeming inability to understand that politics is the art of the possible. Herbert Morrison, a great practical politician, summed up this weakness of the radical left at a Labor conference. A resolution demanding the immediate nationalization of remaining industry—at a time when the country was prosperous and fully employed—was before the conference. Do you think, he asked, that anyone will *vote* for such a program?

VI. *A Quiet Revolution by a Quiet People*

Revolutions begin with infatuation and end with incredulity. In their origin proud assurance is dominant; the ruling opinion disdains doubt and will not endure contradiction. At their completion skepticism takes the place of disdain and there is no longer any care for individual convictions or any belief in truth.

F. P. G. GUIZOT

Revolutions are not made; they come. A revolution is as natural a growth as an oak. It comes out of the past. Its foundations are laid far back.

WENDELL PHILLIPS

THE CHANGES in Britain since 1939 have been revolutionary. Yet because Britain is a nation with a highly developed political sense, the revolution has been fought not at barricades but in ballot boxes. And, seen on the broadest scale, what has happened to Britain and its people at home is part of what has been happening all over the world since 1939. The year that saw the start of World

War II saw the beginning of a terrible acceleration of forces that for fifty years had been slowly, sometimes almost imperceptibly weakening Britain's position.

This book is concerned principally with Britain. But let us look at what has happened to British interests abroad since 1939. The Indian Empire is gone. The lifeline of what remains of the Empire is unraveling in Ceylon, Singapore, Aden, and Cyprus. The rise of the Soviet Union and the United States has dwarfed Britain as a world power, and the imaginative conception of the Commonwealth is not yet, and may never be, an adequate balance to these two vast conglomerations of industrial and military power. Britain's ties with some of the Commonwealth nations—notably South Africa—grow weaker year by year. The remaining colonies are moving toward self-government, as the British always planned, but it is doubtful whether after they leave the Empire nest they will be any more loyal or responsive to British leadership than Ceylon is today.

We are living through one of the most important processes of recent history, the liquidation of an empire that has lasted in various forms for about two hundred and fifty years. It is a tribute to the people who gave it life, to their courage, political flexibility, and foresight, that, despite the changes and the retreats, they are still reckoned a power in world affairs.

History has its lessons. In 1785 Britain had lost her most important overseas possessions, the American colonies, and the courts of Europe rejoiced at the discomfiture of the island people and their armies and navies. A third of a century later the British had organized the coalition that ultimately defeated Napoleon, the supreme military genius of his time, and were carving out a new empire in India, Australia, and Africa.

We need not drop back so far in history. When, shortly before the Second World War, I went to England, it was fashionable and very profitable to write about the decay of Britain. Some very good books were written on the subject, and they were being seriously discussed when this island people, alone, in a tremendous renaissance of national energy, won the Battle of Britain and saved the Western world from the danger of German domination. As generations of Spaniards, French, and Germans have learned, it is unwise to count the British out.

Yet an observer from Mars limiting his observations to the home islands would find reason to do so today. For the Britain of today resembles very little the Britain that, despite the long and, by the standards of that day, costly war in South Africa, greeted the twentieth century proudly confident.

Britain's old position as "the workshop of the world" has vanished. There are now two other Britains—two nations, that is, which depend largely on the production and export of manufactured goods to live. Both these nations, Germany and Japan, are the defeated enemies of World War II, and both of them were bidding for and getting a share of Britain's overseas trade before that war and, indeed, before World War I. The decline in Britain's economic strength did not begin in 1939.

The second world conflict, beginning only twenty-one years after the close of the first, accelerated the decline. Into World War II Britain poured both blood and treasure, just as she had in the earlier conflict. But 1914–18 had left her less of both. British casualties in World War II were smaller than in the first conflict, but the damage done to Britain's position in the world was much greater.

The differences between the Britain of 1939 and the Britain of 1945 affected much more than the international position of the country. A society had been grabbed, shaken, and nearly throttled by the giant hand of war. After that bright Sunday morning in September when the sirens sounded for the first time in earnest, things were never the same again.

I remember an evening in April 1939. It was sunny and warm, and the men and women came out of their offices and relaxed in the sunlight. The Germans were on the move in Europe, but along the Mall there was nothing more disturbing than the honk of taxi horns. London lay prosperous and sleek, assured and confident.

Six years later I came back from Germany. I had been in London much of the time during the war, but now I had been away for over a year, and I found the contrast between that September evening and the far-off evening in April impressive. It was not the bomb damage; there was more of that in Germany. But London and Londoners had broken their connection with the confident past. It was a shabbier, slower world, face to face with new realities.

The impact of the war on the average Briton was greater than on the average American because for long periods the Briton lived with it on terms of frighteningly personal intimacy. Americans went to war. The war came to the British. In the process an ordered society was shaken to its foundations, personal and national savings were swept away, the physical industrial system of the country was subjected to prolonged attack and then to a fierce national drive for increased industrial production. For close to six years the country was a fortress and then a staging area for military operations. By the end of the war and the dawn of an austere peace the nation was prepared psychologically for the other changes introduced by a radical change in political direction.

Mobilization of military and economic forces during the war was more complete in Britain than in any other combatant save possibly the Soviet Union. The result of immediate peril and the prospect of defeat, it began early in 1940. This mobilization was the start of the social changes that have been going on in Britain ever since.

The mingling of classes began. Diana, the rector's daughter, and Nigel, the squire's son, found themselves serving in the ranks with Harriet from Notting Hill and Joe from Islington. In the end, of course, Diana was commissioned in the Wrens and Nigel was a captain in a county regiment, largely but not entirely because of their superior education; however, their contacts with Harriet and Joe gave them a glimpse of a Britain they had not known about before.

Things changed at home, too. The rectory was loud with the voices of children evacuated from the slums of London or Coven-

try, and the squire spent his days farming as he never had before
and his nights with the Home Guard. All over the country, men
and women were giving up those jobs which were unnecessary in
war and venturing into new fields. The assistant in the Mayfair dress
shop found herself in a factory, the greens-keeper was in a ship-
yard.

The old, safe, quiet life of Britain ended. There were no more
quiet evenings in the garden, no more leisurely teas in the working-
class kitchen, no more visits to Wimbledon. People worked ten or
twelve hours a day, and when they ate they ate strange dishes
made of potatoes and carrots, and when they drank they drank
weak beer and raw gin. These conditions were not universal. There
were the shirkers in the safe hotels and the black markets. And,
despite the bands playing "There'll Always Be an England" (a
proposition that seemed highly doubtful in the summer of 1940) and
despite the rolling oratory and defiance of Mr. Churchill, there was
plenty of grousing. It was, they said in the ranks, "a hell of a way
to run the bleedin' war"; or, as the suburban housewife remarked
in the queue, "I really think they could get us some decent beef.
How the children are to get along on this I cannot imagine."

They went on, though. They were bombed and strafed and
shelled, they were hungry and tired. The casualty lists came in
from Norway, France, the Middle East, Burma, Malaya. The
machines in the factories were as strained as the workers. Then,
finally, it was over and they had won. Only a minute number had
ever thought they would be beaten. But they were not the same
people who had gone dutifully to war in 1939. Nor was the world
the same.

"Well, it's time to go home and pick up the pieces," said a
major in Saxony in the summer of 1945. He, and thousands like
him, found that the pieces just were not there any more. The economic drain of the war had made certain that Britons, far from
enjoying the fruits of victory, would undergo further years of unrelenting toil in a scarred and shabby country.

People were restless. They had been unsettled not only by the impact of the war but by the glimpse of other societies. Not until the last two and a half years of the war, when the American Army and Air Force began to flood into Britain, did people become aware of the size, power, and mechanical ingenuity and efficiency of the people who were so inaccurately portrayed by Hollywood. Some saw in Russia's resistance to the Germans and her final sweeping victories proof that the Communist society could endure and triumph no less than those of the Western democracies. Many who understood what had happened to British power during the war were convinced that if the country was to retain its position in the world, it would have to seek new, adventurous methods in commerce and industry and new men and new policies in politics. This conviction was held by hundreds of thousands who had once voted Liberal or Conservative but who in the election of 1945 were to cast their votes for the Labor Party.

The political history of the immediate pre-war period offers a reason for this change. The defeats of 1940 and 1941 were a tremendous shock to Britons. During the war there was no time for lengthy official post-mortems on the alarming inadequacy of British arms in France in 1940 or in the first reverses in the western desert of Libya a year later. But the polemics of the left managed to convince a great many people that the blame lay with the pre-war Conservative governments of Neville Chamberlain and Stanley Baldwin. When in 1945 the chance came to revenge themselves on the Tories, even though Winston Churchill, who had opposed both Chamberlain and Baldwin, was the Conservatives' leader, millions took the chance and voted Labor into office.

The urge for change to meet changing conditions at home and new forces abroad was not universal. The people of the middle class had not yet fully understood what the war had done to Britain's economy and especially to that section of it which supported them. There was very strong opposition to the first post-war American loan in sections of this class, largely from people whose confidence had not been shaken by the cataclysm. The austerity imposed by Sir Stafford Cripps, the Socialist Chancellor of the

Exchequer, was neither understood nor welcomed. The withdrawal from India was hotly opposed—and, it should be remembered, not purely on imperialist grounds. For two hundred years the middle class had provided the officers and civil servants who led and administered the Indian Army and the government of British India. As a class it knew a great deal more about India and the Indians than the union leaders and earnest young intellectuals of Mr. Attlee's government knew. The Socialist speakers and newspapers scoffed at "the toffy-nosed old ex-colonels" who predicted bloody and prolonged rioting between the Hindus and the Moslems once British power was withdrawn. The rioting began, and before it was over the bloodshed was greater than in all the British punitive actions from the Mutiny onward.

None of this generally Conservative opposition could halt or even check a Labor government that had been voted into power in 1945 with 393 seats in the House of Commons as opposed to 216 for the Conservatives and 12 for the Liberals. The Tories were out, the new day had dawned, and the Labor Party, in full control of the government for the first time in its history, set out to remake Britain.

No one in Britain could plead ignorance of what the Labor Party was about to do. Since 1918 it had been committed to extensive nationalization of industry and redistribution of income. Moreover, it came to power at a moment when the old patterns of industrial power and political alignments had been ruptured by war and when voters other than those who habitually voted Labor were acknowledging the need for change.

The 1945 policy statement of the Labor Party was called "Let Us Face the Future." It dotted all the *i*'s and crossed all the *t*'s in Labor's program.

The statement began with a good word for freedom, always highly esteemed by political parties seeking power. But it added an interesting comment. "There are certain so-called freedoms that Labor will not tolerate; freedom to exploit other people; freedom to pay poor wages and to push up prices for selfish profits; freedom to deprive the people of the means of living full, happy, healthy lives."

The statement went on to promise full employment, to be achieved through the nationalization of industry; the fullest use of national resources; higher wages; social services and insurance; a new tax policy; and planned investment. There was to be extensive replanning of the national economic effort and a "firm constructive government hand on our whole productive machinery." The Labor Party's ultimate purpose at home was "the establishment of a Socialist Commonwealth of Great Britain—free, democratic, efficient, progressive, public spirited, its material resources organized in the services of the British people."

In 1948 Harold Laski, the Labor Party's ideological mentor, said in the course of the Fabian Society Lectures that the party was "trying to transform a profoundly bourgeois society, mainly composed of what Bagehot called 'deferential' citizens, allergic to theory because long centuries of success have trained it to distrust of philosophic speculation, and acquiescent in the empiricist's dogma that somehow something is bound to turn up, a society, moreover, in which all the major criteria of social values have been imposed by a long indoctrination for whose aid all the power of church and school, of press and cinema, have been very skillfully mobilized; we have got to transform this bourgeois society into a socialist society, with foundations not less secure than those it seeks to renovate."

Doubtless these ominous words failed to penetrate into the clubs and boardrooms that were the sanctums of the former ruling class. But it was hardly necessary that they should. The businessmen and the Conservative politicians understood Harold Laski's objectives.

Nationalization of industry is the most widely advertised economic result of Labor policies between 1945 and 1951. In assessing its effect on the changes in Britain since 1939, we must remember that neither was it so new nor is it so extensive as Americans believe. The British Broadcasting Corporation was created as

a public corporation as long ago as 1927. Today most manufacturing in Britain remains in the control of private enterprise.

Between 1945 and 1951, however, the Labor government's
policy of nationalization created corporations that today operate or
control industries or services. In two industries, steel and road transport, the trend toward nationalization has been reversed. But the
following list shows the extent of nationalization in Britain today.

Coal: The Coal Industry Nationalization Act received the
Royal Assent in May of 1946, and on January 1, 1947, the assets
of the industry were vested in the National Coal Board appointed
by the Minister of Fuel and Power and responsible for the management of the industry. For a century coal was king in Britain, and
British coal dominated the world market until 1910. Coal production is around 225,000,000 tons annually—the peak was reached
in 1913 with 287,000,000 tons—and the industry employs just
over 700,000 people.

Gas: Under the Gas Act of 1948 the gas industry was brought
under public ownership and control on May 1, 1949. The national
body is the Gas Council, also appointed by the Minister of Fuel
and Power. The council consists of a full-time chairman and deputy
chairman and the twelve chairmen of the area boards.

Electricity: The Central Electricity Authority in April 1948
took over the assets of former municipal and private electricity
supply systems throughout Great Britain with the exception of the
area already served by the North of Scotland Hydro-Electric Board,
another public corporation. But the industry had long been moving
toward nationalization. As early as 1919 the Electricity Com-
missioners were established to supervise the industry and promote
voluntary reorganization. The industry is a big one, employing
approximately 200,000 people, and production in 1954 was over
72,800,000,000 kilowatts.

Banking: The Bank of England, Britain's central bank, was
established in 1694 by Act of Parliament. Its entire capital stock
was acquired by the government under the Bank of England Act of
1946. As the central bank, the Bank of England is the banker to

the government, its agent in important financial operations, and the central note-issuing authority.

Transport: On January 1, 1948, under the Transport Act passed in the preceding year, most of Britain's inland transport system came under public ownership. Nationalization embraced the railways and the hotels, road-transport interests, docks and steamships owned by the railways, most of the canals, and London's passenger-transport system. The public authority then established was the British Transport Commission. Originally the Commission appointed six executive bodies to run various parts of the system: the Railway Executive, the Road Transport Executive, the Road Passenger Executive, the Hotel Executive, the London Transport Executive, and the Docks and Inland Waterways Executive. This generous proliferation of authority affected an industry that employs nearly 2,000,000 workers.

Transport was one of the nationalized industries whose organization was altered by the Conservatives when they returned to power in 1951. Believing that "competition gives a better service than monopoly," the Tories passed the Transport Act of 1953. This returned highway freight-haulage to private enterprise and aimed at greater efficiency on the railroads through the encouragement of competition between the various regions, such as the Southern Region or the Western Region, into which the national system had been divided. The act also abolished all the neat but rather inefficient executives except the Road Passenger Executive, which had been abolished, unmourned save by a few civil servants, in 1952, and the London Transport Executive, which was retained.

Airways: British governments since the twenties have been involved in civil aviation. Imperial Airways received a government grant of £1,000,000 as early as 1924. By 1939 the Conservative government had established the British Overseas Airways Corporation by Act of Parliament. In 1946 the Labor government, under the Civil Aviation Act, set up two additional public corporations: British European Airways and British South American Airways. The latter was merged with BOAC in 1949.

Communications: The government took control of Cable and Wireless Ltd., the principal overseas telegraph service, on January 1, 1947. Thus, the Post Office now operates overseas telecommunications from the United Kingdom and, of course, all internal telephonic and telegraphic systems.

These were the most important milestones on the Labor Party's progress toward nationalization. Viewed dispassionately, they were evolutionary rather than revolutionary. There had been a trend toward nationalization in electricity for some years. Objective investigators had suggested nationalization to aid the failing coal-mining industry, and during the war (1942) the Coalition government had assumed full control of the industry's operations although private ownership retained control of the mines.

We should avoid, too, the impression, popular among the uninformed in the United States and even in Britain, that nationalization meant that the workers took over management of the industries concerned. There was no invasion of boardrooms by workingmen in cloth caps. On the contrary, employees protested that nationalization did not affect the management of industries, and such protests were backed by facts. In 1951, after six years of Labor Party rule, trade-union representation among the full-time members of the boards of the nationalized industries was a little under 20 per cent, and among the part-time members the percentage was just below 15 per cent. Five boards had no trade-union representation.

The nationalization program of the Labor government between 1945 and 1951 nevertheless marked an important change in the structure of British society. The financial and economic control of some of the nation's most important industries was transferred from private to public hands. The capitalist system that had served Britain so well found its horizons limited in important fields.

There is now no important political movement in Britain to undo the work of the Labor government in the fields mentioned above. But as long as a generation survives which knew these industries under private control, harsh and persistent criticism will persist. Some of it is just. The standard of efficiency and comfort on British railroads, for instance, has deterioriated since pre-war days. But in many instances the critics are attacking aspects of the nationalized industries which are the result not of nationalization itself but of the gradual wearing out of much of the nation's industrial plant. Two wars, a long depression, and a prolonged period of economic austerity during which only the most important improvements and construction could be financed have had their effect. Both British industry and the transport system upon which it rests—railroads, ports, highways—need immediate improvement and new construction.

Nationalization, however, was only one means of altering the bases of British society. The historian of the future may consider that the tremendous extension of government responsibility for social welfare was a more important factor in the evolution of Britain. The Welfare State has been a target for critics on both sides of the Atlantic. Its admitted cost, its supposed inefficiency are denounced. British critics, however, avoid a cardinal point. The Welfare State is in Britain to stay. No government relying on the electorate for office is going to dismantle it.

This is not a reference book, but we had better be sure of what we mean by the British "Welfare State" as we consider its effect on the society it serves.

The system is much more extensive than most Americans realize. The government is now responsible through either central or local authorities for services that include subsistence for the needy, education and health services for all, housing, employment insurance, the care of the aged or the handicapped, the feeding of mothers and infants, sickness, maternity, and industrial-injury benefits, widows' and retirement pensions, and family allowances.

The modern John Bull can be born, cared for as an infant, educated, employed, hospitalized and treated, and pensioned at the expense of the state and ultimately of himself through his contributions. This is the extreme, and it arouses pious horror among those of conservative mind in Britain as well as in the United States.

Again, as in the case of the nationalization of industry, we find that much of the legislation that established the Welfare State did not spring from the bulging brows of Sir Stafford Cripps, Lord Beveridge, or Aneurin Bevan, but is the latest step in an evolutionary process. National Insurance is the logical outgrowth of the Poor Relief Act of 1601, before there were Englishmen in America, and the contributory principle on which all later measures in this field have been based first appeared in the National Health Insurance Scheme of 1912.

The present system is big and it is expensive. The national and local governments are spending about £2,267,000,000 a year (about $6,347,600,000) on social services for the Welfare State, and the expenditure by the Exchequer on social services amounts to over a quarter of the total.

Yet, as this is Britain where established custom dies hard, voluntary social services supplement the state services. There are literally hundreds of them, ranging from those providing general social service, such as the National Council of Social Service, through specialized organizations, such as Doctor Barnado's Homes for homeless children and the National Association for Mental Health, to religious groups such as the Church of England Children's Society and the Society of St. Vincent de Paul. The existence and vigor of these voluntary organizations testifies to the wrongness of the assumption that all social work in Britain today is in the hands of soulless civil servants.

Of all the actions taken to extend social services under the Labor government, by far the most novel and controversial was the establishment of the National Health Service, which came into being on July 5, 1948. The object of the National Health Service Act was "to promote the establishment in England and Wales [other acts for Scotland and Northern Ireland came into force simultaneously] of a comprehensive health service designed to secure improvement in the physical and mental health of the people of England and Wales and the prevention, diagnosis and treatment of illness, and for that purpose to provide or secure the effective provision of services."

Before we consider what the service does, let us think of those it was designed to help. The British working class up to 1945 suffered to a considerable degree from lack of proper medical and dental care. Doctors and dentists were expensive, and in addition there was a definite psychological resistance to placing oneself in their care. Health and medicine were not popularized in Britain, as they were in the United States; among the poor there was still a tendency to consider discussion of these subjects as ill-mannered.

There has been some change since the war, but not much. Britons of all classes were surprised, and some of them a little disgusted, by the clinical descriptions of President Eisenhower's illness in American newspapers. But the National Health Service has done much to reduce the old reluctance to visit the doctor or the dentist because of the expense.

Three subsequent acts in 1949, 1951, and 1952 have modified the scheme slightly and have provided for charges for some services. But the National Health Service is otherwise free and available according to medical need. Its availability is not dependent on contribution to National Insurance.

What does the service do? The Ministry of Health is directly responsible for all hospital and specialist services on a national basis, the mental-health functions of the old Board of Control, research work on the prevention, diagnosis, or treatment of illness, the public-health laboratory service, a blood-transfusion service.

These broad general headings cover an enormous organization, the basis of which is the General Practitioner Services, which covers the medical attention given to individuals by doctors and dentists of their own choice from among those enrolled in the service. About 24,000 or nearly all of the general practitioners in Britain are part of the service. Of approximately 10,000 dentists in England and Wales, about 9,500 are in the service.

Again, costs are high. For six years Labor and Conservative

administrations have sought to keep the net total annual cost of the
National Health Service to just over £400,000,000 or $1,120,-
000,000. To limit the drain on the Exchequer it was found necessary to charge for prescription forms, dentures, and spectacles. Like
any welfare scheme, the National Health Service invited malingerers
and imaginary invalids who cost the doctors—and the state—time
and money.

I asked a young doctor in the West Country what he thought
of the scheme. "Well, I don't know if it has contributed much to
the health of my bank statement," he said, "but it has contributed
to the health of the folk around here. People are healthier because
they don't wait until they're desperately ill to see a doctor. And the
care of children has improved tremendously. Perhaps this might
have come naturally under the old system. I don't know. But it's
here now, and we're a healthier lot."

The opposition view was put by an elderly doctor in London
who opined that so great was the pressure on the ordinary general
practitioner from "humbugs" that he never got a chance to do a
thorough job on the seriously ill. The hospitals, he added, were
crowded with people who "don't belong there" and who occupied
beds needed by the really sick.

This controversy, like those over the nationalization of industry, will continue. Again there seems little prospect that any government will modify in any important way the basic provisions of the
National Health Service Act.

In company with the National Insurance, which applies its
sickness, unemployment, maternity, and widows' benefits to everyone over school-leaving age, and the National Assistance Board,
with its responsibility for the care of those unable to maintain themselves, the National Health Service has established the Welfare
State in Britain. Another important function has been largely taken
out of the hands of private individuals and delivered to the state.

What effect did the nationalization of industry and the establishment of the Welfare State have on British society? Obviously,
the first removed from the control of the moneyed and propertied

classes certain powers over the economic functioning of Britain. The second, because of its cost, made certain that the heavy tax rates introduced during and just before World War II would continue. These taxes were paid principally by the middle class, which, at the outset, refused in many instances to use the National Health Service.

The effect was a leveling one. The dominant class was stripped, on one hand, of some of its power to control a large section of the national economy, although, as we have seen, it managed to retain its direction of the nationalized industries. At the same time this class found that it must continue to pay year by year a high proportion of its earned income for the state's care of its less prosperous fellows. The decline in the influence, prosperity, and prestige of the old middle class was definitely accelerated by these two bold advances toward socialism.

From the standpoint of the prestige of this class in Britain and, frankly, of the usefulness of many of its members to the state, the withdrawal of British rule from India and Burma and the steps elsewhere toward the liquidation of the Empire were blows as grievous as the creation of the Welfare State and the nationalization of some industries.

Americans should realize that to Britons the Empire was not simply a place to work and get rich. The people who did the Empire's work usually retired with only their pensions and a conviction (which is not much help when you need a new overcoat) that they had done their duty.

The propaganda of India and Pakistan and of their well-wishers in the United States has obscured for Americans the grand dimensions of the British achievement in India. For a hundred and ninety years, between Plassy in 1757 and the withdrawal in 1947, British rule brought peace and justice to peoples hitherto sorely oppressed by irresponsible tyrants, many of whom were corrupt and decadent. The British stamped out thuggee and suttee, ended the interminable little wars, introduced justice, and labored to build the highways, railroads, and canals that form the skeletons of independent India and Pakistan. All this was done by a handful of British officials and white troops in the midst of the subcontinent's millions.

Parenthetically, it might be remembered that when the British Indian army, which served with the British Army in India, existed, and when the Royal Navy had the strength and facilities to take it where it was needed, there was peace between Suez and Singapore.

The British are proud rather than defensive about their record in India. Even the anti-colonialists of the Labor Party note that free India and Pakistan operate under British political and legal forms. Most of them, even those who knew the country well, regarded withdrawal as inevitable after World War II. But it will take more proof than Mr. Nehru is prepared to offer to convince many Britons with roots in India that the people are happier, that justice is universal, that corruption is declining.

This attitude galls the Indians and their friends, who never liked the British much. But in the great days of empire the British didn't care about being liked. This is a significant difference between the American and British approaches to responsibility and leadership in international affairs. The American visitor abroad worries about whether he and his country are liked by the French or the Egyptians or the Indonesians. The Briton, when the Empire's sun was at the zenith, never gave a damn. What he wanted was respect, which he regarded as about as much as a representative of a powerful nation could win from the nationals of a less powerful nation under economic, political, or military obligation.

"We ran that district with three officials, some Indian civil servants, the police, and their white officers, and we ran it damned well," an official recalled. "There were some troops up the line, but we never needed them. When we made a decision or gave a judgment, we adhered to it. We made no distinction between Moslem and Hindu. There was justice and peace. No, of course they weren't free. They weren't ready to govern themselves. And d'you think they'd have traded those conditions for freedom and communal rioting?"

I asked the official the population of the district.

"Three, three and a half million," he said.

The loss of India and Burma under the first Socialist administration and the consequent decline of British power thus constituted a severe psychological shock to the middle class that had ruled Britain during the last century of British administration in India. Later we shall see the difference it made in Britain's international position vis-à-vis the Soviet Union. Here we are concerned with the effect upon British society at home.

That society contains thousands of men and women who knew and served the Empire and who bitterly resent its liquidation. Usually inarticulate and no match for the bright young men of the *New Statesmen,* they can be goaded into wrath. Gilbert Harding, a television entertainer who has become a national celebrity, found this out. Mr. Harding referred on television to the "chinless idiots" who made that "evil thing," the British Empire. The reaction was immediate and bitter. Mr. Harding was abused in the editorial and letter columns of the newspapers in phrases as ugly as any he had used. There are, it appeared, many who glory in the Empire and in the Commonwealth that has evolved from the old colonies.

Nationalization, the creation of the Welfare State, the withdrawal from India—these were major events that changed the face and manner of Britain. But the effect of the change in British life was evident, too, in the way men lived. The austerity preached by Sir Stafford Cripps may have been necessary if the nation was to overcome the effects of the war. But continued rationing, the queues outside the shops, the shortages of coal, the persistently high taxation all combined to change the life of the middle class. Slowly they realized that the sacrifices and dangers of the war years were not going to be repaid. There was no brave new world. Instead, there was the old world looking much more shabby than ever before.

"You see," people would say, explaining some new restriction, some new retreat before economic pressure, "we won the war." It was a bitter jest in the long, drab period between 1945 and 1950.

There was plenty of grumbling, some of it bitterly humorous.

Lord Wavell, surveying a glittering audience at a royal command performance at Covent Garden Opera House, was told by a friend that the scene reminded him of pre-war days. "The only difference," the great soldier replied, "is that tomorrow we'll be doing our own washing up."

There was, of course, a good deal of snobbery in the middle-class attitude toward the Socialist government and what it was doing. The Conservatives and the dwindling band of Liberals just could not believe that the Socialists were equipped to carry out such vast changes in British life. They noted with sardonic humor the failures in Socialist policy. They found the Labor ministers ineffectual and diffident compared to their own leaders. "We had X and his wife to dinner last week," the wife of an industrialist told me in 1948. "What a pathetic little man! And in such an important post, too. Really, I looked at him sitting there and thought of Winston and Anthony, and Duff, and I felt like crying."

It was during this period that the Labor Party lost the support, temporarily at least, of many of the Conservatives and Liberals who had voted for it in 1945. The reasons for the shift are difficult to ascertain. Certainly many people were affronted by nationalization, especially when it directly affected their interests (though many of them had voted for Labor expecting such changes). The continuation of high taxation, which seemed permanent after the start of rearmament in 1950, alienated others. The ineffectual way in which the Labor government seemed to be handling many of its problems, particularly the coal shortage, affected the political opinions of many. "Damn it, we live on an island made of coal," said one civil servant who had voted for Labor in 1945. "It's monstrous to have a coal crisis. What are they playing at?"

In one field the Labor government won the grudging respect of the Tories: its approach to the problem presented to the West by the aggression of Soviet Russia. Mr. Attlee's dry, precise refutations of Soviet policy might be a weak substitute for Churchill's thundering oratory, but the nation found a paladin in the squat, rolling figure of Ernest Bevin.

Bevin had spent much of his life fighting British communists for the control of the unions. Entering the rarefied atmosphere of international affairs at the top as Foreign Secretary, he brought to his new task the blunt tongue and quick insight he had employed so successfully in the old. Between 1945 and 1950, when the British Labor Party was at the top of its power, Russian Communism was on the march in Europe. It had no tougher opponent than this Englishman.

The Russians recognized him as a prime enemy. In Moscow in 1946 and 1947 the Soviet press denounced and assailed Bevin as hotly as they did any other Western figure. Indeed, the whole Labor government was vilified almost daily. The reason for this savage onslaught on the earnest and industrious Marxists of the British government was obvious. Stalin and his lieutenants had been talking about socialism for decades. Here was a regime that might make it work without throwing hundreds of thousands into labor camps and allowing millions to starve. The anxiety of the rulers of Russia can be compared to that of the proprietors of a black market who learn that an honest shop is going into business across the street.

So this sturdy proletarian, Ernest Bevin, became one of the champions of the West in the cold war and was praised by Conservatives and Liberals. The left wing of his own Labor Party provided most of the criticism. Still cherishing the illusion that the Russians could be induced to drop their hostility to the West through "frank and open exchanges," Bevin's comrades led by Aneurin Bevan attacked his policies and especially his desire to maintain the Anglo-American alliance.

Those who cheered loudest, the people of the upper middle class who detested Russia, were the ones who, in the end, suffered most from the cold war. Britain's rearmament, under the impact of the Communist seizure of power in Czechoslovakia, the Berlin Blockade, and, finally, the attack on South Korea, was a costly business. It began soon after the great expansion of social services had created the Welfare State. Taxes, already high, rose further.

In thousands of middle-class homes the decline from the old

pre-war standards continued. The maidservant gave way to the "daily" who came in once or twice a week to help with the cleaning. The savings for old age were diverted to the rising costs of keeping the boys at school. In a hundred pathetic ways the middle class strove to maintain its standards under the burden of taxation in a Britain it neither liked nor understood.

But to balance this gradual depression of one class there was the expansion of another. The victory of the Labor Party in 1945 encouraged the working class of the nation to seek a richer, fuller life. It opened vistas of a new existence and greater opportunities. It created confidence.

Traveling to Cardiff in September 1945, I talked with a miner's wife, a huge woman who spoke in the singsong accents of the mining valleys of South Wales. She dandled a plump baby on her knee and talked of what life would be like now. "My Dai's not going down the mine like his dad," she told me. "Now that *we* have *our* government, he can be anything he wants, do anything."

British society, despite its fixed barriers between class and class, has always enjoyed considerable mobility. In the past the country gentry and the aristocracy had surrendered power to the merchants and the industrialists. Now the urban working class that had served the merchants and the industrialists believed it had wrested control from its masters. Labor's election victory seemed to prove it.

This breaking down of the old relationship between the classes was a matter of deep concern to many, and their concern went deeper than partisan political feeling. Repeatedly one was told that the worst thing Labor had done was to create class feeling, to encourage class antagonisms in a country that until then had never been affected by them. This was only a half-truth. The class antagonism had been there, all right, but the middle class now was belatedly the victim of the bitterness that a hundred years of slum housing, poor food, and lack of opportunity had created among some but not all of the working class. I write "not all" because there were members of that class who were as disturbed by the growth of class antagonism as any retired colonel in his club. They felt instinctively that the unity of Britain was being sapped by the emergence of a powerful and militant socialist group whose object was change. Most of them had voted for change. But the British are a conservative people. They accept change within the framework of familiar institutions. Extensive reconstruction may go on behind the façade, but the façade must remain untouched.

The hope and confidence born of Labor's victory, however, had a long-term effect upon British society. It encouraged those who had dreamed, like the miner's wife, of a better life for their children. Ambitious mothers aimed higher than a few years of school and a factory job for their sons. Young men who had won commissions during the war decided to remain in the Army or the Navy or the Air Force now that the old barriers were falling and the right accent and the right private income did not matter so much as it once had.

By 1950 the economic and social forces that were to create the Britain of today were in full motion. Paradoxically, the British electorate was moving slightly to the right.

VII. *A Society in Motion*

NEW CLASSES AND NEW HORIZONS

> *There are but two families in the world—have-much and have-little.*
>
> CERVANTES
>
> *Society is constantly advancing in knowledge. The tail is now where the head was some generations ago. But the head and the tail still keep their distance.*
>
> THOMAS BABINGTON MACAULAY

☙

M A R I E L L O Y D, the darling of the music halls, sang a song that contained the deathless line: "A little of what you fancy does you good."

In addition to their evangelism, their occasional ruthlessness, the British have a streak of self-indulgence. This trait was encouraged by the peculiar circumstances of the country after the Conservative victory in the general election of 1951.

It was not a smashing victory. The Conservatives came back to power with 326 seats in the House of Commons as opposed to 295 for Labor and 6 for the Liberals. Yet it is doubtful that even with double their majority the Tories would have wished to undo all the work in the fields of nationalization and social welfare accomplished by the Labor administrations of 1945 and 1950. This was not politically feasible and, with Britain still in the toils of economic difficulties, it would have been unwise to convulse the industrial structure. There was no restoration after the revolution. The Socialists obviously had not attained the goals outlined by Professor Laski, but they had started the nation in that direction.

If economic conditions had deteriorated, the new administration of Winston Churchill might have been short-lived. But the world demand for British products, especially such raw materials as rubber and tin from Malaya, strengthened the economy. So did the gradual rise in British production and the economic improvement in Europe which created a larger market for British exports. After some uneasy months the indices of economic health began to move upward. After twelve years of military, political, and economic strain and anxiety the British were ready for a little of what they fancied. Life around them looked good, and they wanted to take advantage of it. There was a steady return of confidence.

British exports were rising. You could actually go down to the butcher's and buy all the meat you wanted. The Tories really were building all those houses they had promised to build. It was easier now to buy a new car and say good-by to Old Faithful that had served since 1938 or earlier. Taxes were as high as ever, but the government said they would be reduced. And if you had a little money, there was plenty in the shops to spend it on.

During the struggle with austerity after the war the British had been surprisingly sensitive to foreign criticism of their apparent inability to fight their way back to prosperity. Now here was prosperity or a reasonably accurate facsimile of it. Those foreigners had been wrong.

Presiding over their recrudescence of national confidence was the familiar figure of Mr. Churchill. The Prime Minister might lack the acute economic penetration of Sir Stafford Cripps and Clement Attlee's social consciousness, but he was a world figure in a way that neither Socialist could claim to be. When in May 1953 the best-known voice in the English-speaking world proposed a conference at the summit with the new masters of the Soviet Union, the British felt that their leader had enforced their country's claim to a share in the leadership of the West.

Neither the economic nor the political developments of 1951–3 altered the raw facts of Britain's existence: the importance of denial at home to expand sales abroad, the rising competition of Germany and Japan in international markets. But these facts, which had been presented to the people with monotonous regularity under the pedagogical leadership of the Socialists, slipped out of sight. There was money to spend and there were things to buy. And reading about the Queen and the preparations for her Coronation was much more interesting than worrying about the dollar balance.

The Coronation of Queen Elizabeth II was one of the most impressive and romantic spectacles of modern times. It is quite possible that this combination of national pride, religious symbolism, and perfectly performed ceremony will never be duplicated. It is also possible that from the standpoint of national psychology the Coronation did the British a good deal of harm by leading some of them into romantic daydreams at a time when it was essential that they should keep their heads and face the ugly realities of their position.

The young Queen pledging herself to serve her people, the evocation of a glorious past, the survivals of ancient custom, the splendid ceremony in London, and the other smaller ceremonies around the country all exalted values that, although real and important in their place, are only a part, and not the most important part, of a society that must fight to retain economic and political power. People should be reminded occasionally of their place in the historical procession and of the existence of values other than those of the market place. But such reminders are useful only when the people return to their normal jobs with a new vigor and enthusiasm. In Britain the festivities of the Coronation year seemed to drag on interminably.

In the case of the Coronation the monarchy might be said to have overfulfilled its function of arousing national patriotism. Whipped on by the national newspapers and the BBC, patriotic fervor went beyond the bounds of reason and led to an overoptimistic estimate of Britain's position in the world. *We can make this the new Elizabethan age!* chanted the newspapers.

The idea that the subjects of Elizabeth II would emulate their restless, adventurous, enterprising forebears of the reign of Elizabeth I was a pleasing one. But it sounded odd in a nation of whose citizens millions were devoted to security. In 1953, Coronation year, the age of adventure and chivalry bowed resplendent and beautiful before a nation in which the forces that had been working since 1940 were evoking new classes and new ways of life. Neither had physical or mental connections with the heroic past of aristocratic rural England or with the old middle class.

In preceding chapters we have encountered some of the forces that changed British life: the leveling effect of the war, the Socialist victory of 1945, the extension of nationalization of industry and of the social services, the decline in the economic well-being of the old middle class. Now in the mid-fifties, as a result of these forces and two others—full employment and rising wages—a class new to modern British history has emerged.

Over the years between 1940 and 1955 there was very little unemployment in Britain. The percentage of unemployment in 1940 was 6.4. Thereafter, under the special circumstances of the war, the percentage fell until in 1944 it was only 0.6. In the post-war years it rose slightly, but the highest figure was 3 per cent in 1947.

Simultaneously, wages rose. Using October 1938 for the base figure of 100, weekly average earnings in the principal industries rose to 176 in 1943, 229 in 1949, and 323 in 1954.

The new class resulting from these changes and the earlier political ones is composed mainly of the manual workers of British industry, better housed, better paid, and more secure than ever before in their history.

Definition of the new class from either a geographic or an economic point of view is difficult. In the 1930's there was an extensive redistribution of the British working population. Industries, heavy and light, began to spring up in places like Oxford and in the heart of hitherto largely rural counties like Berkshire and Northamptonshire. Tens of thousands of workers left their homes in slum areas or drab working-class neighborhoods and moved to new jobs in new industries. In the six years before the start of World War II more than 2,000,000 new houses were built in Britain. This was important in the resettlement of the industrial population. Equally important was the fact that over 500,000 of them were built and let by local government authorities who in turn were helped by the central government.

Subsidized housing had come to stay. In the decade since the war more than 2,000,000 new houses have been built. Of these about 1,600,000 are owned by local governments, which let them at low rents made possible by government subsidies.

Another development that benefited the new class was the advent of the New Towns. These are self-contained communities outside the great centers of population, complete with industries, schools, churches, hospitals, and public services. They are intended to draw people from the cities and conurbations, already too large, and establish them in the countryside.

The idea is old. Ebenezer Howard proposed it in 1898 and the proposal was promptly attacked as the spawn of the devil and his socialist friends. It was not until 1903 that Letchworth, the first of the New Towns, was established. But World War II impressed on both Socialist and Tory the wisdom of dispersing the industrial population, and in 1946 the House of Commons approved the New Towns Act. Today there are fourteen New Towns in Britain, eleven of them in England. None is complete, although workers are moving into them by the thousand.

Harlow, which occupies ten square miles of Essex, is the most advanced of the New Towns. Its present population is about 30,000. The target is around 80,000. The cost of this vast resettlement scheme is high. Thus far it has been about £112,000,000, approximately $313,600,000. Estimates indicate that more than double that sum will be needed to complete the New Towns.

The New Towns are by all odds one of the most interesting and imaginative developments in modern Britain. Their social and political consequences are almost incalculable. For the New Towns will continue to grow and to house a new class whose political and economic power will be a dominant factor in British society.

They will not be completed overnight. In most cases the rate of growth depends on the willingness of industry to build in the New Towns. Exceptions are towns like Newton Aycliffe and Peterlee in the North of England which have been built to house miners and their families. On the whole, however, industrial support has been encouraging. With the establishment of a new industry in a New Town more houses are built and schools, churches, shops, and parks constructed.

In the process hundreds of thousands of people are leaving the working-class sections of the Clyde or South Wales or London, trading tiny, old-fashioned flats or houses for well-designed houses. The children are going to schools that are new and not over-crowded. They are playing in fields rather than city streets.

But the New Towns are not the only factor in the emergence of the new class. In addition, there has been a steady increase in the construction of low-rent housing estates by local authorities. Incidentally, the people of the New Towns are sharply critical of ignoramuses who confuse them with the people of the housing estates. The housing estates are most often built on the fringes of big cities; the tall—for Britain—apartment houses rising in Wimbledon, outside London, are an example.

Each housing estate, when completed, siphons off some hundreds or thousands of Britain's slum population. In some cases, notably in east London south of the Thames, new housing estates have been built in the wastes left by German bombing.

As a consequence of these efforts by both Labor and Conservative governments to resettle the working class, Britain's slums are slowly disappearing. Of course many square miles of them remain, and any newspaper can publish photographs showing conditions of appalling filth and squalor. Yet a great deal has been done to destroy the slums. There remain, of course, the miles and miles of old working-class districts, shabby and dull, but these are part of the landscape of any industrial nation and it is probably impossible for any government, British or American or German, to eliminate them entirely.

The people of the New Towns, of the housing estates, and of the working class generally enjoy full employment and higher wages than they have ever dreamed of in their lives. Admittedly, prices have risen steadily since the war. But rents have not. In Norwich, for instance, there were in 1956 eight thousand council houses that rented at seven shillings, or ninety-eight cents, a week. The manual worker in British industry often pays only a nominal rent. The Welfare State has relieved him of the burden of saving for the education of his children or for medical care.

A skilled worker in industry may have a basic wage of £12 ($33.60) or £13 ($36.40) a week. Overtime work may raise the total to an average of £15 ($42.00) for a week's work. A worker at a similar job in a similar industry before the war was extremely fortunate if he made £4 a week.

Under these circumstances the buying spree on which the British people embarked in 1953 was inevitable. The new class had no need to save. The state took care of its welfare, and taxes were taken at the source under PAYE (Pay As You Earn). Workers had been fully employed for more than a decade. Now at last the shops were full, and the hucksters of installment buying, known in Britain as "buying on the Never-Never," were at every door.

One investigation of life in the New Towns revealed a typical weekly budget for necessities. The family spent £5 10 *s.*, or about $15.40, for food and household necessities. Rent and local taxes cost £2, or $5.60. Lighting and heating cost 10 *s.*, or $1.40, while the same amount went to clothes and repairs. Cigarettes took a pound, or $2.80, and the weekly installment on the television set was 15 *s.*, or $2.10.

Few things demonstrate more strikingly the change in the status of the British manual worker than his insistence on a television set as a "necessity." Cars, radios, and, earlier, gramophones were available only to the middle class or wealthy in pre-war Britain. For the first time they are within the range of the manual worker.

Few families budget the considerable sum spent each week on beer, the obligatory trips to the local movie theater, or gambling either through football pools or bets on horse races. But it is not unusual in these new circumstances to find men who spend £2 or £3 a week for such purposes. "Why the bloody hell not?" a worker in Liverpool asked. "I've got me job and I don't 'ave to worry." The permanence of his job and of high wages had become an accepted part of his life. He was one of those who had not been moved by the Labor Party's dire forebodings of unemployment and the dole under Conservative rule. To him these were as shadowy and distant as the Corn Laws and Peterloo.

The new class has money, security, and leisure: this is the promised land. According to theories of some reformers, the worker, freed from the oppression of poverty, should be expanding intellectually, worrying about the future of Nigeria rather than the football fortunes of Arsenal. My opinion is that the opposite is true, that with the coming of the good life the worker has gradually shed his responsibilities (some of these, in fact, have been stripped from him) and has lost the old desperate desire to improve his lot and make himself and his class the paramount political power in the land.

There is no need to save, for the state provides for all eventualities the worker can foresee. There is no compulsion to ensure that the children get an education that will enable them to rise above the circumstances of their parents. For the circumstances are so good, so unimaginably higher than those into which the fathers and mothers of this class were born, that there seems to be nothing further to be sought. Why should a boy be given a good education —"stuffing 'is head with a lot of nonsense 'e'll never use" was the way one father put it—when he can make £10 a week after a few years in a factory? The schools are there, they are free, but when the time comes the boy can leave the school and take up a man's work in the factory.

There seems to be a conviction among working-class mothers that a girl needs a little more schooling to fit her for an office job. But the men of the class, proud of the money they are earning and the "rights" their unions have won, see no virtue in an office job or the higher education that fits one for it.

For the manual worker has found security, and that is what he is interested in, that is what he has sought through the long, bitter history of industrial disputes in Britain. He is not interested in and he does not share the standards of the old middle class or even of the artisan class that preceded him.

Charles Curran, in a brilliant article on "The New Estate in Great Britain" in the *Spectator,* put it this way: "One word sums up the New Estate: the word 'security.' It is security in working-class terms, maintained and enforced by working-class methods. The traditional values of the middle and professional classes form no part of it; among wage-earners these values are meaningless.

"To the middle-class citizen, economic security is a goal to be reached primarily by personal effort. It is a matter of thrift, self-help, self-improvement, competitive striving. But the manual worker sees it differently. To him, any betterment in his conditions of life is essentially a collective process—something to be achieved not by himself as an individual but in company with his fellows. He will organize for it, vote for it, strike for it, always with them. It is 'Us' not 'I.' Eugene Debs, the American Socialist leader, put this attitude into one sentence when he said, 'I don't want to rise from the ranks; I want to rise with them.' "

In this psychological situation it is ludicrous to appeal for New Elizabethans among the men and women of the new class. For they have no great admiration for individual enterprise, for risk or sacrifice. Among the many men I have talked to in the New Towns, I never met one who was interested in saving enough money to buy his own small business, to strike out for himself. The ideal seemed to be a community of equals protected from economic dangers by full employment and high wages, politically lethargic, unstirred by Socialist or Tory. Everyone earned about the same amount of money, spent it on the same things, and appeared to think and talk alike.

Yet theirs is a nation that desperately needs the imaginative, inventive mind if it is to overcome its economic difficulties.

The paramount emphasis on security found among manual workers may be regrettable. But in view of Britain's past it is natural and understandable. These, after all, are the descendants of farm laborers who worked twelve hours a day and lived in hovels. The grandfathers and grandmothers of the young people in the New Towns knew the dank, dirty poverty of the slums of London and Liverpool. There must be among the miners at Peterlee men and women whose female ancestors dragged coal carts through mine tunnels on their hands and knees.

The new class begins with a strong bias in favor of the Labor Party. It is never allowed to forget the inhumanities of the past or the long struggle of the unions against entrenched capital. It is reminded at every election that all it has today is a result of the efforts of the Labor Party. This is not true, but we are talking about politics. Finally, in every new housing development or New Town there must be an aging group who remember with fierce-eyed resentment the long periods of unemployment and the marginal existence that were the lot of many working-class families a quarter of a century ago.

The Welsh, in particular, have never forgotten. And hundreds of thousands of bitter, talkative, excitable Welsh workers have left South Wales in the last twenty years to work in other parts of Britain, carrying with them their hatred of the Tories and their zeal for "the movement." When Aneurin Bevan, that most Welsh of Welshmen, describes the Tories as lower than vermin or genially compares them with the Gadarene swine, he is expressing a sentiment strongly held by a considerable percentage of his fellow countrymen.

The geographical redistribution of the working class altered the political map of Britain. Housing estates and New Towns introduced solid blocs of Labor votes into traditionally Tory constituencies. This was a factor in the Socialist victory of 1945 and it is still a factor today. The constituency of Melton, for instance, was long considered a safe Liberal seat. Then it became equally safe for the Conservatives. But the advent of a housing development and several thousand new votes made this rural constituency insecure. The influx of a new type of voter is one of the main reasons why this must now be considered a marginal constituency by the Tories.

But the effect of the geographical redistribution is being matched and balanced in many constituencies by the effect of their new economic status upon the voters of the working class. They now have something to conserve: jobs, good wages, pleasant homes. This does not mean an immediate conversion to Conservatism. Among many, particularly the older age groups, the memories of the past are still strong. But the achievement of a new economic status has resulted in a lessening of the fervor and energy for the Socialist cause. A class that puts security above everything else is not likely to be won by a Labor platform that endorses more nationalization and the ensuing upheaval in the British economy. Its younger members, many of whom have never been jobless, are unimpressed by dire prophecies of the return of the bad old days under Tory rule because they themselves have never experienced such a period.

Nor should we forget that in each general election the Conservative Party wins a substantial share of the working-class vote. Even in the catastrophe of 1945 the Conservatives estimate they won between 4,000,000 and 4,500,000 votes among manual workers. In 1951 about 6,000,000 electors of this group voted Tory.

Of course the vote for Labor rose too: it is estimated that in the general election of that year 52 per cent of the working class voted for Labor. But Labor was defeated by the coalition of middle-class and working-class votes for the Tories.

Nonetheless, the Tories continue to gain in the areas where the new working class has reached a new economic status. In 1945 the Labor Party won Chislehurst in Kent, normally a safe Conservative seat. The influx of working-class voters was the principal cause. Ten years later Chislehurst was safely back on the Conservative side.

The Conservative Party is thus faced with a difficult question. Like all major parties, it is a coalition of various economic and social interests. In the last decade a new interest, that of the working class, has become vital to the party. But the Conservative government's efforts to meet the wishes of that group, particularly its insistence on the continuation of the Welfare State, clashes directly with the interests of the old middle class, which has suffered a loss of social prestige, economic standing, and political influence at the hands of the working class.

The rebellion among Conservative voters of the middle class against the government's policies, reflected in their refusal to vote in by-elections, cannot go unchecked without damaging the Conservatives. That this is fully realized by the party leaders was shown by the warnings they gave the Tories against seduction by political groups of the extreme right.

What kind of people are the new working class? You will not find them portrayed in the novels of Angela Thirkell or, indeed, any other English novelist popular in America. But veterans of World War II may recognize them as the slightly older brothers of the British soldier they knew in Africa, Italy, and France.

They are not at all reserved; reserve is the province of the upper-middle-class Briton. They are friendly, incurious, and polite. For the first time in history they are satisfied with themselves and with their lot.

I mention this as a curiosity. When I first went to England to work before the war I was struck by the powerful interest shown in the United States. An American in a working-class pub was bombarded by queries about the organization of the unions, John L. Lewis, the absence of a labor party in the United States politics, the techniques of mass production in industry. The young men were eager to know and anxious to improve.

Today one encounters the same politeness but less interest. After the preliminary and obligatory question about the "Yank corporal" named Jackson who lives in Chicago and do you know him, the talk is likely to trail off into inconsequentials. The English, as opposed to the Scots, Welsh, and Irish, are a people notably difficult to arouse and, equally important, difficult to quiet once they are aroused. But in recent years the pubs have been quiet. The new working class has what it and its predecessors wanted. It is not excited either by the prospect of Tory rule or by the infiltration of the British Communists into the union structure.

It would be aroused, however, by any policy that appeared to endanger its new position. That is certain. And consequently both major parties will be circumspect in their approach to the new class.

Socially, the new class is modern. Increasingly it is making use of new techniques in living which were out of the economic range of its fathers and mothers. The old family life built around the kitchen and the pot of tea on the stove has been replaced by one built around the television set.

For the first time in their lives the young people of the New Towns and the housing estates have enough room in their homes to plan and build. The three-piece bedroom suite is as important as the television set as an indication of economic status. The "do it yourself" craze that swept the United States did not "catch on" among the working class in Britain for the simple reason that its members had always done it themselves. A great deal of the painting and decoration and some of the furniture-making is done by the man of the house in his spare time.

The class is not notably religious. The Catholics and the Methodists support their churches, but the response to other faiths is not ardent. The British are not "a pagan people," as some critics have charged, but there certainly is little enthusiasm for conventional religious forms.

The working class is a definable class. Thus it takes its place in the graduated ranks of British society. Within the class, however, there is very little snobbery. I have mentioned one instance: the resentment of the dwellers in the New Towns when they are classed with the people of the housing estates. But in a community in which all the men work in the same or similar factories and in which everyone knows almost to the penny what everyone else makes, pretense of economic superiority is difficult.

Here is the new British workingman. He moved to a New Town or a housing estate from a slum or near-slum. If he is in his late thirties or forties, he fought in the war and his wife knows more about the effect of high explosives, flying bombs, and rockets than most generals. He is living in what is to him comparative luxury: a living room, a clean and, by British standards, modern kitchen, a bedroom for the children, a modern bath and toilet. He can walk or cycle to his work, and if the weather is fine, he comes home for lunch. In the evening there is "the telly" or the football-pool form to be filled out or the new desk he is making for the children's room. Some two or three times a week he drops in at the "local," the neighborhood pub or bar, for a few drinks with friends from the factory. Even here his habits are changing. The actually potent "mild and bitter" or "old and mild" that was his father's tipple has been replaced by light ale—"nasty gassy stuff" the old-fashioned barmaids report.

It is a quiet life but to our subject a satisfactory one. He reads the *Daily Mirror* rather than the *Daily Herald,* which was his father's Bible, but he is only occasionally aroused by international problems. He did get excited about the idea of arming "those bloody Germans," but when the leaders of both the Conservative and Labor parties accepted the necessity he went along with German rearmament. But he was never particularly happy about it. In general, however, he is not interested in world affairs. There are one or two fellows at "the works," he will tell you, who get excited about China or Suez or Cyprus. Here it should be noted that he is more nationalist than internationalist. He doesn't like it when British soldiers are killed by the bombs of Greek Cypriotes, chiefly because the Army is no longer a professional force but one composed largely of conscripts of National Service. Young Tom from down the street, a nice lad, has gone out there with the Green Howards.

There he is: content, complete, complacent. His contacts with the rest of the world, British or foreign, are limited, and this is especially true of his contacts with the old middle class.

The old middle class itself is intensely interested in this new kind of working class. Partly this is true because the new class is blamed for many of the reverses that have fallen upon the middle class. Partly it is because of political spite. Partly it is jealousy. Whatever the dominant reason, the feeling is there, and the middle class, harking back to the first Socialist boasts in 1945 about remaking bourgeois Britain, will tell you: "They started it."

This class (here we are talking about the professional men, civil servants, Army, Navy, and Air Force officers, the higher but not the highest ranks of business and industry, the clergy of the Church of England, and the retired pensioners of these groups) fights hard to resist the uniformity that the last fifteen years have imposed upon it. It finds itself unable to organize to win higher salaries, and it knows that the taxation of the last decade has closed the gap between it and the new class of industrial workers. Finally, its more intelligent members are aware that it too is being challenged from within—that there is arising in its ranks a new group which from the economic standpoint can claim to be middle class but which has very little in common now, socially or politically, with the old middle class. Yet, as both groups claim a certain superiority over the class of manual workers, it is safe to predict that the two groups will unite and make common cause in defense of their standards. Interestingly, this is already happening in the field of education, where the sons of the physicists, engineers, and scientists who are among the leaders of the new middle class are going to the public schools that were one of the solid foundations of the old middle class.

Such schools, incidentally, are one of the bones of contention between the political leaders of the Labor Party, which represents the majority of the working class, and the old middle class. This class has pressed the Exchequer for a tax allowance for public schools—i.e., private education. The Socialists replied that such an allowance would be a private subsidy to a system that spreads inequality. To this the Tories of the old middle class retorted that part of the British freedom was the right of the parent to decide how and where his child was to be educated. They added a reminder that if the new working class were to save a bit on installment payments for television sets and the football pools, it too could send its sons to public schools. The answer, of course, is that the new working class cares little for schools, public or national.

The change in the composition of the middle class brought about by the introduction of new members reflects a change in Britain's industrial life and, to some extent, her position in the world. The administrators, managers, and technicians of the new industries such as plastics and electronics, the leaders in the newspaper, television, radio, and movie industries are becoming as important as the lawyers, judges, general officers, retired pro-consuls who once led the class. Just below these leaders is a steadily increasing group of newcomers to the class who have worked their way out of the working class since the war. Industrial designers and chemists, buyers, advertising men, production engineers—all these have come to the top.

This group reflects modern Britain and her problems. The colonial governor is less important to it than the expert on foreign markets. The scientist is infinitely more necessary to the country's progress than the soldier.

There is an important difference in income between the new entries into the middle class and the professional men who formed its backbone in the past. On the whole, the incomes of the new group are a good deal higher. It is engaged, for the most part, in industries, businesses, or quasi-public organizations that are expanding. Moreover, many of its members augment their incomes with expense accounts.

But these differences in types of activity and in income are only the beginning of the differences between the two segments of the middle class.

Many members of the new group have just arrived, pushed to the top by the necessities of war or of Britain's long economic struggle. The percentage of public-school graduates is lower than in the established middle class. Attention to that class's recognized totems is much less. The new group is less concerned with the Church of England, the Army and the Navy—the Air Force and the production of new weapons are, however, its special province —the Foreign Office and active politics. These it has left largely to the established middle class, and frequently the interests of the two groups clash. For example, the conflict within government between the traditionalist view of the Navy as vital to Britain's defense and the view that all that matters is the big bomber today and the intercontinental ballistic missile tomorrow is essentially a clash between two groups in the same class.

The new group is not primarily managerial, although managers make up a considerable percentage of its total. It includes a great many creative workers, architects, scientists and engineers, and a surprisingly high percentage of men who have risen without the aid of the Old School Tie.

The group has had less education and less leisure than the old middle class, and, consequently, its approach to culture is different. Its interest in the arts is limited, its taste in literature tends toward Nevil Shute rather than Thackeray. But it has a furious curiosity about Britain and the world: it devours magazine articles and books. Like the new working class, it has reached income levels that seemed out of sight fifteen years ago, but, unlike the new working class, it is not content to rest in its present position. For it knows enough of the world and the country to doubt that the present security is enough.

The middle class in Britain over the centuries has developed a marvelous capacity for altering while maintaining roughly the same façade. This process is going on now. The sons of the new group within the middle class are going off to public schools and Oxford and Cambridge rather than to state schools and the red brick provincial universities that trained their fathers. But because this group has an abiding interest in technical education, its members are anxious for the spread of such education in the old classical schools.

It should be noted that the trend toward the public schools and the great universities is not due entirely to snobbery. As an industrial engineer told me, "That's still the best education in the country, and my son's going to have it." He himself was the product of a state school and a provincial university. Obviously he enjoyed talking about his boy's public school.

Consequently, the two groups within the middle class are mixing slowly. But the old middle class is on the defensive; its standards are not those of the new group, and with the continued rise of the new group this defensiveness probably will remain. As Britain's world political and military responsibilities decline, the men and women charged with overseeing her new position as an exporting nation—in which salesmanship and industrial techniques are paramount—will find their importance increasing.

Once again we find a new group that, like the new kind of working class, has very little to do with Merrie England. Its roots are less deep. It is not intimately concerned with the institutions that the old middle class served. In its outlook toward the world it is much more realistic and modern. Yet it is gradually assuming the forms of the old middle class—the schools, the regiments, the clubs. These institutions inevitably will change as a result of the admission of the new group. However, if the outward form remains unchanged, the British will be content.

Politically the new group within the middle class began its

adult life well to the left of center. In the ten years since the war it has gradually shifted to the right. Young Conservative ministers like Iain Macleod and Reginald Maudling represent the ideas of the group, although they themselves are not of it. In general, the group admires tidy planning and crisp execution in government. Its shift away from Socialism probably began when many of its members realized that the execution of Labor's economic plans left a good deal to be desired and that some of the party's radicals were cheerfully advocating other plans—the further extension of nationalization, for instance—that might wreck an already delicately balanced economy. But the new group's support of the Conservative Party is far removed from the bred-in-the-bone, true-blue Conservatism of the old middle class. It is on the right at the moment because the Tories offer the greatest opportunity to the activities it represents.

The old middle class, based mainly on the professions and government service, is thus under pressure from the new middle class and from the new working class. Its importance in British society is diminishing because the former has a closer connection with what is immediately important to Britain's survival and because the latter will no longer accept leadership by the old middle class. It is important to note, however, that the ties between the new middle class and the new working class are more substantial. Many of the new middle class have risen from the urban working class in a generation. In regard to the technical aspects of industry, the two groups speak the same language.

The influence retained by the old middle class should not be underestimated, however. Especially in the countryside the lawyer, the vicar, the retired officer who is the local Justice of the Peace continue to wield considerable authority. And in clinging to traditional forms through two wars and the long night of austerity, the middle class has demonstrated its essential toughness.

The old middle class still reads *The Times* of London, that great newspaper, although you are liable to be informed in country drawing-rooms that *The Times* is "a bit Bolshie nowadays."

The forms and felicities of British life are encouraged and supported by the old middle class. The Church of England, the local Conservative Party fete, the gymkhana, the voluntary social services, the Old Comrades Associations of regiments owe their continued life to unstinting aid from the men and women of this class. It has had its periods of blindness (Munich was one), but it has never doubted where duty lay. When the war began in 1939—or, as its members would say, "when the balloon went up"—it sent away its sons and daughters and settled down to man the Home Guard and the civil-defense services. It suffered bombing and austerity, but it made certain that when the boys and girls came home there was a dance at the yacht club—some Polish sailors lived there during the war, and everyone pitched in to put it back in shape—and all the food the rationing would allow.

The positive characteristics of this class are impressive: its courage, its desire that each generation have a wider education and a greater opportunity, its cool calmness in the face of danger, its willingness to accept as a duty the responsibility for the lives of untaught millions living in famine and poverty and to labor for their welfare, its acceptance of the conviction of duty well done as the suitable reward for a lifetime of work. To me these seem to outweigh the pettiness, the snobbery, the overbearing self-confidence. No nation can do without such positive characteristics, and it will be a sorry day for Britain if the change in the middle class eliminates their influence on the country.

We Americans are fond of thinking of Britain as a settled, caste-ridden society. But at least two groups, the new middle class and the resettled working class, are on the move or have just moved into a new status, politically, economically, and socially. Moreover, one large class, the middle class, is in the process of changing. British society is much more mobile than it appears from the outside because of the Britons' desire to retain traditional forms while the substance changes.

As these changes take place, the value of many old indications of class change also. Accent remains one of the easiest methods for placing a Briton, but it is no longer an infallible guide. The effect of the BBC upon British speech has been considerable, and today the clerk in an obscure provincial shop may talk, if not in the accents of Eton, at least in a pleasant voice that reveals only a trace of provincial accent. The disappearance of old robust provincial accents would be a loss. And an acute ear in London can still, like Shaw's Professor Henry Higgins, place a Londoner in Wimbledon or Barnes or Stepney. It is the conviction of many Socialists that equality will never reign in Britain until there is a universal accent.

Clothes, too, are a much more accurate indication of class in Britain than in the United States. The derby or bowler is the almost universal headgear of the upper-class male in the city, with the cap for the country. The workingman affects a soft hat, sometimes a Homburg and often a cloth cap. The mass production of clothing came later in Britain than in the United States, but today the miner can be as warmly clothed as the banker. The difference lies in the styling given the banker's clothes by his London tailor. Then, too, the banker may be far more negligent in his dress than the miner: it is a mistake, if not a crime, in Britain for a member of the upper class to be too well dressed.

Nancy Mitford and Professor Alan Ross have made Americans aware of the infinite variations of U (upper-class) and Non-U (non-upper-class) phraseology in Britain, but many of the distinctions so carefully drawn are changing. A young lady of my acquaintance habitually uses "serviette" instead of "napkin," a crime Miss Mitford ranks just below arson and beating an old woman with a stick. As she goes to an expensive and very U school, the young lady was queried about her choice of words. No one, she reported, had ever heard of Miss Mitford at her school, and what did it matter anyhow?

There has been no mention of the aristocracy in this long chapter, which will probably offend readers whose views on Britain have been formed by the Merrie England school of writing. The fact is that the aristocracy does not rate a great deal of space in a book dealing with modern Britain.

The real aristocracy of Britain was composed of the great landowning families whose power began to decline with the rise, at the start of the nineteenth century, of the great industrial and commercial families. The remaining British servants of the old school —the best judges extant of who is and who is not an aristocrat— are inclined to look down their noses at the pretensions of Johnny-come-latelies who earned their titles by services, usually financial, to political parties, or by the proprietorship of chain stores. To them the people who count are the old families and the old names —Derby, Norfolk, Salisbury.

Inheritance taxes, the import of foreign foodstuffs, reckless spending all contributed to the reduction of the aristocracy's position. One reason why the institution of monarchy is supported by most and tolerated by some Socialists is that the Crown does not command the immediate allegiance of a large, influential, and moneyed aristocracy. There is no court party between the Crown and the people. The rulers of Britain have become progressively more popular with the common man as the influence of the real aristocracy declined. Of course, that influence has been exerted in a different way. Two recent Conservative Prime Ministers have been of aristocratic birth. Sir Winston Churchill was born the grandson of a duke; he was offered a dukedom on his retirement in 1955 and characteristically refused it. Sir Anthony Eden comes of an aristocratic North Country family one of whose members was a colonial governor in Maryland. They headed a Conservative Party that was middle class rather than aristocratic.

A few members of the old aristocracy strive to continue life as their fathers and grandfathers knew it, but they fight a losing battle. The opening of the great country houses to the public, the most desperate expedients to cut down spending so that the heir can enter the Guards and the daughter enjoy a proper introduction to London society cannot compensate for the taxation and for the changes in the character of British society and in the world.

The aristocracy, the real aristocracy, makes its presence felt in modern Britain only when such men as Lord Salisbury or Lord Mountbatten leave the peaceful countryside and contend with the active body of Britons.

The moment of a significant decline in the aristocracy's position has seen a gallant defense of it in literature. Both Miss Mitford and Evelyn Waugh have expounded its virtues of courage and responsibility in war. The "damn your eyes, follow me, I'm going to do what's right" idea always appeals powerfully to those who reject thinking for themselves. It is easy for an author to poke fun at the sober civil servant or the earnest trade-unionist dropping his *h*'s, but in modern Britain they are far more important than Lord Fortinbras.

For, as we have seen, this is a society in the throes of change. New groups are rising to the top just as, and frequently because, Britain's survival demands new habits, new enterprises. Individual members of the declining classes who adapt themselves to the changing times will survive. Lord Salisbury, bearer of an ancient name, presides over Britain's entry into the age of nuclear fission. But those who cannot adapt will slowly disappear.

In all this change there is strength. Britain's hope for the future lies in her ability, proven in the past, to change to meet new conditions. The nation that has emerged since 1945 is the product of greater changes than Britain has ever known. There are weak spots—the lack of individual enterprise on the part of the working class is certainly one. But the changes so bitterly resented by many are the best reason for optimism concerning Britain's destiny in this century's struggle with totalitarian powers.

VIII. *The British and the World*

The tumult and the shouting dies;
The Captains and the Kings depart.

RUDYARD KIPLING

We have no eternal allies and no perpetual enemies; our interests are eternal, and those interests it is our duty to follow.

LORD PALMERSTON

MORE THAN any other Western European nation, Britain has been involved in mankind. Geography placed these islands on one of the main routes between the Old World and the New. Ambition, avarice, and absent-mindedness combined to create the greatest of modern empires. Knaves and heroes, sinners and saints, fools and wise men took the blunt Saxon tongue across the snarling seas and into silent jungles. Now the Empire nears its end. But the drain of two world wars and the changes in the world make it more vital than ever to Britain that she remain a leader of international intercourse—a trader, a diplomat, a financial clearing-house for much of the world.

In discussing Britain's relations and attitudes toward other peoples, the whole field of international relations and diplomacy, we enter an area in which the British feel they are experts. This is a view hotly opposed by the piously patriotic operatives of the U.S. Department of State, but perhaps there is something behind the complacent British assumption. It is difficult otherwise to understand how this comparatively small island people built a world empire and held it despite the attempts of some of the greatest conquerors of modern times to seize it.

One of the most interesting contrasts in British life is that between the nation's world-wide interests and responsibilities and the strong strain of xenophobia in the national character. "Niggers begin at Calais" is only one expression of the Englishman's dislike for all foreigners, Froggies, Eyeties, Boches, and Russkis. I remember a slight shock at hearing one of the most eminent of British statesmen ask what "the Froggies" were up to. Similarly, the British working class, supposedly friendly to its comrades in other lands, has been remarkably cool toward inclusion of Polish or Hungarian refugees in its ranks.

There is a strong strain of isolationism in Britain. Usually dormant, it flowered late in 1956 after condemnation of the United Kingdom by the United States and other members of the United Nations. In periods of crisis the British have often been alone. In 1940 the surrender of France left the British without a major European ally. Physically this was a grievous blow. Psychologically it rallied the people. In the past there has been considerable agitation in British politics against imperialism. Overseas investment and new export markets in overseas colonies made imperialism important. But the "Little Englanders" persist. Their heir is the man who wants the British government to get out of the United Nations, NATO, SEATO, and the rest, and concentrate on Britain.

Britain's relations with the rest of the world are most important to us in the United States in six major areas: the Soviet Union and the Communist satellites in Eastern Europe; Communist China;

Western Europe; the Middle East; and, lastly and most important, the United States.

Few aspects of Britain's position in the world are as little understood in the United States as relations between the Commonwealth and the mother country. This is a failing that irritates the British. "Do you know what they asked me in Chicago?" a British author said. "They asked me why we didn't stop taxing the Canadians to buy jewels for the Queen!"

Ignorance is not confined to the United States. One British diplomat who had dealt with Russian diplomats and officials for years reported that it was not until the summit conference at Geneva in the summer of 1955 that the Russians showed any glimmering of understanding of what the Commonwealth was and how it worked.

The Commonwealth evolved from the Empire. Its original members were the older colonies settled by Britons and Europeans: Australia, New Zealand, Canada, and South Africa. Its newer members are Asian or African peoples whose countries were parts of the Empire and are now sovereign within the Commonwealth; these include India, Ceylon, Pakistan, and Ghana. It is a matter of fact that in the years since 1945, while the supposedly anti-imperialist Russians have been establishing the rule of the red star over 100,-000,000 souls, the British have created out of their Empire sovereign states with populations of over 500,000,000.

The Commonwealth is not "run" by anyone. But Britain, as the mother country, as the source of political forms and constitutional ideas, financial support and industrial exports, can claim to be the first among equals. The ties that bind the members of the Commonwealth to Britain vary in strength. And the ties between such Commonwealth members as South Africa and India are virtually nonexistent. The common purpose of preserving peace and the necessity of discussing common problems bring the leaders of the Commonwealth together in London periodically for conferences.

Despite the absence of a central ruling power, the system

works fairly well. In Britain and among the older members of the Commonwealth there is a strong loyalty, almost a reverence, for the idea. The political orators who describe the Commonwealth as "a great force for peace and civilization" are speaking to a responsive audience. Because there is no central power, Americans are prone to doubt the strength of the ties that connect the nations. But it may be that today the very absence of such a power strengthens the Commonwealth.

Strong economic links exist between the United Kingdom and the members of the Commonwealth. As a basis there is the sterling area, in which all the Commonwealth countries except Canada are joined with Burma, Iceland, Iraq, the British Protected States in the Persian Gulf, the Irish Republic, Jordan, and Libya. These countries contain one quarter of the world's population and do one quarter of its trade.

Membership in the sterling area or sterling bloc, as it is sometimes called, means that the greater part of the overseas trade of member countries is financed in sterling. The members maintain their foreign reserves largely in the form of sterling and maintain a fixed relationship between their own currencies and sterling. For the most part, they sell their earnings in foreign currency to the United Kingdom Exchange Equalization Account for sterling, and they can purchase for sterling such foreign currency as they need. The members also sell gold in the London market for sterling, and the United Kingdom's purchases of gold are held in the Exchange Equalization Account. The gold and dollars in this account constitute the central gold and dollar reserves of the sterling area.

The sterling area thus is an important means of maintaining Britain's position as the banker of the Commonwealth and as the center of financial transactions. It is also one of the chief markets for British exports, taking roughly half of Britain's export total. Of the Commonwealth countries, Australia is by far the biggest buyer. In 1955 Australia bought from Britain goods valued at £286,400,-000, or about $801,920,000—just under 10 per cent of Britain's

total export trade. Four of the five next biggest buyers of British
goods were also Commonwealth nations: South Africa, third; Canada, fourth; New Zealand, fifth; India, sixth. The United States was
the second-largest purchaser, taking 6.6 per cent of Britain's total
exports.

Britain, of course, buys extensively within the Commonwealth.
In the same year she imported goods valued at £1,888,200,000,
or about $5,286,960,000, from the Commonwealth and the Irish
Republic. This amounted to over half of Britain's total imports.

There are numerous irritations and imperfections in the conduct of this great world trading concern. The Australians and New
Zealanders, for instance, complain often that British capital shies
from investment in their countries.

The huge British investments for the development of countries
overseas were among the most damaging losses in two world wars.
As the nation slowly recovered its economic health in the post-war
years, overseas investment was encouraged by successive governments. Many Commonwealth officials say that, although private
borrowing for development has been encouraged, much more could
be done.

The Capital Issues Committee, an independent group of seven
men experienced in finance, commerce, and industry, approved in
1953 to applications for the investment of £40,000,000, or about
$112,000,000, for Commonwealth development. The next year the
figure rose to £48,000,000, or about $134,000,000. Compare this
with the annual net investment overseas of about $504,000,000 in
the years 1951–3. Evidently the Australians and New Zealanders
have cause for complaint.

In contrast to commercial ties that transform credit in London
into new factories in western Australia, there is the emotional tie
mentioned earlier. The Crown's mysterious power to draw peoples
as dissimilar as the Australian cattleman and the Brighton clerk
into a community of patriotic loyalty cannot be denied. Whether in
the next decade or so the same sort of connection can be established

between the Crown and such sensitive newer members of the Commonwealth as India and Ceylon is one of the most delicate questions facing British statecraft.

A host of other institutions—some official, others the work of private individuals captured by the Commonwealth conception—strive to keep the relations between Britain and the Commonwealth countries happy and firm. In such dissimilar fields as the theater, literature, and sport there is much more contact among the countries of the Commonwealth and Empire than Americans realize. A British rugby football team tours Australia or South Africa, a West Indian cricket team visits Britain. British theatrical companies still make the long but financially rewarding trip to play in Australia and New Zealand. British authors tirelessly roam the provinces of Canada or India, discoursing at length upon the merits of the mother tongue and its literature.

Many young Conservative Members of Parliament are convinced that the Commonwealth is the great twentieth-century instrument for maintaining and extending British prestige. They see it expanded from its present form to include the Scandinavian countries and others in a world confederation that will be not *a* third force in the world but *the* third force. They do not, however, discount the problems that plague the Commonwealth now.

An economic problem is the filtration of American capital into the Commonwealth. The British recognize the enormous potential of American overseas investment, and they wonder what would happen to their position in a Commonwealth country where the United States invested heavily and purchased products with a free hand. The knowledge that the United States could, if it wished, literally buy out the Commonwealth is a patriotic incentive for greater British investment.

Two political problems are South Africa and Ceylon.

The National Party in South Africa is moving toward the establishment of a republic and the progressive weakening of political and economic ties with Britain. Complete independence of the Crown and the Commonwealth probably is the ultimate South

African aim. This would be a grievous blow to the strength, both economic and political, of the Commonwealth.

Ceylon has shown signs of moving in the same direction. One of the first actions of the government of S. W. R. D. Bandaranaike, the leader of the Sri Lanka Freedom Party, was to ask the British to leave the great naval base at Trincomalee. This was a severe shock to the British and a damaging blow to the position of the Western world in the Indian Ocean. At the subsequent Commonwealth Conference an agreement that allowed the British to remain temporarily was negotiated. But the restlessness of Ceylon within the Commonwealth and the desire of many of its leading politicians to divest themselves of all connections, cultural as well as political, with the British are a bad omen for the future.

The British attitude toward the Commonwealth and Empire is a curious mixture of indifference and interest, snobbery and friendship, ignorance and knowledge. But the general approach has improved greatly since before the war. The British know they need their friends and markets overseas, and the old brusque approach to Commonwealth and Empire problems has changed.

So has the social attitude. Not long before the war an elderly and aristocratic lady told me she always "considered Americans as colonials." She thought she had paid us a compliment. Today such a remark would not be made.

The idea of a world-wide Commonwealth is imaginative and attractive. But the efforts to sell it to the people of Britain, with the exception of the almost daily exhortations of Lord Beaverbrook's newspapers, are depressingly feeble. The English Speaking Union and other organizations are devoted to the cause of strengthening Commonwealth relations, but such organizations usually preach to the converted. The great mass of public opinion has yet to be stirred. The British of all classes are much more likely to be moved by events in France than by events in Canada or Nigeria.

"They certainly have a different idea of dealing with the Russians here," said the young wife of an American diplomat in 1954. "Why, they have track meets with Russians running in them, and they talk about how they're going to get the Russians to agree to this or that. Folks at home think all the Russians have horns and tails."

She was describing the British ability to live with a problem while thoroughly understanding its dimensions and dangers. Since 1945 the leaders of Britain, Socialist and Tory alike, have been fully aware of the dangers to Western freedom of Russian Communist imperialism. This statement may evoke criticism from some stout Republicans who regard the British Labor Party as an offspring of the Communist Party. But the facts are that it was a Labor government that sent troops to Korea, that carried on a long and successful campaign against the Communists in Malaya, that joined the Royal Air Force with the United States Air Force to build the air bridge that broke the Berlin blockade, and that passed what was then the largest peacetime armaments bill in British history. All these measures were part of the general effort to bolster the defenses of Western Europe against Soviet aggression.

These exertions were a severe burden on a country whose economy was already in difficulties and whose resources were strained. They were undertaken because they matched the resolution of the leaders of the Labor Party. They were heartily endorsed by the Conservative Party, then in opposition, and were continued by that party when it came to power in 1951.

The point of difference between the British and Americans was that at the height of the cold war the British never moved toward abandonment of normal diplomatic intercourse and welcomed any move by either side which promised closer contact and friendlier relations with the Soviet Union.

Socialist and Tory governments pursued this dichotomy in policy with almost complete freedom from political interference. The British, an island people dependent on international trade, strive in any crisis to maintain communications with their enemies and thus retain a means through which negotiations can be carried out. They will go to great, often shaming lengths to avoid war. Once it comes, they wage it with earnest intensity and fight it to the end.

In periods of danger such as followed the influx of Soviet power in Europe, British politicians usually assume a bipartisan attitude. This does not mean that the opposition of the time refrains from criticism of the government policy. It does mean that opposition speakers use restraint. During the period of maximum strain with Russia, no politician shrilled a warning against talking with the Russians about Berlin or Korea, or predicted that the admission of Russian high-jumpers to a track meet would undermine the nation. The British never gave up on the situation; they did not like it, but they thought that any means of finding a way out should be used.

This was, as I have noted, a period of danger. The bipartisan approach broke down completely over Suez. When Sir Anthony Eden ordered intervention in Egypt the danger was real but indistinct. It was also a long-term economic danger arising from threat to the country's oil supplies rather than the immediate military danger represented by the Soviet Union's military strength in East Germany and elsewhere in Central Europe accompanied by Russian diplomacy and subversion. Russian military power already had won its foothold in Egypt. But the Labor Party refused to regard this power as an immediate threat and consequently rejected it as a reason for the adoption of a bipartisan approach.

The British people have never been so violently anti-Russian as the Americans. There is a distinction between anti-Russian and anti-Communist. Communism has had few more bitter opponents than Ernest Bevin or Herbert Morrison, two leaders in the post-war Labor government. They represented elements of the movement which for decades had been fighting in the unions and in the constituency parties to prevent the Communists from winning control of the Trades Union Congress and the Labor Party. But neither the leaders nor the led could be called anti-Russian.

The war alliance with the Soviet Union meant far more to Britons than the military co-operation between the Soviet Union and the United States during the same period meant to Americans. The British attitude was rooted in the situation of June 1941 when the Germans turned east and attacked the Soviet Union.

The British had then been fighting the Germans and the Italians single-handed for a year. Their cities had been bombed, their armies and navies grievously punished in France, Norway, Libya, and Greece. Each month the German submarines in the North Atlantic were bolder and more numerous and the toll of shipping losses was higher. Most Britons knew they had stout friends in the United States, but the wiser also recognized the strength of isolationist sentiment. And, although American industrial mobilization was gaining momentum, that would not avert another Coventry tonight or another Dunkirk tomorrow.

Suddenly all this altered. Russia, which had sided with Germany for two years and had gobbled up parts of Finland, Poland, and Romania as her reward, was invaded. Overnight the British became willing to overlook the despicable role Russia had played in the first two years of the war. Here, at last, was an ally. An ally, moreover, that fought, that was undergoing the same punishment Britain had known.

Naturally this warm admiration for the Russian war effort and this sympathy for the Russian people offered an opportunity for the British Communists, who exploited it to the utmost. Propaganda from the Soviet Union portrayed life there in glowing terms. The British working class was informed that this was a working-class war—a few months earlier the Communists had been calling it a capitalist war—and that side by side the British and Russian "brothers" would fight it to a successful conclusion.

The propaganda would not have made much headway, however, had it not been for the basic strain of admiration and sympathy which existed. The decade of cold war which included the rape of Czechoslovakia, the Berlin blockade, and the Korean war obviously altered the British working-class attitude toward Russia. But some of the old wartime feeling remained. It is there yet in the minds of the working class, tucked behind the football scores and the racing tips: the Russians didn't let us down, they went on fighting, they must be like us, they can't want another war.

The changes in Soviet leadership and tactics since the death of Stalin have affected the British approach to Russia and Communism. In Britain, as elsewhere, the immediate danger has receded. The East is slowly opening up. This means a great deal more to Britain than to the United States.

Trade is the answer. The British want to expand their trade with the Soviet Union and with China. Again, as in their diplomatic relations, this does not mean that they approve of Communism in either country. But they live by trade, and they must take it wherever they find it. To British industrialists and British ministers the Soviet Union and Eastern Europe represent a market for industrial products and a possible source of raw materials. However, they are wary of Russian methods of business. The initial approach has been circumspect. The British do not wish to throw everything onto one market; they would infinitely prefer an expansion of trade with the United States. Nor will they sell to the Soviet Union one or two models of each type which the industrious Russians can then mass-produce for themselves. Finally, although Britain and other European nations are restive under embargo restrictions on the sale of certain strategic goods, the Conservative government has no intention of breaking these restrictions under the encouragement of Mr. Khrushchev's smile.

The visits to Britain of a succession of delegations from the Soviet government and of three top-ranking ministers—Nikita Khrushchev, First Secretary of the Communist Party, Premier Nikolai Bulganin, and Deputy Premier Georgi Malenkov—fanned British interest if not enthusiasm.

Much has been written about the effect of these visits on the British public. Indeed, the faint hearts in Congress seemed to think that they would result in the immediate establishment of a Communist regime in Britain. But it appeared to many who had frequent contacts with "Krush and Bulge," as the British called them, that the greatest effect of the visit was on the Russians themselves. Like

Malenkov before them, the Communist boss and the head of the government encountered a prosperous, vigorous democracy. To anyone accustomed to the crudity and ugliness that express Russia's raw strength, industrial Britain was a revelation. Here were huge, new, clean factories set in the midst of comfortable towns enclosed by green fields and parks.

"We'll have all this one day in Russia," Khrushchev said to one of his hosts. "But it takes time."

The British poured out to see the visitors. But it was symptomatic of the maturity of public opinion that in London and the other great cities, the Communists failed to generate any wild enthusiasm for the Soviet leaders. On the contrary, they were met in most cases with stolid, disapproving silence interspersed by volleys of boos.

Yet because the British were never so excited about the possibility of war with the Soviet Union as were the Americans, there is and will be in Britain greater willingness to accept the Russians at their own valuation. Also, the British working class is far more interested in the Soviet Union than American labor is.

To the American workingman there is nothing especially novel in the description of huge enterprises breaking new ground in virgin territory. Americans have been doing that sort of thing for a century. But to the Briton, accustomed to an economy severely circumscribed by the geographical limitations of his island, these Soviet enterprises have the fascination of the unknown. So he marvels over the pictures and the text in the magazines issued by the Russian and satellite governments.

This propaganda is intended, naturally, to divert the reader's mind from the innumerable cruelties that have accompanied the building of the Soviet state by impressing him with a glowing account of the results. Here, as elsewhere, the Russians underestimate their critics, of whom the British workingman is one. People do not easily forget cruelty, even if it has not been practiced on them.

"Certainly, I'm a trades-union man *and* a good socialist," a printer said to me during the Khrushchev-Bulganin visit. "That's why I 'ate these bleeders. What they've done to the unions in Russia wants talking abaht, chum. Know what I 'ates most about them? It's them arsing around our country with a lot of coppers with them, the bleeders. We don't want none of that 'ere."

Finally, we come to a factor of great importance in molding British attitudes toward the Soviet Union. This is the large group of teachers, writers, editors, movie-directors, and radio and television workers who have been powerfully influenced either by Communism or by the results of a Communist society in the Soviet Union. Proportionately, this group is larger than its counterpart in the United States. It has never been drastically reduced in numbers by the pressure of public opinion. Outside of the "sensitive" departments of government, no great stigma is attached to membership in the Communist Party in Britain.

Politically, Britain is deeply and justly concerned with the liberties of the subject. Consequently, any discrimination by the government against Communists evokes the wrath of politicians and public bodies unconnected with Communism. This is true even when the government seeks to eliminate a known Communist from a "sensitive" department. The question is not whether Communism threatens Britain. The British know that it does, and they are prepared to fight it. But Britain's place in world society, it is reasoned, would be threatened even more if the liberties of the subject were endangered. The view that only a truly free society is capable of defeating Communism transcends party lines in Britain.

It is important to remember that the powerful influence of Communism on this heterogeneous group has affected it in two ways. Such people as Malcolm Muggeridge, the editor of *Punch,* were once sympathetic to Communism and are now among its best-informed and sharpest critics. In Britain, as in the United States, there are apostates who have turned from Communism and who now attack it. But their attacks, though often brilliant, command less attention in Britain than in the United States. This may be because the British never were so excited about the cold war as we were in the United States (after all, they were grappling with pressing economic problems). It may be because the British have scant respect for those who betray causes and then make money out of it.

On the whole, however, the group influenced by the Soviet Union exerts its influence to create friendlier relations between Britain and the Soviet Union. In its attitude toward the United States this group is sensitive, critical, and quite often abysmally ignorant.

The virtues and defects of the Soviet Union and the United States thus are weighed in public by an influential group that has already been tremendously impressed either by communism as a political creed or by the industrial, military, or diplomatic achievements of the Soviet state. They are receptive to news of Russia and, in many cases, remarkably uncritical. Indeed, they are generally less skeptical and critical in their approach to the Soviet Union than they are to the problems of Germany or the United States. One of their favorite sayings is "Let's try and keep an open mind about Russia."

In the battle for men's minds, this is a serious situation. It means that a considerable proportion of what Britons read, of what young Britons learn, of what the whole nation sees or hears through mass communication media is prepared by people whose attitude toward Russian claims and policies is less skeptical than it should be. On the other hand, the danger has been exaggerated by anxious Americans.

Since 1950 these fields of endeavor have been invaded by a group of young men and women much more favorably inclined to conservatism and modern capitalism than the group influenced by Russia. Some of them have been to the United States and are able to refute the anti-American charges of the other group with firsthand knowledge. Most of them developed intellectually in the period when the Russian danger overshadowed Europe, and they are not prone to make excuses for the Soviets.

Moreover, they are strongly influenced by the marked recrudescence of national feeling in Britain. Perhaps this is a revulsion from the internationalism of the group influenced by Russia. Perhaps it reflects a desire to do something about Britain's waning prestige in the world. Sometimes it indicates a new and welcome preoccupation with the political possibilities of an enlarged Commonwealth. Whatever the cause, it adds to the vitality of British thought. And it is healthy for the country that its young people should be interested in British development of nuclear energy rather than in Magnetogorsk or TVA.

The British attitude toward Communist China is unaffected by emotional memories of a war alliance, as in the case of the Soviet Union, or the sense of guilt regarding the conquest of China by the Communists which affects some Americans. Chiang Kai-shek was never a public hero during the war, as Tito and Stalin were. The London representatives of the great Anglo-Chinese trading firms might portray Chiang as the hope of the West in China, but the British people were not convinced.

Although the British military effort in the Korean war was considerably larger than Anglophobes would have Americans believe, the war's effect on the British was a good deal less. There has never been any sustained public outcry against Britain's recognition of the Chinese government. The danger of a Communist invasion of Formosa did not stir the British. When such an invasion seemed likely, the Conservative government faced a difficult situation: would the British people, in the event of war between China and the United States, have followed the Americans into the conflict?

The present British interest in Communist China is largely commercial. No one entertains the happy belief that the Communist regime can be overthrown—certainly not by Chiang and his aging forces. What the British want from Comrade Mao is more trade. If they get it and trade expands, the process will reflect not a national attraction to Communism but a restatement of the familiar British position that theirs is a trading nation which, in its present circumstances, must find commerce where it can.

There would be no great opposition to China's entry into the

United Nations. Again, this would not reflect admiration for communism. For many reasons the British doubt the effectiveness of the United Nations. One reason is that a nation of over 500,000,-000 people has no representation in the UN's councils.

The relationship between the French and the British is a fascinating one. For nearly a thousand years these two peoples have faced each other across the channel. During that period, in Britain at least, there has developed a curious love-hate relationship. By turns loving, exasperated, and enraged, the British think of the French as a man might think of an affectionate but wayward mistress.

In June of 1940, when the world between the wars was being shaken to bits, the fall of France shocked and saddened the British as did no other event of those terrible days. I remember that while waiting in the Foreign Office, the morning after my return from France, I saw an elderly official, a man with a brittle, cynical mind, walk down the corridor with tears streaming down his face. There was no recrimination. All he could say was: "Those poor people —God, how they must be suffering!"

Few enemy actions during the war distressed the British as much as the decision to attack the French fleet at Oran. Few postwar diplomatic achievements gave them more pleasure than the re-establishment of the old alliance with France. The rise and fall of French governments, the convulsions of French politicians are watched in Britain sometimes with anger and harsh words but never without an underlying sympathy.

Perhaps because of the alliance in two world wars or perhaps because France offers such a complete change from their own islands, the British know France very well, far better than they know the United States or some nations of the Commonwealth. This is true of all classes of Britons.

The elderly doctor or retired officer of the middle classes will spend his holidays at an obscure resort on the coast of Brittany. Before the war a Continental holiday was one of the indications of middle-class status. Today the Continental holiday is within the financial reach of the working class. The conductor on the bus I sometimes take to work was full of his plans this spring for "me and the missus" to motorcycle from Boulogne to the Riviera. Thousands like him tour France in buses or spend vacations not in Blackpool but in a French seaside resort.

The national attitude ranges from tolerance to affection. I do not believe, however, that the British respect the French as they do the Germans or the Russians. The mutiny in the French Army in 1917, the catastrophe of 1940, the Anglophobia of the Vichy government ended, probably permanently, popular British reliance on France as a powerful ally in world affairs. When the Suez crisis arose in 1956 and the governments of Sir Anthony Eden and Guy Mollet hastened to reinvigorate the alliance, their efforts awoke little response in Britain. "Now that we're in this thing, we have to go on and win it," a friend said. "But think of being in it with the French, especially these French—Mollet, Pineau, and Bouges-Manoury." He made a sound more customary in Ebbets Field than in a London club.

The British are amused by the French (the French, of course, are even more amused by the British). Sometimes it seems that every Englishman of a certain age and financial position has his own "secret" village where the Hotel de la Poste provides a good dinner for five hundred francs. Britons have great knowledge and affection for France born of contact in two wars, but they do not rely on the French.

For other reasons the British hesitate to rely on the Germans. Two generations of Britons have learned that the Germans are a tough, resolute, and courageous people, characteristics admired in Britain. But the British groups devoted to furthering friendship between the two peoples are fighting a losing battle. There is among all classes in Britain an underlying distaste for the Germans. This feeling is not often expressed, but it is there, as it is in most countries in Western Europe. The attitude is a factor in the relationship between Western Europe and the key question facing the continent as a whole: Germany's ultimate reunification.

The Germans, a singularly obtuse people in judging the reasons for foreign attitudes toward Germany, are inclined to believe that British mistrust is tied to the two world wars and the decline of British power. This is inaccurate. British mistrust and dislike of Germany have political rather than military roots. Both the Kaiser's imperialism of 1914 and Nazi imperialism in 1939 were seen not as overwhelming threats to Britain alone but as dangers to the democratic system of the West under which she had flourished. The horrors of the concentration camps, the solemn lunacies of Hitler and his court, the death of personal and political liberty—all these were factors more important than military posturing. Finally, the British do not consider the Germans politically stable, and they are suspicious—perhaps too much so—of German ambitions and intentions.

Repeatedly this has affected British politics. The great prewar debate in foreign affairs was waged between those who, like Churchill, were not willing to trust the Germans and those who, like Chamberlain, were. Since the end of World War II the international political issue that generated the most heat in Britain was the debate over the rearmament of Germany. One effect of this debate was the emergence of the Bevanites in the Labor Party as a political force. Aneurin Bevan believed that German rearmament would unite the pacifists, old anti-fascists, and others as no other issue could. He was correct. The leadership of Clement Attlee was gravely endangered for a time when the party officially supported arms for the nation's former enemies.

The State Department and other American officials have taken the position that British opposition to German rearmament was the product of wild-eyed agitators on the left and had no popular support. This was an inaccurate, even a dangerous attitude. Field Marshal Lord Wavell opposed it. So did Viscount Norwich, who as Alfred Duff Cooper had allied himself with Churchill in the latter's long fight against the appeasement policy of Chamberlain and Baldwin.

For the time being, the issue is dead. Germany is being rearmed. But the excitement the issue provoked testified to the abiding British uneasiness about Germany. This concern centers upon the prospect that West Germany will someday succumb to Russian enticement, be united with East Germany, and leave NATO. A permanently divided Germany may be a danger to peace, but few Britons outside the Foreign Office see it that way. Two wars have come out of a united Germany.

The attitude of the upper-class Englishman toward people of the same class in Germany has altered since the war. Before World War I, and in the long week-end between the wars, upper-class Germans and Britons mingled a good deal. Ties of affection and respect were created. "I can't stand this feller Hitler," you were told, "but I know old Von Schlitz, and he's a first-rate chap. You can trust the Prussians." But in the end Von Schlitz and his friends, with a few honorable exceptions, threw in their lot with the Nazis. When the British see old Von Schlitz nowadays they wonder what deceits, what cruelties, what moral compromises he has countenanced to survive and prosper.

Seen from this background, the British acceptance of a Western policy that rebuilt German industry into Britain's leading competitor for export markets and created a strong state in the Federal Republic of West Germany was a remarkable victory of the head over the heart. The policy was accepted because the British saw that the Soviet Union under Stalin was the greater, more immediate threat. Any relaxation of that threat is bound to affect the British attitude toward Germany and her ambitions.

The mutual affection of the British and the Italians was interrupted but not broken by the second war. To a somewhat dour, unemotional people the Italians and their land have an irresistible attraction. Even when the war was at its worst the British regarded the Italians with rueful perplexity: how could such an amusing, gracious people be so deluded by Mussolini? Surely everything would be all right once Mussolini was eliminated.

Characteristically, when he was eliminated many British objected to the summary nature of his execution. They would not blink an eye when military necessity required the destruction of the German city of Kassel. But they did not like the picture of their old enemy, who had vilified them and attacked them when it hurt the most, strung up by his heels outside a gas station.

Now all is forgiven and almost forgotten. Each year the earnest tourists pour southward to Rome, Florence, Venice. In the autumn they come home to their fog-shrouded islands bringing with them memories of long, sunny days.

The British attitude toward Italy and the Italians is symbolized by their view of Italian Communism. They are not oblivious to the dangers of Communism in Italy or elsewhere. But they find it difficult to regard the Italians, communist, fascist, or republican, as serious factors in world affairs. As only a few Italians seem to desire such a position, and as the British are too polite to discuss the matter, all goes well.

The traveling Briton has lost his old status in Europe. The British tourist with his limited allowance of francs, marks, or lire is no longer the "milord" of the nineteenth century. That role, with its privilege of being the target for every taxi-driver's avarice, now belongs to the Americans.

During the peak years of the cold war between 1945 and 1953, Western Europe was threatened by military attack from Russia. The power to whom the Europeans looked primarily was not Britain but the United States. It is a disheartening reflection that, despite this military dependence, successive American administrations failed to create the reservoir of trust which would induce the nations of Western Europe to accept our policies and follow our lead once the Russians altered their tactics.

Despite their precarious economic situation, there has been a revival of British prestige and influence in Western Europe. To some Americans Britain may appear a small, almost insignificant power. But to a small European nation Britain, with its bombers, its atomic and hydrogen bombs, its thriving new industries, presents a different picture. Another factor is the gradual movement of Britain toward some form of union with the Continental nations, as evidenced in the Macmillan government's approach to a common European market. Finally, there are doubts about wisdom of United States policy, especially as it is practiced and elucidated by John Foster Dulles.

Western Europe was not impressed by the statesmanship of Mr. Dulles at two serious crises: one arising from the possibility of Western military intervention in Indochina, and the other emerging after the collapse of the European Defense Community. Nor was Mr. Dulles's attitude toward America's closest allies, the British, in the period of British and French intervention in Egypt calculated to create the impression that the United States, as an ally, would remain true in good times and bad.

Nowhere has British prestige and influence declined more rapidly as in the Middle East. Yet nowhere are Britain's economic interests greater.

Recent events have emphasized the economic connection between Britain and the Middle East. But the ties that connect a group of islands set in the cold waters of the northern ocean with the arid, sunny lands of that area were established long before the discovery and exploitation of oil reserves made the Middle East vital to Britain's economic life. Sidney Smith, Abercromby, Nelson, Gordon, T. E. Lawrence—a whole battalion of British heroes won fame in the area. The empty deserts and clamorous cities have exercised a fascination on Britons for more than two centuries, have called explorers and scientists, missionaries and merchants eastward. Nor was the Middle East's strategic importance to Britain born with oil. Nelson destroyed the French on the Nile, Kitchener triumphed at Khartoum, and Montgomery fought at El Alamein because the land bridge between Asia and Africa and later the Suez Canal were considered vital to the existence of Britain as a world power.

Centuries of involvement in the Middle East resulted in a strong British bias in favor of the Arabs. No such favoritism was extended to the Egyptians as a people, although certainly the British were at first as willing as the Americans to trust Colonel Abdel Nasser of

Egypt. This bias, amounting in some cases to a blind affection, played its part in the formulation of British policy especially in the years when the state of Israel was taking shape. One example is the fact that the British consistently underrated Jewish military ability and overrated that of the Arabs.

Egypt's seizure of the Suez Canal on July 26, 1956, was a punctuation point in the long history of Britain's involvement in the Middle East. No British government could permit control of the canal to be vested in a single country, especially a country so openly hostile, without going to the utmost lengths to break that control. Given the shipping and pipeline facilities of the summer of 1956, the passage of oil tankers through the canal was essential to Britain's economic life.

Even when the program for the industrial use of nuclear power has been completed, oil will remain important to the British economy. The British government of the day was angry with Colonel Nasser, it was worried by Soviet infiltration in Egypt. But the primary cause of Britain's intervention in Egypt was that she could see no other way of securing freedom of passage through the canal. Reliance on oil was an elemental fact of Britain's position as a world power; it is extraordinary that the administration in Washington was so surprised when Britain took steps to insure her oil supply.

The influence of Britain in the Middle East at the time of intervention in Egypt was extensive. Tiny states on the Persian Gulf and on the south side of the Arabian peninsula behind the Aden protectorate were managed, if not ruled, by a few scores of officials from London. Iraq, Britain's firmest friend in the Middle East, benefited from British technicians and advisers. In Egypt and Jordan and Syria, Britain's prestige had fallen. But as late as January 1956, when I toured the Middle East, there was an evident respect for Britons and for British power, a respect which often was difficult to reconcile with the actual dimensions of that power.

In terms of oil, Britain took a great deal out of the Middle

East. From an altruistic standpoint, the return was small. But it is important to remember that British power there did not take the same form as in British colonies. The British could not order schools to be built or irrigation works to be started; they could, and did, advise such works.

They were the first power—the United States will be the second—to encounter the jarring fact that the improvements which a big oil company brings to a nation promote nationalism. In the end, peoples are not content with oil royalties, clean company towns, and new schools. They want all the money, not merely royalties, and they want to build the towns and schools themselves.

The decline of British power in the Middle East coincided with the entry into the area of a new power, Soviet Russia. One of the oddest aspects of the relations between the United States and the United Kingdom was the calm—almost the indifference—with which the administration in Washington viewed the entry of Russia into the Middle East. As late as November 1956, *after* the British had destroyed large numbers of Soviet aircraft and tanks in Egypt, the State Department was undisturbed by intelligence reports that Russia had agreed to make good the Egyptian losses with new arms shipments.

Because of their economic involvement in the Middle East, the British undoubtedly will persevere in their efforts to maintain influence in the area. Early in 1957 all the cards were stacked against them.

One advantage of a long and stormy experience in international affairs is that it allows a nation to look with equanimity on reverses. After the withdrawal from Egypt in December 1956, many Britons thought they would make a comeback in the Middle East. No argument, neither Arab enmity nor the advent of American and Russian power, could shake this belief. They did not mean, of course, that they would come back along the lines of nineteenth-century colonialism. The British recognize that the days of British rule from the citadel in Cairo are as dead as Thebes. But with that placid confidence which is one of their most irritating characteristics, they predicted that in the future, as in the past, they would play a major role in the area.

When I protested that this was not the view in Washington or, probably, in Moscow, a soldier-administrator laughed and said: "Oh *they* thought we were finished in 1940." But it is in the Middle East that British hopes and ambitions conflict directly with those of the United States. And relations with the United States are another story—or at least another chapter.

IX. *The Atlantic Alliance*

STRENGTHS AND STRESSES

*If I were an American, as I am an Englishman, while a
foreign troop was landed in my country I never would
lay down my arms—never! never! never!*

WILLIAM PITT, EARL OF CHATHAM

*His Britannic Majesty acknowledges the said United
States, viz., New-Hampshire, Massachusetts-Bay, Rhode-
Island and Providence Plantations, Connecticut, New-
York, New-Jersey, Pennsylvania, Delaware, Maryland,
Virginia, North-Carolina, South-Carolina, and Georgia
to be free, sovereign and independent states; that he treats
with them as such; and for himself, his heirs and succes-
sors, relinquishes all claims to the government, property
and territorial rights of the same, and every part thereof.*

TREATY OF PARIS, SEPTEMBER 3, 1783

THE ALLIANCE between the United States and the United
Kingdom is a paradox. This intimate association that has fought
wars and carried out the most delicate and intricate diplomatic
tasks is not based on any single treaty or agreement. It is a paradox
because, although roundly attacked from the outset by powerful

groups in both countries, the alliance has grown steadily in strength toward a position in which it is almost invulnerable to political attack.

This situation is a tribute to the hardheaded appreciation of facts which lies beneath the political oratory and posturing on both sides of the Atlantic. For the alliance is not the result of the intrigues of Anglophiles along the eastern seaboard of the United States or of the Machiavellian diplomacy of Britons eager for a handout; it is the result of mutual self-interest. In the dangerous world of the mid-twentieth century it is the best hope of survival for both nations.

Americans, in the plenitude of power, often ask one another why they need alliances, and why, in particular, there should exist any special relationship with Britain. One way of answering the question is to consider our situation if the United Kingdom were neutral in the world struggle with the aggressive totalitarianism of the East. There would then be no United States Air Force bomber bases in Britain. The British naval bases with their facilities in Britain and the Mediterranean would no longer be open to the United States. The United Kingdom would not be a member of the North Atlantic Treaty Organization. The British divisions that have helped hold Germany since 1945 would have been withdrawn. British hydrogen bombs and atomic bombs and the long-range bombers built to carry them would not be on our side. The position assumed by the United States at diplomatic meetings would no longer be supported by the leaders of a stable, experienced power still possessing considerable influence in many parts of the world.

Finally, the United States could not rely in times of crisis upon the backing of fifty million people speaking the same language and adhering to similar political beliefs—people who are resolute, ingenious, and brave in war, progressive and industrious in peace.

Certainly the alliance is not to everyone's taste. There are and there always will be urgings in both countries to "go it alone." There are politicians and statesmen who would place each nation's re-liance on other allies. But custom, usage, common interests have combined to create the situation; the problem is to see that the alliance works and to realize its potential in the world.

No one would contend that the United Nations or NATO or the South East Asia Treaty Organization or any one of half a dozen smaller associations is not important. But examination shows that all these rest on the basic union of American and British interests. If that goes, everything goes.

It follows, therefore, that the popular attitude in Britain toward the United States and Britain's relationship in international affairs to the United States is of the utmost importance to both countries. Understanding it calls for a thorough appreciation of Britain's position in the world, not as we Americans see it but as the British themselves see it.

To begin with, let us try to answer that familiar and inevitable question: "Isn't there a good deal of anti-Americanism in Britain?"

If the question refers to personal dislike of Americans as in-dividuals, the answer is no. Of course if an American in Britain is noisy and impolite he will be told off. Britons should expect the same treatment in the United States under similar circumstances.

Americans as individuals are not disliked in Britain. But an American must be prepared to encounter searching inquiry and often sharp criticism about the policies and programs of the United States government. He will learn that some institutions in the United States of which we have a high opinion do not similarly impress the British. Certain groups within British society view vari-ous aspects of life in the United States with reactions ranging from hostility to hilarity. This is natural. You cannot expect a socialist to be enthusiastic about capitalism, especially when capitalism is so obviously successful. Nor can you expect a British conservative to rejoice in the transfer of world power westward across the Atlantic.

So, inevitably, there are discussions and debates when Americans and Britons meet. Long may it be so. For this freedom to argue problems is the very essence of the alliance. It is a means of ironing out the difficulties that arise. It also emphasizes the common ground on which we stand, which, put at its simplest, is a mutual belief in the principles of democratic freedom.

In Germany I often encountered men of education and intellectual probity who were convinced that a modern state should not have a democratic form of government and that to encourage democracy was inadvisable, even dangerous. In Britain or the United States one often meets men and women who rail against the occasional inanities of democratic government and deplore its weaknesses. But it is most unusual to meet someone, save a member of the small band of communists or fascists, who believes that the British or American people could or should live under any other system. Differences must be worked out and *are* worked out under the cover of this common acceptance of democracy. This belief does not sound impressive until you talk about the same subject with a middle-class Frenchman, a German professor, or a Soviet diplomat.

Although of course there are plenty of people in Britain, as there are in the United States, who are profoundly uninterested in the alliance or in any other aspect of international affairs, it can be a salutary experience to talk about Anglo-American relations with Britons. Often you encounter candor, honest curiosity, and, sometimes, shrewd judgment.

Such conversations go a long way toward killing the old idea that Britons—or, specifically, the English—are an aloof, chilly lot. Aloofness was and, to some extent, still is a middle-class characteristic. But, like so many other things in Britain, behavior in public has changed in the last fifteen years. The time has not come when Britons in a railway compartment will exchange telephone numbers and photographs of their children, but the old social isolation is breaking down.

The questions and criticisms that the American encounters are a good sign. They testify to the average Briton's understanding of the interdependence of the two countries. As long as the alliance flourishes there will be and should be such exchanges. They are a source of satisfaction, not offense.

Moreover, the questions are necessary. There is a dearth of serious news about the United States in the popular British press, although the remotest village will be informed of Miss Monroe's chest measurements. *The Times* of London, the *Manchester Guardian,* and the *Daily Telegraph* do an excellent job of reporting the United States within the limitations imposed by the paper shortage. The popular press, however, is something else.

There are, I believe, three factors that contribute to British questionings and criticisms about United States policies and statesmanship. These are:

(1) McCarthyism, by which the British mean the political attitude in the United States which begins at a perceptible trend toward ideological conformity and, at its worst, imitates totalitarian measures;

(2) the United States's leadership of the free world, which has been transferred from Britain in the last fifteen years. Doubts on this score are fed by statements of American leaders, often belligerent and uninformed, which raise the question of whether the United States administration understands either its enemies or its friends;

(3) the trade competition between Britain and the United States and the trade barriers to British imports raised by the United States.

It is difficult to say which of these is the most important factor in forming British attitudes toward the United States. For a variety of reasons McCarthyism was certainly the most important in the first five years of this decade.

Not many Britons understand the emotional involvement of a large proportion of Americans in the Far East and its problems. Nor was the impact of the Korean War upon the United States fully appreciated in the United Kingdom. Finally, the British, although they stoutly opposed communism, were never so deeply concerned with communist infiltration in government. Perhaps they should have been. The point here is that for a number of reasons they were not.

Consequently, neither those who report and edit the news in Britain (with a few exceptions) nor their readers were prepared for McCarthyism. A good many otherwise well-informed people were shocked when at the height of the McCarthy period Professor D. W. Brogan, one of the most stimulating and knowledgeable British authorities on America, pointed out that there had in fact been a considerable amount of subversion in the United States government and that there was ample proof of Soviet espionage.

The gradual reduction of the Senator's importance and power pleased the British. This was not because he had been a good deal less than friendly in his comments about them—they are not markedly sensitive to foreign criticism. The reason was that many Britons saw in the methods of Senator McCarthy and some of his associates a threat to the heritage of individual liberty and equal justice under the law and, ultimately, to the democratic government that is the common ground on which the alliance is based.

The scars McCarthyism left on British popular opinion are deep. Months after the Senator's star had faded, many people were only too ready to believe that terror still reigned in the United States and to discount the presence of a large body of moderate opinion that strongly disapproved of extremism either of the left or of the right.

McCarthyism, of course, was a godsend to the British communists in their efforts to turn the working class and the intellectuals against the United States. They exploited his methods and his speeches to frighten those who doubted the strength of American democracy. Their propaganda was directed chiefly at the industrial workers, whose good will the United States needs in Britain and, indeed, everywhere in the world. This, said the Communists, is fascism. This, they said, is what we warned you would happen in the United States. Look, they said, here's an elderly general as President and McCarthy running the country. Doesn't it remind you of Hindenburg and Hitler? they asked. What freedom would you have, they inquired, in a country where McCarthy considers socialists the same as communists? How long would your trade-union organization last?

This may sound absurd to Americans, but it was dreadfully important, and it can become dreadfully important again. Senator McCarthy did the good name of the United States more harm in Britain than anyone else in this century.

McCarthy did not have many friends in Britain. But it is symptomatic of the importance attached to good relations between the two countries by Britons that at the height of the anti-McCarthy uproar some Englishmen attempted to point out that after all there were other forces in the United States and that the wild pictures of fascism rampant in Washington painted by left-wing journalists were, to put it mildly, slightly exaggerated.

Such assurances made little headway. Many Britons, as I have said, discerned in the Senator a threat to the basic liberties of the American people and hence to the health of the alliance. Many more were profoundly ignorant of the real situation in the United States largely because they are profoundly ignorant of the American system of government and how it works. There was, finally, the extreme sensitivity of the British working class to anything that its members consider to be capitalist reactionary action. In Britain the memories of the fight against an organized and powerful reactionary group for the rights of labor are vivid. As we have seen, they are nourished by the speeches of Labor propagandists and politicians. There is also a strong flavor of internationalism within the Labor movement. Given these factors, it was easy enough for many thousands of working-class people to believe that McCarthy represented the same forces they had seen arise in Italy, Germany, and Spain to impoverish labor and smash the power of the unions.

This group paid little attention to—if, indeed, it even heard—the arguments of Americans and Britons that, while McCarthy was deplorable, some measures had to be taken against Communist espionage in the United States. Such arguments were drowned in the uproar raised by the left wing in Britain over the plight of some poor devil of a schoolteacher who had been a member of the Communist Party for a few months fifteen years ago and who now was being put through the wringer by Senator McCarthy and his fellow primitives. Finally, the British public as a whole—and particularly the British working class—was not so aroused emotionally by the cold war as Americans were, and there was far less hatred and fear of the Soviet Union.

American critics of Britain have suggested that if the United Kingdom had been as deeply involved militarily in Korea as the United States was, this attitude toward the Communist bloc would have hardened. I doubt it. The British are accustomed to casualties from wars in far-off places. They do get angry and excited about casualties among their troops from terrorism. The hanging of two British noncommissioned officers by Jewish terrorists in Palestine during the troubles there produced more public bitterness and animosity than did the grievous casualties suffered by the Gloucestershire Regiment in its long, valiant stand against the Chinese in Korea.

The attacks on British policies and British public figures by Americans disturb those who are concerned with the future of the alliance. I do not think that the effect of these upon the general public is so great as is generally believed. Some newspapers feature reports of these attacks and reply in editorials that are stately or bad-tempered according to the character of the newspaper. The attacks themselves, however, do not produce excessive anger among ordinary people. To repeat, the British are not sensitive to foreign criticism. One reason is that they retain a considerable measure of confidence in the rightness, even the righteousness, of their own position—a characteristic that has galled Americans and others for years. (Incidentally, it is a characteristic they have passed on to the Indians. Mr. Nehru in his high-minded inability to see any point of view but his own is not unlike the late Neville Chamberlain.) A second reason is that this generation of Britons has been insulted by experts. Secretary of State Dulles, Senators McCarthy, Knowland, and Dirksen can say some pretty harsh things. But, compared to what the British have heard about themselves from the late Dr. Göbbels or the various Vilification Editors of *Pravda* or *Izvestia*, American criticisms are as lemonade is to vodka.

Mr. Dulles's unpopularity among the British results not from his taste for inept phrases but from the belief widely held among leading politicians and senior civil servants that on two occasions— the formation of the South East Asia Treaty Organization and the negotiations with Britain after Egypt had seized control of the Suez Canal—he told them one thing and did another. Such beliefs strongly held by responsible people trickle downward.

This evaluation of Mr. Dulles's diplomacy is one cause for British worry about the United States's leadership of the free world. The idea that the British do not accept the transfer of power westward across the Atlantic is superficial. They may not like it, but they do accept it. Yet the idea has great vigor. An American editor of the highest intelligence once said: "These people will never get used to our being in the number-one position!" I think they *are* used to it. But acceptance has not ended their doubts and criticisms about how we exercise the tremendous power that is ours, or their resentment of United States suggestions that Britain is finished and no longer counts in the councils of the West. The British do not mind when Senator Knowland accuses them of feeding military matériel to the Communist Chinese. They do mind when in an international crisis the State Department treats Britain as though she were on the same level as Greece.

For, whatever the alliance means to Americans, to Britons it has meant a special relationship between the two countries under which the United Kingdom is entitled to more consideration than she often receives. It was the realization that the United States did not recognize this special relationship which touched off the wave of criticism and doubt during the Suez crisis.

From the welter of words loosed in that period—speeches, Parliamentary resolutions, editorials, and arguments in pubs—a central theme affecting relations between Britain and the United States emerged. The decision of the United States administration to condemn British action in Egypt and to vote with the Soviet Union against Britain in the General Assembly of the United Nations smashed the conception of the alliance held by millions of Britons. This sorry development is quite unaffected by such considerations as whether the British government should have ordered intervention or whether the United States government should have been as surprised by intervention as it was.

The British regarded the alliance as one in which each partner was ready to help and sustain the other. They felt that the administration's actions mocked a decade and a half of fine talk about standing together. Traveling through Britain early in 1957, I found "that United Nations vote" was a topic which arose in every conversation and to which every conversation inevitably returned. Some could understand the logic of the United States. But very few understood how, in view of the past, we could bring ourselves to vote against Britain.

Whatever Washington may think, the British believe they deserve special consideration because of their present exertions and past performances. They point out, accurately, that the United Kingdom has put more men, money, and matériel into NATO than has any other ally of the United States. They assert that, although there have been differences between the two powers, Britain has sustained United States policy in Europe sometimes, as in the case of German rearmament, at the cost of great political difficulty. An alliance, they say, should work both ways.

Britons are thankful for American generosity after World War II. But their gratitude is affected by a powerful psychological factor often overlooked by Americans, one that strengthens the British belief that their country merits a special position in America's foreign policies. This factor is the British interpretation of the role played by their country in two world wars.

It is an article of popular faith in Britain that the nation twice went to war in defense of smaller powers—Belgium in 1914 and

Poland in 1939—and that the United States, whose real interests were as deeply involved as Britain's, remained on the sidelines for thirty-three months of the first war and for twenty-seven months of the second war.

Americans find it tedious to be told by the more assertive Britons how their beleaguered island stood alone against the world in 1940. The American conviction that the war really began when the Japanese blew us into it at Pearl Harbor is equally tedious to Britons. Nevertheless, the British did stand defiantly alone. They whipped the *Luftwaffe,* and they took heavy punishment from German bombs. They fought hard, if often unsuccessfully, in the Western Desert, Greece, Crete, Abyssinia, and Syria. All this went on while we across the Atlantic began ponderously to arm and to argue at great length whether the Nazi dictatorship really was a threat to freedom.

These events affected those Britons who are now moving toward the direction of the nation's destinies. The cabinet minister of today or tomorrow may be the destroyer seaman, tank-commander, or coal-miner of 1940. However deplorable the attitude may seem from our standpoint and from the standpoint of some individual Britons, the British people believe something is due them for their exertions. The wiser leaders, speaking from both the left and the right, advise their countrymen to forget the past and think of the future.

How they will think of their international future is a different matter. For the first time since 1940 there is now a strong sentiment in Britain for going it alone. There is also a revulsion against all forms of international association, starting with the United Nations and extending to NATO and SEATO. To anyone who understands the pride and toughness that lie at the center of the British character this is understandable. They have never been afraid of being alone.

In considering British dissatisfaction with the place accorded their country in the American outlook, it should not be thought that this reflects lack of liaison between the two nations on the lower echelons of diplomacy. The co-operation between the United States Embassy officials and the Foreign Office in London ordinarily is very close. So is the co-operation between the British Embassy diplomats in Washington and the State Department. To repeat, it is in situations like the crises over Cyprus and Suez that the British feel they are treated by the State Department and the administration not as the most powerful and reliable of allies but as just another friendly nation.

This concern over Britain's place within the alliance is sharpened by doubts over the ability of the United States to exercise leadership in a manner that will secure both the peace of the world and the maintenance of the interests of the West.

Such doubts arise generally from the wide differences between what American policy really is and what various spokesmen for the United States say it is. Let us consider two statements by John Foster Dulles, a man who, when he became Secretary of State in 1953, was admired and trusted by professional British diplomats and by politicians interested in international affairs.

At one point Mr. Dulles spoke of "massive retaliation" against any enemies of the United States in the Far East. The remark made a great splash in the headlines of the world, and in the view of the British it was totally useless. The Russians and Communist Chinese leaders, they argued, realized that the United States had nuclear weapons and would be prepared to use them in the event of war. As both nations are dictatorships and as the government controls all communications media in each country, there was no prospect of Mr. Dulles's warning being relayed effectively to the Russian and Chinese masses whom it might conceivably impress. But it was relayed to all those people in the world, especially in the Asian world, who in any case consider the United States as a huge, powerful, and possibly aggressive nation. The British were appalled by the effect of the statement on India. There, as elsewhere, it was well ventilated by the Communists and other enemies of the United States as an example of America's devotion to belligerence.

Earlier in his busy career as moral lecturer for the West,

Mr. Dulles had spoken of the possibility that the defeat of the European Defense Community plan in the French National Assembly might provoke an "agonizing reappraisal" of the United States policy toward Europe. Again the result was quite different from that desired by the Secretary of State. The National Assembly rejected EDC, just as everyone interested in the matter, with the exception of the Secretary of State, Dr. Adenauer, M. René Pleven, and M. Jean Monnet, knew it would. The United States did not immediately begin any "agonizing reappraisal" of its position in Europe because quite obviously it could not do so at the time. It had to keep its troops in Europe, it had to rearm Germany, it had to sustain the NATO alliance because these are the essentials of a foreign policy that is partly the result of American initiative and partly the outcome of our response to the challenges of the times.

In both cases it slowly became plain that neither the Congress nor the people of the United States were prepared for massive retaliation or even agonizing reappraisal. The reappraisal did start in 1956, but it was the result of very different factors: the rising costs of nuclear weapons and the necessity in both Britain and the United States of reducing armament expenditures and taxes, the change in the tactics of Soviet foreign policy, the reassurance (largely illusory) given the West by the summit conference at Geneva in the summer of 1955, which convinced many that the need for heavy armament expenditure was receding. This reappraisal may be agonizing, but it has nothing to do with the one the Secretary of State was talking about.

The crisis in European affairs caused by France's rejection of EDC was solved largely by British initiative and diplomacy. Today most Britons interested in international affairs feel that this feat has received too little recognition in Washington. Sir Anthony Eden, then Foreign Secretary, pulled the forgotten Brussels treaty out of his pocket—or, more accurately, out of the soap dish, for he was bathing when he thought of it—and hied off to Europe to sell the treaty to the interested governments as an instrument under which Germany could be rearmed. Sir Anthony was eminently successful in his sales talks. Mr. Dulles remained aloof for the first few days, thinking dark thoughts about the French. He had been advised by high State Department officials that Eden didn't have a chance of selling the Brussels treaty idea. When it became evident that Sir Anthony was selling it and was being warmly applauded even by the Germans for his initiative and diplomatic skill, Mr. Dulles flew to Europe. It looked very much to the British as though he wanted to get in on the act.

Many Britons felt that Mr. Dulles let Sir Anthony and the Foreign Office do the donkey work in patching up European unity in the autumn of 1954 and in negotiating a settlement in Indochina that spring. The Secretary of State and the administration were ready to take a share of the credit for success, but were only too eager to remain aloof from failure. Only the patience, experience, and forthrightness of General Walter Bedell Smith, then Under Secretary of State, enabled the United States to cut any sort of figure at the conference on Southeast Asia.

Such a policy of limited liability in great affairs is not in accord with either the power of the United States or the principles preached by Mr. Dulles and others.

Another American phenomenon that annoys and occasionally frightens the British (and, incidentally, many other allied and neutral states) is the belligerent loquacity of our generals and admirals. The American public is not particularly aroused when someone in the Pentagon announces that we must be on our guard and must build enough heavy bombers or atomic cannon or aircraft-carriers to blow the Kremlin to Siberia or even farther. The public is pretty well sold, perhaps oversold, on defense. Besides, the public is much brighter than the generals or the admirals or their busy public-relations officers think it is—bright enough to realize that behind these dire prophecies of doom, these clarion calls for more weapons, the services may be having some trouble in squeezing the treasury. The citizen reads the first few paragraphs and turns to the sports pages to see what Mantle did yesterday.

The situation is far different in the United Kingdom or in France or Italy or even Germany, to name only our allies.

The British people live packed on a relatively small island, and it has been estimated that six hydrogen bombs dropped in Britain would be the knockout. Consequently, the people do not like loose talk about nuclear bombing. They have a shrewd suspicion that they, and not the talkers, will be the first target.

Such apprehensions may be exaggerated. But there is sound thinking behind British insistence that such announcements by our military spokesmen damage the cause of the West and the good name of the United States among our allies and, equally important, among the growing number of states now neutral or near neutral in the struggle between East and West. For many reasons, geographical, military, political, even religious, these states abhor war and violence. Russian propagandists recognized this attitude at the outset of the cold war and have played upon it with great skill. And they have been helped immeasurably every time Senator Blowhard or Admiral Sternseadog suggests that we should blow hell out of the Russians or the Chinese.

These manifestations of combativeness may be helpful in reminding the Russians of United States power. But the Russians are not our primary concern: we are their enemies, whatever the surface policy of the Soviet government. Our primary concern in this new period when the cold war is being continued by more complex and subtle means than blockades and *coups d'états* is the new nations we have helped bring into being.

It is in relation to this approach, I believe, that the British question our judgment. Particularly those officials and politicians who deal with foreign affairs are not immediately concerned with the prospect of Communist revolution in Italy or France. They estimate that the leaders of the Soviet Union would avoid such upheavals in the present state of world affairs because revolution would sound the alarm bells in every Western capital and prevent the Soviet Union from accomplishing a more important objective:

the steady weakening of the regional alliances—NATO, SEATO, the Baghdad Pact—which have been laboriously constructed by the United States and the United Kingdom to contain Communist aggression and to provide a safer, richer life for the peoples of the allied states. Simultaneously, the Soviet Union, through diplomatic, political, and cultural agencies, will make every effort to pull the neutrals, great and small—India, Egypt, Indonesia—onto their side.

It is in this arena, one where diplomatic skill and economic assistance are more important than military power, that Britain believes the West must exert its strength. Both diplomats and politicians are convinced that in the next five years there must be a thorough overhaul of the political planning and military arrangements made by the West in the period 1949–55. They question whether this can be done if the principal emphasis in defense circles in the United States remains on the prospect of an imminent war.

A point arising from this discussion is that the British themselves are unused to the spectacle of a soldier or sailor pronouncing on issues of national policy. In Britain the warrior, retired or serving, is kept in his place. If the government wants the advice of Field Marshal Montgomery it asks for it and gets it in the privacy of the cabinet rooms.

In the field of foreign affairs the British maintain that the tremendous physical power of the United States and our immense resources do not automatically guarantee that in the exercise of our power we will always be right. Leaders of both parties feel that the United States government, particularly President Roosevelt and his advisers, misread Soviet intentions lamentably in the period 1942–6, and that consequently Allied strategy strove only for victory and not for a stable peace after victory. The political tides that sweep the United States every two years give American foreign policy an aspect of impermanence, even instability, which weakens United States influence in the world. There is a feeling that United States diplomacy would benefit from fewer press conferences and more private negotiations.

Naturally, these criticisms can be irritating, especially if they are delivered in the Pecksniffian tones characteristic of many British officials. But history will judge, I believe, that this transfer of power westward across the Atlantic has been carried out with great good sense and dignity. It may also hold up to scorn the present generation of Americans if they fail to avail themselves not only of the physical strength but also of the diplomatic experience and skill of a nation wise in the ways of the world. This is not a time for Americans to be too proud to listen.

Such considerations belong to the stratosphere of Anglo-American relations. An American living in Britain will soon be brought down to earth in any conversation with British business-men.

Repeatedly he will be asked why the United States bars British imports through high tariffs, why there is discrimination against British bids for contracts in the United States, why Senators and Congressmen belabor the British on one hand for trying to expand their trade with the Soviet Union and on the other hand do all they can to block the expansion of British trade with the United States.

"Trade Not Aid" is the British goal in their economic relations with the United States, which is Britain's second-best market. In 1954 we bought goods valued at £ 198,800,000 ($556,640,000) from Britain. But this represented only 6.6 per cent of the total United Kingdom exports, and in 1938, long before the export drives, when Britain still counted on her overseas investments to help finance her own imports, the percentage was 5.4 per cent.

So, although both nations recognize this trade's importance to Britain—it is her principal source of dollar earnings—the increase in the trade has been relatively small.

The inability of British exporters to sell competitively in the United States because of tariff protection provokes sharp criticism. The Republican administration of 1952–6 was attacked in the editorial columns of newspapers that are usually most friendly to the United States, for, despite the reassuring speeches of President Eisenhower, British industry still claimed it was being denied access to American markets by the tariff restrictions.

Certainly the tariff does bar many British imports. It may be, however, that many of them, perhaps a majority, would not be able to compete with similar American products. There is a great deal of ignorance about the American market among British industrialists and some reluctance to assume the long and complex job of analyzing a particular market. I know of one manufacturer of women's handbags who has built up an extremely profitable business in the United States largely through a thorough study of the market on frequent visits to this country. I also know of other larger firms that have failed to exploit their potential American market because they would not change their methods or their product to meet the market's demands. Beyond this, they could not understand the importance of servicing their product and of maintaining continuous relations with middlemen and buyers.

We have seen that Aneurin Bevan and other politicians of the extreme left are wedded to the idea that successive Labor and Conservative governments have danced to Washington's tune. There are many who would deny undue political or diplomatic influence by the United States on Britain; indeed, many in America would say the shoe was on the other foot. But no one could discount the growing influence of American customs and ways of living upon the people of Britain. Part of this is the direct result of the popularity of American movies and the continued presence of American troops. Part comes from the fact that British manufacturers are rather belatedly turning out the household devices which have revolutionized living in the United States. This and the ability of the new working class and the new middle class to buy in abundance has led to a change in the living conditions of millions.

Ignorance of the political system and international objectives of the United States is still fairly widespread. In some important respects, however, there is today among the people of England a greater knowledge about the people of the United States than there ever was in the past.

Before the entry of the United States into World War II, for instance, there was a strong conviction in Britain that ethnically we were the same people. The mass of Britons expected us to be as British in our background and national outlook as the people of Australia or New Zealand. The war corrected that impression. The army that came to Britain was composed of men of diverse ethnic stocks, and the people among whom they lived learned that Americans could have names like Magliaro, Martinez, or Mannheim and still be good Americans. This shocked both the Americanophobes who thought of us as "Anglo-Saxons" unchanged since the administration of Thomas Jefferson and their political representatives who envisaged us as openhearted and openhanded former colonials only too eager to help out the "mother country." But in the long run this clearer, more realistic view of modern America has had a good effect on relations between the two countries.

Similarly, the presence among Britons of several million young men representing the United States removed some illusions built up by years of steady attendance at the local movie house. We were not all rich, we were not all gangsters or cowboys, we did not all chew gum. Americans worked just as hard, worried just as much, and had the same hopes and dreams as Britons did. The period of the big buildup in 1943 and 1944 before the Normandy invasion was marred by saloon brawls between Americans and British and by friction on both sides. But this is outweighed, I believe, by the fact that the same period contributed greatly to the two peoples' knowledge of each other.

When the United States Air Force sent forces to Britain at the peak of the cold war, it was assumed by many that this process would continue. But the present contingent is minute compared to the millions of Americans who moved through Britain during World War II. Moreover, its members are more professional. They do not have the opportunity or the inclination for close contact with British homes. They want what professional soldiers want the world over: a bellyful of beer and a girl. They get both.

The senior officers of the United States Air Force units in Britain and well-intentioned Britons, zealous for the improvement of relations between the countries, spend a great deal of time worrying about the behavior of the airmen and their treatment by British civilians. The time is ill spent. It is the nature of young men far from home, in or out of uniform, to drink, to wench, and to fight. Here and there they may encounter tradesmen eager to make an extra shilling out of the foreigner. But such profiteering does not seem to be on the same scale as that practiced by the good people of Florida or Texas or Kansas upon their own countrymen in uniform during World War II.

In many superficial respects Britain is more Americanized than before the war. There are hamburger joints near Piccadilly Circus and Leicester Square, and the American tourist can buy a Coke in most big towns. A pedestrian in London sees windows full of "Hollywood models" and "Broadway styles." In the years immediately after the war, working-class youth copied the kaleidoscopic ties and broad-shouldered, double-breasted plumage of the American male. Today, still following styles set in America, he is adopting the more sober appearance of the Ivy League, and the button-down shirt has made its appearance in High Holborn. This is a curious example of styles traveling west and then east across the Atlantic, for the Ivy League dresses as it believes—or, rather, as its tailors believe—English gentlemen dress. Now the working-class young man in Britain is imitating "new" American styles that are themselves an imitation of the styles followed by his own upper class. Whatever the fashion in the United States, this class clings manfully to the dark suit, the starched collar, and the derby in London, and to tweeds in the country.

Obviously the movies made in America have had an enormous effect on the British way of life. For a number of reasons the effect has not been altogether good. Accuracy in portraying the American scene is not one of Hollywood's strong points. A couple of generations of young Britons matured nursing an idealistic view of the United States as a wonderland where hippy stenographers lived in high-ceilinged houses, wore luxurious clothes, drove big, powerful cars, and loved big, powerful men. There was almost invariably

a happy ending to the minor difficulties that beset hero and hero-
ine of an American film.

Realism was restored to some extent by the advent of the American soldier. Very few of the GI's resembled Mr. Robert Taylor,
and their backgrounds were quite different from those portrayed on
the screen. There were, of course, some fast talkers who could and
did make a pig farm in Secaucus sound like a ranch in California,
but, on the whole, the American soldiers came from civilian surroundings no more exciting than Leeds or Bristol. The movie-going
public now views pictures about home life in America with a more
skeptical eye.

The series of American films about juvenile delinquency, drug
addiction, dipsomania, and other social evils created a problem
for those interested in presenting a balanced view of the United
States to Britons. Great efforts were made by the United States
Information Service to demonstrate that the ordinary American
did not begin the day with a shot of heroin or send his boy to a
school that would make Dotheboys Hall seem like a kindergarten.

These efforts were inspired to some extent by the manner in
which the Communists exploited such films as genuine reflections of
life in the United States. Both the comrades and the USIS were
wasting their time. The British public can be agonizingly apathetic,
but it is not stupid. I never met anyone who thought these films
represented the real America or who believed the Communist contention that they did. The fact is that the ability of the United
States to make and show such pictures testifies to the strength of
America. When the Russians produce an epic about the slave labor
that built the White Sea-Baltic canal or an exposé of the corruption that riddled Soviet industry in the war and immediate post-war
years, we can begin to worry.

The theater since the war has exercised an important influence
in bringing America to Britain. Starting with *Oklahoma,* a series of
Broadway musical shows dominated the London stage for a decade.
One of the minor occupations of British critics is grumbling about
the shortage of "real" British musicals. But even the grumpiest

have been won over by the music of Richard Rodgers and Irving Berlin and the lyrics of Oscar Hammerstein II.

British taste is not always in accord with our own. *South Pacific* was not the critical success in London that it was in New York. The British loved *Guys and Dolls*—they had lost their hearts to the late Damon Runyon in the thirties—but they did not like *Pal Joey,* in which John O'Hara gave a much more realistic picture of the seamy side of American life.

But the accent has been on musicals. Very few serious American plays have successfully invaded London. In this field the traffic seems to be the other way.

The comics, invariably described in left-wing publications as "American Horror Comics," have been another medium for the spread of American culture in Britain. Like the movies, they have their critics, and, like some movies, they are used by the Communists to demonstrate what fearful people the Americans are.

The reader will notice that British Communism, although of almost negligible importance as a political party, is active in promoting differences between the two nations. The Communists know very well that the relationship between the United States and the United Kingdom is the strongest link in the Western chain; if they can break it, the rest will be easy.

I have been at pains to point out the issues over which governments and peoples on both sides of the alliance differ and those aspects of our national behavior which occasionally worry and concern the British. It should be emphasized that the areas of ignorance in the British attitude toward the United States are of minor importance compared to the ignorance of the average Frenchman or the average Indian. British misconceptions about the United States can be corrected and Communist attempts to exploit these misconceptions defeated because the British public does know something about the United States. This knowledge may be slight, but it is enough to build on.

Over the years there has been a change in attitude on the part of young people which I find disturbing. When I first came to Eng-

land in the late thirties I encountered a good deal of curiosity about
the political and social aspects of the American system. Young people wanted to know about American opportunities for education,
about technical schools, about the absence of a class system. Today
such interest as is displayed centers mainly upon the material
factors in the United States.

Perhaps what I encountered nearly twenty years ago was the
lingering afterglow of that period in our history when we stood as
a promise and a hope to the peoples of the world. Certainly many
of the egalitarian aspects of American society admired in pre-war
Britain have been slowly introduced into British society. A cynic
might even suggest that they know us better now. At any rate, I
meet fewer young people who are sure they would like to live in
America and be Americans.

Ignorance of the United States lies at the root of many of the
criticisms of our country one hears in Britain. This is being overcome to some extent by the work of the USIS, but the task is a
serious one. Beyond such obvious difficulties as the shortage of
newsprint which limits the amount that responsible newspapers can
print about the United States, there is another important obstacle
to better relations. This is the fact, that although Americans travel
to Britain each year in tens of thousands, the prospect of the average Briton seeing our country is remote. The British treasury doles
out dollars with a sharp eye on the gold and dollar reserves, and
a large percentage of the transatlantic travelers are businessmen
selling British exports to the United States. This is something, but
it is not enough.

The industrial working class is the most numerous and politically important in Britain. It is also the least informed about the
United States. Scholarships for Oxford and Cambridge students at
Harvard or Princeton and visiting professorships for English dons
do not, as a rule, help this class. The ideal would be an exchange
system under which hundreds of working-class men and women
from Bradford, Manchester, Liverpool, and the back streets of
London were given the opportunity to see America plain. The

English Speaking Union in the United States and the United Kingdom is attempting to bring this about.

Only through such contact, I believe, could the picture of the United States built up by some Labor Party politicians be erased. There remains a dangerous lack of understanding not only of our political system but of what mass production and greater productivity in the United States have done for the average workingman here. Newspaper articles, television series, books help, but it is a thing that must be felt as well as seen. It can be felt only in the United States.

The attention paid to differences and difficulties should not obscure the value that Britons place on their relationship with Americans. Materially, Britain's interest in maintaining the relationship is much the greater; undoubtedly they need us more than we need them. But here we must remember the national character of Britain. The British have been an independent people for a thousand years. Even when the fortunes of the nation have been at their lowest ebb, the people have been outspoken in defense of what they considered their rights. The earliest Continentals who traveled to England lamented the blunt independence of the yeomen and the absence of subservience among the noisy city crowds.

Some sociologists have concluded that all this has changed and that the industrial revolution and other social changes have transformed the British from the rowdiest and most belligerent of nations into law-abiding conformists. The national boiling-point, they report, is high.

Certainly a superficial view of the British working class in its high noon of full employment, security, high wages, and new housing would seem to confirm this conclusion. Personally, I doubt that the turbulent passions which sent Britons out to singe the beard of the King of Spain and to make rude noises when Hitler proposed peace in 1940 are spent.

Phlegmatic, often apathetic, sentimental but not emotional, they are a people capable of great outburts of political action. They should not therefore be considered a people prepared to follow docilely and blindly where the United States leads. The failure to recognize the presence in British character of this fundamental, unruly independence even when it was flourished in their faces is one of the principal reasons why President Eisenhower and his administration were surprised by Britain's intervention in Egypt in the autumn of 1956. Granted that the President was involved in the election campaign, it is mystifying that a man of his experience in dealing with the British failed to see the signs pointing toward independent action.

As early as August of that year letters in *The Times* urged an independent course for Britain and France in the Middle East. One letter signed by Julian Amery, then a Conservative back-bench Member of Parliament, ended with the reflection that if the two countries followed such a course and took action independently of the United States, it would not be for the first time. That *The Times* would give space to letters of this sort was a sign that the Establishment recognized the ideas they contained. In September, when the Chancellor of the Exchequer visited Washington, he made it clear to the most important of his hosts that Britain would not take the Egyptian seizure of the Suez Canal lying down—that if this was to be a struggle for Britain's existence, his country would prefer to go down with the guns firing and the flags flying. During that same month Sir Anthony Eden had written to President Eisenhower in terms which to anyone familiar with British official phraseology said that if Britain did not get a satisfactory settlement of its difficulties over the Canal through the United Nations, other action would be necessary. In speech after speech, especially at the Conservative Party Conference on October 13, the leaders of the government carefully stated that they did not exclude the use of force as a means of settling the Suez problem.

The British government badly miscalculated the Eisenhower administration's reaction to intervention in Egypt. It expected benevolent neutrality from a trusted ally. It got pressure and criticism. But this miscalculation may have been natural under the circumstances, for it can be argued that Britain did not expect the

United States administration to be surprised. It had, after all, given abundant direct and indirect warnings that force might be used as a last resort. How much of the administration's anger, one wonders, was based in the realization that it had been told what was going to happen—if only it had stopped to read again and think?

British diversions from co-operation in policy over Suez or anywhere else are, to a considerable extent, the result of the circumstances governing the existence of the United Kingdom—circumstances that are as different from our own as could be imagined. Here is an island absolutely dependent on world trade. Westward lies the continental United States, with a continent's natural resources at its disposal—an almost completely self-sufficient power. The difference is inescapable and permanent. We must expect the British to react sharply whenever a vital part of their trade is endangered. In 1956 the harsh equation was "Suez equals oil, oil equals British production, British production equals the existence of the United Kingdom." Likewise, we must expect the British to expand, within agreed limits of strategic restrictions, their world trade. This is particularly true of trade with Communist China.

In this connection we might remember that, to the British, diplomatic recognition is not a mark of approval, and that if there is a possibility of dividing the Soviet Union and the Peiping regime, it can be exploited only through diplomatic channels. Diplomatic attempts to wean China away from Russia may fail. But they are worth trying. Can they be tried successfully without the co-operation of both the United States and the United Kingdom? I think not. In any case, the task this generation faces of preserving Western freedom in defiance of the Communist colossi is difficult enough without discarding this diplomatic weapon.

An alliance flourishes when it is based on realism. Realism involves knowing your ally and understanding his motives. In war the strategic reasons for an alliance are laid bare; the motives are there for all to see. In peace, when international relations are infinitely more complex, the task of maintaining an alliance is consequently more difficult. In this chapter I have cited salient aspects of American political life and government policy which have irritated and angered the British. The differences over the Suez crisis were the last and most important of these. That issue generated a great deal of anger, and some harsh and brutal truths were spoken on both sides. I think that from the standpoint of the future of the alliance this was a good thing. It forced the British, I believe, to adopt a more realistic attitude toward the United States and United States policy, and it will lead them to take more, not less, diplomatic initiative in the future.

There will be other differences in foreign policy between the two countries, for differences are inevitable in the relationship between two parliamentary democracies. Indeed, they are a strength. It is because the British are an independent, outspoken, hardheaded people that they are good allies. It is because British governments think for themselves and enjoy the services of an experienced, incorruptible, intelligent civil service that their support is welcome and necessary in the contest with the East.

And we know—at least, we should know—that if the worst comes the British are stout fighters, ready, once every effort to preserve peace has failed, to fight with all they have and are.

I carry with me as a talisman the memory of a conversation at Supreme Headquarters, Allied Powers Europe, during the darkest days of the war in Korea. An American general officer, a man of the highest professional qualifications, suggested to a small, intimate group that, with more and more American power diverted to the Far East, the Russians might jump in Europe.

"It will be pretty tough for you people," he told a British lieutenant colonel, an amiable, rather rakish character. "They'll offer you a chance of getting out. If you don't take it, they'll tell you they'll blow London and half a dozen other cities off the map. They'll probably tell the French the same sort of thing. What do you think your people will do?"

"What do you think we'll do?" the lieutenant colonel answered. "We'll tell them to go to hell."

Beneath the political bickering, the unrelenting self-criticism, the pessimism there exists now, as there did in 1940, a fiery spirit. The British will never be vassals. Nor will they ever be easy allies. But if this alliance fails, there is little left on which an enduring peace can be built.

X. The British Economy and Its Problems

Annual income twenty pounds, annual expenditure nineteen nineteen six, result happiness. Annual income twenty pounds, annual expenditure twenty pound ought and six, result misery.

CHARLES DICKENS

It would be madness to let the purposes or the methods of private enterprise set the habits of the age of atomic energy.

HAROLD LASKI

WE MUST now take a closer look at the British economy as it is today. This is a big subject, one well worth a long book. It is my purpose in this informal estimate of our ally to sketch the fundamentals of the present economic situation and to deal briefly with some of the factors in it. Earlier we have encountered the Trades Union Congress and the emergence of a new working class. We have seen that Britain is changing behind the mask of tradition. In this chapter we will see that the change in the national economy is progressing perhaps even more rapidly than the change in the structure of society and politics. And, of course, all three changes are closely related and interdependent.

The British Empire, which half a century ago stood at the apex of its economic power, was built on coal. Largely because of the extent of her coal resources, Britain got a head start in the industrial revolution, which originated in England. An organized coal-mining industry has existed in Britain for over three hundred years, or three hundred years longer than in any European country. Not only was there enough coal to make Britain the world's workshop, but until about 1910 British exports dominated the world export market. In the peak production year of 1913 the industry produced 287,000,000 tons, exported 94,000,000 tons, and employed 1,107,000 workers. Contrast these figures with those for 1955: 221,600,000 tons produced, 14,200,000 tons exported, 704,-100 workers.

Three centuries of mining means that the majority of the best seams are worked out. Each year coal has to be mined from deeper and thinner seams. Each year the struggle to raise productivity becomes harsher. There are huge workable reserves; one estimate is 43,000,000,000 tons, which, at the present rate of consumption, is more than enough to last another two hundred years. But this coal will be increasingly difficult to mine. Moreover, certain types, such as high-quality coking coal, will be exhausted long before 2157.

In the reign of King Coal all went well. Britain built up a position in the nineteenth century which made her the world's leading manufacturer, carrier, banker, investor, and merchant. By the turn of the century, however, other nations, notably the United States and Germany, were challenging this position. Nevertheless, Britain was able to withstand competition up to the outbreak of World War I through her huge exports of coal and cotton textiles and through her ability to take advantage of the general increase in world trade.

Coal and the industrial revolution, it should be remembered, gave Britain something more than a head start in production: they enabled her to train the first technical labor force in the world. The traveler in Eastern Europe, the Middle East, and Asia will soon realize that the British Empire and British influence of half a century ago were built not on gunboats and redcoats but on the products of British factories and on the bewhiskered expatriates, many of them Scots, who tended locomotives in Burma and saw-mills in South America. They, too, as much as the booted and spurred heroes of Kipling, were builders of empire. This advantage, at least, Britain has not lost. Today she still possesses a large force of highly skilled labor.

The economic problems that developed into a whirlwind in the forties of this century first became serious in the years after the close of World War I. British textiles had to compete in Asia with textile products from India and Japan which were produced at a much lower cost because of low wages. Oil and coal from new European mines challenged Britain's lead in coal exports. At the same period there was a fall in the demand for many of the heavy industrial products that British factories had supplied to the rest of the world; locomotives, heavy machinery, cargo ships. The politico-economic dogma of self-sufficiency developed in nations that for long had been British customers. They began to protect their own growing industries with tariffs, quotas, and other re-strictions.

But the effect on the British economy of this decline in ex-ports was cushioned by income from investments overseas and by a substantial improvement in the terms of trade. During the twenties and early thirties British industry began to contract for the first time in centuries. Unemployment averaged 14 per cent between 1921 and 1939. By September 1939, however, the economy, stimu-lated by the armament program, increased production, and greater industrial investment at home, began to improve. Britain faced the Second World War on a secure economic basis. Indeed, there were persuasive gentlemen in the London of that Indian summer of peace who tried to persuade you that economic strength alone could win the war.

When Americans think of the effect of World War II on Britain we are apt to think in terms of bomb damage and ships sunk. Certainly these were important parts of a generally disastrous picture, but the whole is much more impressive than the parts.

The inability to continue industrial maintenance and make replacements under the hammer of war, shipping losses, and bomb damage ran down the British economy by about £3,000,000,000. At the present rate of exchange this amounts to $8,400,000,000. The present cost of rebuilding ships and houses and factories is, of course, infinitely higher due to the upswing in labor costs and material prices since 1945.

This loss was accompanied by a drastic change in Britain's world trading position. To begin with, she lost almost all her overseas assets—those investments which had cushioned the shock of the falling export market and whose income had largely paid for imports. The terrible appetite of war—a ship torpedoed, a division lost, a factory bombed—devoured them. Over £1,000,000,000 worth of overseas investments ($2,800,000,000 at the current rate of exchange) were sold to pay for war supplies. Of this amount, £428,000,000 (about $1,198,400,000) represented investments in the United States and Canada.

Yet even this expenditure of the carefully husbanded investments, the results of thrift and financial foresight, did not suffice to pay for nearly six years of war. Britain also accumulated overseas debts to the amount of £3,000,000,000, or, at current rates of exchange, $8,400,000,000. When the money was borrowed, the pound sterling was pegged at $4.03 and the dollar equivalent of the external debt was closer to $12,000,000,000.

The emphasis on armaments and the priority given arms-producing industries, the arrears of industrial maintenance and replacement, the concentration of manpower in the services and industries of national importance for the winning of the war, and the shortage of shipping all reduced Britain's export trade during the war years. By 1944 exports had fallen to less than one third of their 1938 volume.

This meant that, in some cases, nations whose economy had been less strained by the war were replacing British sellers in these markets. In other instances, nations long dependent on British exports began to make their own products. When the British were prepared to return to normal export trade, the markets were not so extensive as they had been before the war.

The war affected Britain's financial position in two other respects. At its end the real value of the gold and dollar reserves of the nation had been reduced to about one half of the pre-war level. But the physical destruction of the war had increased Britain's dependence, and that of other sterling-area nations and other countries, upon supplies of all kinds from the United States. Yet the dollar earnings by these countries were not enough to pay for their supplies.

Finally, and perhaps most important from the standpoint of a country that must live by trade, the terms of trade changed. The price of raw materials imported into Britain rose sharply after the war. By 1948 about 20 per cent more goods had to be exported than in 1938 to pay for the same amount of imports.

As a result of these changes in her position, Britain emerged from the war as an empty-handed victor. The banker of the world was deeply in debt. The market places of the world were crowded with other nations, and her own goods were few in number and out of date. Shabby, tired, undernourished, the island people, not for the first time, began the long road back.

The road chosen was longer and more arduous than it might have been because the British, government and people, Socialist and Tory, did not wish to abandon their position as a world leader. War might have impoverished them, circumstances might have made them dismiss the maid and do their own washing up, but to an incurious world they turned a brisk and confident face. For years the world had recognized that the British never knew when they were licked. Now, it seemed, they did not know when they were broke.

They knew, all right. On visits to London during the years I spent chiefly in Russia and Germany I would meet friends in the services or the ministries. "We're in a hell of a mess, old chap," they said, "but we'll work out of it somehow." No one seemed to know just how; but no one doubted it would be done.

The first problem then—and it is the first problem today—was the balance of payments. Exports had to be increased quickly, for the terms of trade continued to be against the United Kingdom. It was in the years 1946–51 that American aid counted most. Loans from the United States and Canada, it is estimated, paid for about 20 per cent of the imports of the United Kingdom between 1946 and 1950.

Simultaneously, the drive to increase exports made headway. The country, and especially the industrial worker, was, in the modern jargon, made "export-conscious."

"Export or die"—the slogan may have seemed exaggerated to some, but it was, and is, an accurate statement of Britain's position. British exports had recovered their pre-war volume by 1947, only two years after the end of the war. Three years later they were two-thirds higher than in 1947. Thereafter, as Germany and Japan began their remarkable economic recovery, exports rose more slowly. But they did rise, and by 1954 they were 80 per cent higher than in 1938.

The upswing in exports was accompanied by two other processes. The pattern of industrial production for exports began to change. Textiles were no longer a dominant export product. Instead, emphasis shifted to the engineering industries: electric motors, factory machinery, electronic equipment, precision instruments, chemicals, and shipbuilding. At the same time, imports—including importation of some raw materials essential to the export trades—were severely restricted, and consumer rationing at home directed British production to foreign markets.

Five years after the war Britain had made great strides toward recovery. There was in that year a surplus of £300,000,000, or $840,000,000, on the balance of payments. But the Korean War, which began in June 1950, was a serious setback for Britain's economy. The country, resolved to play its part, began to rearm. At the same time there was a world-wide rush to stock raw materials, and this forced up the prices of the imports Britain needed for her export trade. The satisfactory balance of payments in 1950 became a deficit of £403,000,000 by 1951.

Import prices began to fall after 1951, and in the next three years there was a balance-of-payments surplus. This recovery was accompanied by a steady rise both in industrial production and in the real national product.

The average rate of increase in industrial production from 1946 to 1954 was 5 per cent, while the real national product increased by 3 per cent. The nation used this increased output, first, for exports; second, to make good the capital losses of the war years by new investment; and, finally, for rearmament. Those who wonder at the rocketing German economic recovery after 1949 and the relative slowness of British economic advance should ponder the fact that in 1950–3 defense expenditure gobbled up *approximately half* of the British total output.

The rationing and other restrictions held over from the war held personal consumption at bay until 1954. Wages rose, but these were offset by a sharp increase in prices, which by 1952 were about 50 per cent above those of 1945. After that year, however, earnings rose more rapidly than prices. With the end of wartime controls after 1952 the standard of living, especially that of the industrial working class, rose perhaps more rapidly than it had ever done before.

The increase in production, the end of rationing, the rises in wages and prices, and the boost in internal consumption all took place against a background of full employment. In the United Kingdom unemployment averaged less than 2 per cent of the working population in 1946–54.

This, then, is the short story of British recovery since the war. By the summer of 1956 the Central Statistical Office could announce that from the beginning of 1946 through the end of 1955 the national output of goods and services had increased in volume by one third. Reckoned in monetary value, the increase was even greater: the figure for 1946 was £8,843,000,000 ($24,480,400,-000), while for 1956 it was £16,639,000,000 ($46,589,200,000). The difference between the increase in value and the increase in production is due to the continuous rise in prices since 1946.

These are impressive figures. But no one in authority in Britain believes that the nation can rest on them. The double problem of maintaining exports abroad and defeating inflation at home remains.

The two are closely related. In 1950 Britain had grabbed 26 per cent of the world market for manufactured goods. German, Japanese, and other competition has now reduced the British share to about 20 per cent, the pre-war figure. To maintain it, Britain must continue the export drive, and this, in turn, involves the attack on inflation.

Inflation began at the time when the British people were emerging from years of war and post-war austerity. There was more money, and suddenly there was plenty to buy as one by one the controls on raw materials, building licenses, food, and clothing disappeared. By 1955 cars and other products that should have gone for export were being sold in bulk in Britain, and gasoline was being imported for them. Industries that should have been almost totally devoted to export trades were producing for a lucrative home market.

The "squeeze" applied by the Conservative government early in 1956 to halt the buying boom is not, as so many Britons hope, a temporary affair. Until British industry can increase its production and adjust itself to the demands of world-wide competition, the country will have to restrain its home purchases in the interests of overseas sales. The preservation of the present standard of living depends directly on exports. If this hard fact is rejected by the British people, then the economy will deteriorate rapidly.

Those interested in the future of Britain, both Americans and British, have been looking at the nation's industry for a decade and sadly shaking their heads. It is too traditional, it is unenterprising, its workers don't work as hard as the Germans or the Japanese, it is restricted by the trade unions or the employers, monopolies and trade rings stifle it. There is a little truth in each of these accusations. But if all were true or even one completely true, how is the sharp increase in volume of production and the general economic recovery to be explained?

Early in 1956, about eleven years after the last Allied bomber flew over the Ruhr, German steel production outstripped British steel production. This caused a good deal of "viewing with alarm" in Britain, much of it by people who failed to realize that before the war Germany yearly produced about five million more tons of steel than Britain. The health of the British economy today does not rely primarily on its output of basic products such as steel or coal but on the nation's ability to sell its manufactured products.

If the number of employees is taken as a criterion, the most important of these manufacturing industries are: (1) engineering, shipbuilding, and electrical goods, with 1,695,000 employees; (2) motor and other vehicles, 934,000; (3) textiles, 898,000; (4) food, drink, and tobacco, 654,000; (5) precision instruments and other metal goods, 531,000; (6) clothing, 524,000; (7) metal manufactures, 519,000; (8) manufacture of wood and cork and miscellaneous manufacturing industries, 472,000; (9) paper and printing, 445,000; (10) chemicals and allied industries, 402,000.

All of these industries contribute to the export drive, including food, drink, and tobacco. There has been no overwhelming demand for such Northern delicacies as toad-in-the-hole or Lancashire hot pot from British markets, but the demand for Scotch whisky seems to be holding up reasonably well.

These industries are the meat and potatoes of the British economy. Since the war there has been a steady increase both in production and productivity (output per man in industry) in these industries. Fortunately for Britain, the greatest rises in over-all production have taken place in the engineering-shipbuilding-electrical-goods group, the vehicles group, and the chemicals group.

Productivity was a more serious problem. Lack of maintenance and capital investment during the war, antiquated machinery, the understandable physical weariness of a labor force that had been working at top speed since 1939 all contributed to a relatively low rate of output per man year in industry compared with the United States.

In 1948 the Labor government took an important step to meet the problem when it formed the Anglo-American Productivity Council. Its goal was to increase productivity in Britain through study of manufacturing methods in the United States. Teams representing management, technicians, and shop workers went to the United States to study American methods. They returned to boost British productivity.

The effort did not stop there. An independent body, the British Productivity Council, was established in 1952 to continue the work. Represented on it are the British Employers' Confederation, the Federation of British Industries, the Trades Union Congress, the Association of British Chambers of Commerce, the National Union of Manufacturers, and the nationalized industries. Under the aegis of the Council, Local Productivity Committees have been formed and the exchange of information and visits between groups from industrial firms have been encouraged.

The Council is a good example of the British approach to a national problem in modern times. The nation's difficulties have gradually, but not entirely, eased the old enmities between some employers and workers. Aware of the extreme seriousness of the situation, they are working together to boost productivity, and they are making headway. Employer-worker consultation is becoming the rule. When the rule is broken by either side there is trouble.

The increase in productivity has been steady. Taking 1948 as the base year with a figure of 100, output per man year in industry rose to 105 in 1949. Save for 1952, when there was a slight relapse, the figure has improved steadily ever since.

Production has shown a corresponding rise. The general index of industrial production, using 1948 as the base year of 100, rose from 114 in 1952 to 121 in 1953 and then jumped to 136 for 1955. But production leveled off in 1956. As that year ended, the expectation was that 1957 would see a new rise in production as the capital investment of the previous five years began to show results.

These figures are one answer to questions often asked abroad: "Why don't the British boost production? Why don't they work?" The answer is that they have boosted production and they are working. Early in 1957 the factory where Jaguar cars are made was almost entirely destroyed by fire. Great efforts by both management and labor put the factory back into production two weeks later. Production and productivity are rising fastest, of course, in the new industries such as electronics. But the economy is burdened by elderly industries such as coal-mining, where extra effort by labor and management cannot, because of existing equipment and conditions, produce dividends in production as they would elsewhere.

Britain's long predominance in both industry and commerce, especially during the last half of the nineteenth century, fostered a lack of enterprise and lethargy in management that is highly unsuitable to the nation's present economic situation. This attitude lingered until the period after the last war when the situation became plainly desperate. Changes of styling and packaging abroad failed to impress British business. "We make a much better product than some of this flashy foreign stuff," one was told loftily. "Let them have their fancy wrappings."

Memories of the golden days of the last century also encouraged a conservative attitude toward change in business methods or the routine of production. Some of the larger industries, however, emerged from the war intent on drastic changes, and others, less progressive, were forced to change by the increased competition for export markets and by the new necessity of using the restricted quantities of raw materials to greatest advantage.

Industrial engineering, including work study, work simplification, plant layout, and planned maintenance, has become a primary concern of industrial management. Many of the managers—the managerial class is about half a million strong—are much more interested in new methods of industry than are the workers. Any innovation that seems to disturb the happy condition of full employment and high wages can provoke discontent among the workers. The more progressive unions are doing their best to explain and advocate change. It is in the middle ranks of labor's officer class, the ranks most interested in the emotional support of "the lads," that the strongest resistance to change is located.

Management in industry, therefore, is beginning to assume some of the importance and standing that it attained long ago in the United States. Facilities for training in management are increasing, although the majority of today's managers never received any special training. Trade unions, employers' associations, and individual concerns are pressing forward with training schemes.

There is a relationship between this development and the arrival in British society of the new middle class. Many of the leaders of this class are in management work in industry and commerce. As their position is solidified by Britain's increasing reliance on the export industries they serve, their social and economic importance is bound to increase. In the past their social position has been well below that of the lawyers, doctors, soldiers, and civil servants who were the elite of the old middle class. That, too, is changing.

Gross fixed capital formation recently has been at about 14 per cent of gross national expenditure. By 1954 its volume was 17 per cent above that of 1938 and about 30 per cent greater than in 1948.

In 1951 and 1952 the government responded to the pressing needs of defense and exports by taking measures to curtail certain kinds of investment. In 1953 and 1954 the policy was reversed, and incentives for investment were written into the Budget. But the wave of home buying in 1955 made it necessary for the government again to impose restraints on investment. In particular it sought moderation in capital outlay for municipal and local building and improvements and a deceleration of investment programs in private industry.

These and other actions taken at that time were the result of the Conservative government's preoccupation with the balance of payments, the nation's gold and dollar reserves, the inflationary trend in the national economy, and the need for investment and expansion in the export industries. These objectives will dominate the economic approach of any government, Socialist or Tory, that achieves power in Britain in the foreseeable future.

British industry has many problems of finance, of production and productivity, of management. But to an outsider it appears that the gravest problem of all is the indulgence by the two main partners in industry, labor and management, in restrictive practices. By preventing the most effective use of labor, technical ability, or materials, or by reducing the incentive for such use, these practices gravely damage the industrial efficiency of the country. Restrictive practices seem to many competent observers a far greater danger to the British economy than strikes.

It is important to understand that such practices are almost as prevalent among management as among labor. Each group has the same basic motivation. They seek a reasonably stable economic life free from the strains and stresses of competition. The psychological explanation may be unspoken desire to return to the old easy days of Britain's unquestioned economic supremacy.

The employers' restrictive practices are less widely advertised than those of the workers. Their classic form is the price-fixing agreement which insures that even the least efficient manufacturing firms will have a profit margin. To maintain the price-fixing system, employers maintain private investigators and courts of inquiry; they can and do discipline the maverick who breaks out of the herd.

One expression of the employers' approach is the tender of contracts identical to the last farthing. Britain in 1955 lost the contract for the Snowy River hydroelectric plant in Australia largely because the eight British firms among the twenty that submitted tenders all submitted exactly the same amount. In New Zealand nineteen out of twenty-six companies bidding for an electric-cable contract submitted identical figures.

The practice is embedded in British industry. Legislation to combat it was introduced into the House of Commons in 1956, but objective experts on the subject believed the legislation fell far short of the drastic action necessary.

Restrictive practices are only too evident in the larger field of relations between the worker and the boss. The importance of problems in this area of conflict is multiplied by their political implications and by the fact that Britain, like other countries, is entering a new period of industrial development. The industrial use of nuclear energy for power and the advent of automation can produce a new industrial revolution in the homeland of the first industrial revolution. But this cannot improve the British economy—indeed, the revolution cannot really get under way as a national effort—without greater co-operation between organized labor and employers and managers.

Throughout this book there have been references to organized labor and to the Trades Union Congress. Now we encounter them in the special field of industrial relations.

Organized labor in Britain is big. There are 23,000,000 people in civil employment, and of these over 9,000,000, nearly the whole of the industrial labor force, are union members. They have an enormous influence on the economic policy of any British government; they are, according to Sir Winston Churchill, "the fourth arm of the Estate"; in the view of Mr. Sam Watson, the tough, capable leader of the Durham miners, they are "the largest single organism in our society."

But organized labor is not a single force, an orderly coalition of unions. It is an extraordinary mixture. Politically some of its leaders are well to the right of the left-wing Tories although they vote Labor. One important union and a number of smaller ones are dominated by Communists. The Transport and General Workers Union has 1,300,000 members; the National Amalgamated Association of Nut and Bolt Makers has 30. Some unions are extremely democratic in composition. Others are petty dictatorships. Many are not unions in name. If you are civil-service clerk, for instance, or even a member in good standing of the Leeds and District Warp Dressers, Twisters and Kindred Trades, you join an association.

The Trades Union Congress is the most powerful voice in British labor. Only 186 of about 400 unions are affiliated with it, but as these 186 include almost all the larger ones, the TUC represents nearly 8,000,000, a majority of the country's union members.

The outsider's idea of the typical trade-unionist is a horny-handed individual in a cloth cap and a shabby "mac." But there are 1,500,000 white-collar workers, including 500,000 civil servants, among the unionists affiliated with the TUC.

The tendency of the white-collar workers to affiliate with the TUC probably will continue. In March of 1956 the London County Council Staff Association decided to apply for affiliation. We can expect that the clerical workers in this type of union will exert increasing influence within the TUC and upon its Council. The TUC's claim to represent the industrial working class thus is being watered down by the admission of the white-collar workers' unions. As this class of worker generally believes that the industrial workers' pay has risen disproportionately and that inflation has hurt the office worker more than it has the industrial worker, the new composition of the TUC may produce sharp internal differences. At any rate, the old position of the TUC as the spokesman only for the industrial worker is a thing of the past.

The TUC is a powerful voice. But it is only a voice. It has great responsibilities and little formal power. It can, for instance, attempt to moderate demands for higher wages and urge restraint, but it cannot prevent any union from pressing such demands. The TUC can advise and conciliate when a strike begins, but it cannot arbitrarily halt one. When two member unions are in a dispute—and such disputes can seriously damage both the national economy and labor's position in British society—the TUC can intervene, but too often its intervention is futile. Each union is self-governing. The TUC's influence, nonetheless, is enormous. The restraint shown by the major unions after the war and during the war on the question of wage increases was largely due to the influence of the TUC.

The general growth of responsibility on the part of many unions can also be attributed, to a great extent, to the missionary work of the TUC.

In recent years the General Council of the TUC has moved toward assuming a stronger position in the field of industrial strikes. It has tried to show the workers that the strike is a two-edged sword that wounds both worker and employer. The TUC maintains that the strike, the workers' great weapon, should not be used indiscriminately because of the damage a strike by one union can do to other unions and to the national economy.

At the 1955 TUC conference the General Council won acceptance of a proposal that it intervene in any case of a threatened strike when negotiations between the employers and the unions seem likely to break down, throwing the members of other unions out of work or endangering their wages, hours, and conditions. This is a significant step forward. Formerly the TUC could move only after negotiations had broken down and a deadlock had been reached. In other words, the TUC acted only at the moment when both sides were firmly entrenched.

But this advance does not improve organized labor's position in regard to the problem of restrictive practices, a problem that is as serious as strikes or threats of strikes.

The *Daily Mirror* of London, that brash, vigorous tabloid which is the favorite newspaper of the industrial working class, published an inquiry into the trade unions in 1956. Its authors, Sydney Jacobson and William Connor, who conducts the column signed "Cassandra," traced the origin of restrictive practices back to 1811, when bands of workers known as the Luddites broke into lace and stocking factories and smashed the machinery. "The suspicion toward new methods has never entirely died out in this country," they wrote, "and although sabotage of machinery is rare (but not unknown) the protests have taken a new direction—the slowing down of output by the men themselves and the development of a whole series of practices that cut down the production of goods and services."

Any reader of the British press can recall dozens of instances of restrictive practices by labor. One famous one concerned the floating grain elevator at Hull, an east-coast seaport. This elevator, which cost £200,000 ($560,000), was kept idle for two months because the Transport and General Workers Union insisted that it should be worked by twice as many men as the Transport Commission thought necessary. The Transport Commission, incidentally, represented a nationalized industry.

And there was the union that fined a milkman £2 for delivering milk before 7:30 a.m.

The unions are quick and brutal in their punishment of those who break their rules. Indeed, today, when there is full employment and the unions generally enjoy a prosperity and power undreamed of by their founders, they are more malicious than in the old days when they were fighting for their rights. The principal weapon against an offending worker is to "send him to Coventry." No one speaks to him; he eats and walks home alone. Ronald Hewitt, a crane-driver, endured this for a year. He had remained at work, obeying his union's rules, when his fellow workers, who belonged to another union, went out on strike. Hewitt was a person of unusual mental toughness. Another worker sent to Coventry committed suicide.

Many of these punishments are the outcome of situations in which unofficial strikes send out the workers. Those who remain and who are punished are accused of being "scabs" because they obey the union's rules.

All union leaders publicly acknowledge the great importance of increased productivity in British industry. But the methods of boosting productivity often seem to some union leaders to strike at the principles for which they have fought so long. For instance, an increase in output is regarded by the veterans solely as a traditional means of increasing the profits of the employers. Moreover, increases in productivity often involve the introduction of new machines and layoffs for some workers. To the short-sighted, appeals for greater productivity thus seem calls to smash the job security that is the fetish of the industrial working class. This sort of union leader just does not seem to grasp, or to want to grasp, the principle that increased productivity is a general good benefiting workers, employers, and unions.

Efficiency is not the sole god of British industry, as is evident when one studies the weird system known as "demarcation" in the shipbuilding industry. To install a port light under this system requires the labor of a shipwright to mark the position of the light, a caulker to indicate and make the hole for the light, another driller to make the surrounding holes, and another caulker to fix the bolts and chain. In addition, a foreman for each of the trades supervises the operation. Interunion disputes arising out of such unnecessarily complicated operations frequently result in a stoppage of work and a delay in the filling of export contracts.

The most alarming example occurred at Cammell Laird's, a shipbuilding company, in 1955 and lasted until well into 1956. New ships were being built—for dollars—and the strike began over a difference between woodworkers and sheet-metal workers. The new vessels were to have aluminum facing in the insulation. Formerly the woodworkers had done this sort of work, and they claimed rights over the new job. But the sheet-metal workers said that, as aluminum was metal, the job was theirs. The two groups and management finally reached an agreement. Then the drillers of the Shipwrights' Union entered the affair and a new strike developed.

The construction of the ships was delayed for six months and more. The ability of Cammell Laird's or other British shipyards to offer foreign buyers a firm date for completion of ships became a matter of doubt. About 400 workers were dismissed as redundant. About 200 strikers found work elsewhere. Thousands of other jobs were jeopardized. There was not the slightest indication that those who inspired the strike took much account of its effects on their country's future.

As a result of the application of the demarcation principle in shipyards—you drill holes in wood, we drill holes in aluminum— wage costs are often as much as 6 per cent higher than normal.

The innate conservatism of union leaders and the rank and file in shipyards, industrial plants, and factories has been proof against the missionary work of critics extolling the far different approach of American labor. The leaders are often unmoved by figures which show that increased productivity by the American labor force has resulted in a far greater national consumption. In many cases neither the union leader nor the union member will accept the idea that new machines and new methods mean more efficient production, lower costs, and higher wages.

British union leaders often counter that the American worker has no memory of unemployment and depression. This is, of course, untrue. Indeed, in many instances political and economic it seems that British labor has made too much of its experiences, admittedly terrible, in the depression of two decades ago. American labor, by eagerly accepting new processes and machines, has attempted to insure itself against the recurrence of a depression. British labor has not.

Industrial disputes affect the British economy's ability to meet the challenge of the new industrial revolution. Disputes between union and union are especially important. In 1955 there were three national strikes. All were complicated by interunion friction.

Another complicating factor in industrial relations is the slow disappearance, under the pressure of increased mechanization, of the system of wage differentials in British industry. These differentials represented a reasonable difference between the wages of skilled and unskilled workers. With their disappearance, skilled workers in one industry have found themselves earning less money than unskilled workers in another. One cause is the ability of the big "general" unions to win wage increases. Another is the practice of demanding wage increases solely on the basis of the rising cost of living.

Naturally the disappearance of differentials has led to hot disputes among workers and unions. In this atmosphere it is difficult for either the union leaders or the employers to urge increased productivity and harder work. "Everyone is furious with everyone else," an industrialist in the Midlands said. "They start with me, but they are pretty mad at each other, too."

In this interminable war between labor and management, the former wields a weapon of enormous potency—the strike. Labor acknowledges its disadvantages, but the right to strike is fiercely guarded. The whispered suggestion that strikes might be made illegal unites the labor movement as does nothing else. Labor needs the strike as its ultimate weapon: the hydrogen bomb of British industrial relations. And because of the peculiar economic conditions in Britain, the employer finds himself almost weaponless. He can still dismiss an unsatisfactory employee, if he has a good reason and can convince the employee's union that it *is* a good reason. But dismissal does not mean much in an era of full employment.

Right-wing critics on both sides of the Atlantic have contended for a decade that British economic difficulties are rooted in strikes and other industrial disturbances. There is something in this, but, as H. L. Mencken would have said, not much.

From 1946 through 1954 the days lost through strikes in Britain ranged from a low of 1,389,000 in 1950 to a high of 2,457,000 in 1954. Due to strikes in the newspaper and railroad industries and on the docks, 1955 was an exceptionally bad year: 3,794,000 working days were lost. The figures look big, and of course it would have been much better for Britain if they were half as large. But let's put them into perspective. The figure for 1955, admittedly high, represents a loss of less than one day's work per man in every five years' employment. The loss to production through industrial accidents is eight times as high.

Both sides know that a strike is a costly business: costly to labor, to management, to the union, to the nation. In many cases the threat of a strike has been enough to force the employers to give way. Inevitably, the higher cost of production resulting from the new wage rates is passed on to the consumer. The merry-go-round of rising prices, rising wages, and rising costs spins dizzily onward. Overseas the buyer who is choosing between a Jaguar or a Mercedes finds that the price of the former has suddenly risen, so he buys the German car rather than the British one. This is what the economists mean when they warn British labor and industry about pricing themselves out of the export market.

As we have seen, the industrial worker is doing pretty well in Britain, even if the rise in prices is taken into consideration. The average weekly earnings for all male adult workers, according to the records kept by the Ministry of Labor, show a rise from £3 9s. 0d. in 1938 to £10 17s. 5d. in 1955—an increase of 215 per cent. The coal-miners who were earning £3 2s. 10d. in 1938 are now earning a weekly wage of £13 18s. 6d. The figure does not represent wealth by American standards, for it amounts to approximately $38.99. But it is high pay by British standards, and when the low cost of subsidized housing and the comparatively low cost of food are taken into account it will be seen that the British miner is living very well.

The miner's view is that he does a dirty, dangerous job, that he has never been well paid before, and that if a union does not exist to win pay rises for its members, what good is it? The miners and the union members in the engineering industry belong to strong unions able to win wage increases by threats of a strike. Once these increases are granted, other smaller unions clamor for their share of wage rises. The merry-go-round takes another turn.

Government attempts to urge restraint, through the TUC, upon the unions customarily fall afoul of the snag that each union believes that it is a special case and that although other unions can postpone their demands for higher wages until next year, it cannot. So one union makes a move and the whole business begins again. If the increase is not granted, there is a strike or a threat of a strike. The national economy suffers, class antagonism increases, and export production is delayed. For such is the interdependence of the British industrial machine and so great is the drive for exports that any industrial dispute that reaches the strike stage inevitably affects exports.

A modern strike is like a modern war. No one wins and everyone loses. A classic case is the Rolls-Royce strike of 1955, which involved not only employers and union labor but, eventually, the Roman Catholic Church and the Communist Party. The cause of the strike was a conflict between restrictive practices and a stubborn workman named Joseph McLernon, who worked at the Rolls-Royce factory at Blantyre in Scotland as a polisher of connecting rods.

The workers in Joe's shop feared that, in view of reduced work, some of their number might be let out. So they agreed to share their work by limiting bonus earnings to 127 per cent of the basic rate. McLernon, however, refused to limit his overtime. He polished as long and as hard as ever and refused the assistance of another worker. For this, McLernon was reprimanded by his union, the General Iron Fitter's Association.

Joe had been working for Rolls-Royce for twelve years. The firm is considered a good employer. But its managers were men of conviction. They objected to the union picking on Joe and said so. Three months later the union expelled McLernon.

Enter the Communists with many an agonizing cry about the solidarity of labor. They demanded that Rolls-Royce fire McLernon on the grounds that he no longer belonged to the union. The employers refused, and immediately all the other polishers stopped work. Joe kept right on. By the end of the day the entire factory labor force of 600 men was out on strike.

The Amalgamated Engineering Union's local branch then entered the picture. After a few days another 7,500 workers at the Hillington and East Kilbride factories had struck.

Was it a strike? Certainly, said the General Iron Fitter's Association. The Electrical Trades Union, dominated by Communists, recognized the strike as official in accordance with its rule of recognizing all strikes involving electricians as official until they are declared otherwise. The Amalgamated Engineering Union, after much soul-searching, decided to back the strike and approved strike pay for its members. Negotiations between the Employers' Federation and a committee representing the various unions got nowhere.

The Roman Catholic Archbishop of Glasgow then issued a pastoral letter warning the workers against Communism. McLernon is a Catholic. But so were many of the workers who wanted him fired.

The strike dragged on for seven weeks. The strikers lost over £700,000 ($1,960,000) in wages. By the time the strike was over, no one on the strikers' side could disentangle the objectives of the various groups that had called it. Rolls-Royce export contracts were delayed. The Royal Air Force failed to get delivery on time of some important machines. Other industries also involved in the export trade and in national defense were slowed down. The unions had maintained solidarity at a tremendous cost. But when the strike collapsed, Joe McLernon was still at his job, polishing away. He alone could be termed a winner. Rolls-Royce, the unions, industry, and the nations were losers.

The Communist intervention in the Rolls-Royce strike symbolized its current role in Britain. This is to win control of key positions in the British unions so that the Communist Party will be able to paralyze British industry in the event of an international crisis or a war. To achieve this ultimate objective, the Communists obviously intend to establish a stranglehold on the communications and defense industries.

This is the real Communist danger in Britain. Active political campaigning by the Communist Party has been fumbling, misdirected, and notably unsuccessful. Neither the old colonel from Cheltenham who classes the sprightly dons of the Labor Party with "those damned Bolshies" nor the Bible Belt Congressman who confuses British Socialist politicians with Russian Communists is on the right track. The danger of Communism in Britain lies in the unions. So does the defense against the danger.

The pattern of Communist success is uneven. Communists lead the Electrical Trades Union, ninth-largest in the country, with a membership of about 215,000. Because electricity is everywhere in modern industry the union's members are everywhere. And although probably not more than one in every sixty members of the

ETU is a member of the Communist Party, the party completely runs the union.

Here is a curious sidelight on Communist methods. The ETU is weak financially, perhaps the poorest of the ten largest unions. But it spends money freely on "education." The ETU has its own Training College at Esher, where its more ambitious members can be trained to further the interests of the Communist Party and to silence the voices of critics and doubters. Although the non-Communist members of the ETU consider the college as a valuable device for the advancement of the worker, the institution plainly is a training school for Communists and their creatures in their prolonged war against the British economy.

One of the basic concepts of British Socialism is the solidarity of the working class. Acceptance of this concept makes it difficult for the industrial worker to think of the Communist, who comes from the same town, speaks with the same accent, wears the same clothes, as an enemy. There is a pathetic ingenuousness about workers who try to tell the visitor that the Communists "are just the same sort of blokes as us except they've got a different political idea."

The *Daily Mirror* team in its portrayal of the trade unions devoted a chapter to "The Communist Challenge." Significantly, a large part of the chapter provided an incisive and illuminating illustration of just how the Communists move to gain control of a union.

Where else are the Communists strong? They are in control in some areas of the National Union of Mineworkers. Arthur Horner, the Secretary of the Union, is a Communist. But they are being fought hard in the NUM by men like Sam Watson, who heads its Durham region.

The connection in the Communist mind between the control of the NUM and the ETU is obvious. Control of these two unions would enable Communists to halt the flow of coal and electric power to Britain's factories. Not much more is needed to cripple a nation's economy.

But the Communists press on. They establish cells in the aircraft industry. They work industriously at fomenting trouble on the docks, especially in the ports—such as London, Liverpool, and Glasgow—through which most of the exports pass. Already the threat to block coal and power can be augmented with a threat to halt defense production and exports. It is improbable that the Communists are now powerful enough to carry their program to a triumphant conclusion. But they are on their way.

How do they work? Very much as they do elsewhere in Europe. In Britain, as in Germany or Italy or France, the Communists care very little about better pay or better working conditions for union members. Their objective is power, power that will enable them to push the interests of the Union of Soviet Socialist Republics. And, to repeat, they have learned that for them power in Britain is obtainable only through control of the unions and not through Parliament.

The Communists try to establish cells in every important factory in Britain. These cells maintain contact with the district secretary of the Communist Party, who knows from the cell exactly what sort of work the factory is doing. Little wonder that Soviet visitors are incurious about the details of British production when they are shown British factories. The information obviously is safely filed in Moscow.

When an industrial dispute develops in a factory, the Communists seek to widen the area of dispute and to involve as many unions as possible. They also do their best to bring the recognized non-Communist leaders of organized labor into disrepute. One method is to organize support for demands that the Communists know the management cannot accept. When a strike organized on this basis fails, the Communists point out to the union members that the leadership is weak and hint that a more "dynamic"—i.e., Communist—direction would benefit the union.

The Communist drive to break the power of the unions and thus to spread industrial discontent is assisted by the character of some union leaders. In many instances leaders are elected to hold their jobs for life, and after years of power they become dictatorial.

It is a favorite Communist charge that the union bosses are "in" with the employers, and that as long as their jobs are safe they will do nothing to upset the present situation.

In the trade unions, as elsewhere in British society, the war alliance with the Soviet Union inspired sympathy with the people of Russia and admiration for their resistance to the Nazis. These sentiments altered under the impact of the cold war, and they altered faster at the top levels of the labor movement than anywhere else. The Trades Union Congress in 1948 attacked Communist activities in the unions in a pamphlet called *Defend Democracy* and followed this with another pamphlet, *Tactics of Disruption*. In 1949 the TUC quitted the World Federation of Trade Unions, which is dominated by the Communists, and helped establish the International Confederation of Free Trade Unions. A year later the TUC barred Communists and fascists as delegates to the annual conference of Trades Councils.

Meanwhile, the leaders of the TUC strove to explain the true nature of the Communist challenge to free unions, and to emphasize the refusal of the Communists to accept democratic principles in the unions or anywhere else.

All this has had some effect, but not enough. The TUC has thus far failed to shake the average industrial worker out of his lethargy. Safe in the security arising from full employment and high wages, he does not take the Communist challenge seriously. And now that many of the basic objectives of the labor movement have been won, he does not work so hard to protect them as he did to win them.

In this atmosphere Communist successes are inevitable. For it is the members of a Communist cell in a union or a factory who are prepared to talk all night at a meeting, to vote solidly as a bloc in support of one Communist candidate while the non-Communists divide their votes among three or four candidates. In many cases the non-Communists will not even turn out to vote—it is too much trouble, especially when they can watch the "telly" or go to the dog races.

The official leadership of the unions faces a formidable task. It must first educate the rank and file on the true nature of Communism. After that, it must organize anti-Communist action in the unions. Here they encounter a real obstacle in the minds of the rank and file. In the past, reaction in Britain and elsewhere has lumped Communists, Socialists, and trade-unionists together. To many a unionist, anti-Communism seems, at first inspection, to be an employers' trick to break the solidarity of the working classes. Of course the Communists do all they can to popularize and spread this erroneous idea.

The Communists in Britain seem to have been moderately successful in establishing themselves as a national rather than an international force. When Frank Foulkes, the General President of the Electrical Trades Union and a member of the Communist Party, asserted: "This country means more to me than Russia and all the rest of the world put together," few challenged this obvious insincerity.

We must accept, then, that Communism within the trade unions is a far more serious threat to the welfare of Britain than Communism as a political party. It is on hand to exacerbate all the difficulties in the field of industrial relations which have arisen and will arise during a change from obsolete economic patterns to the new patterns by which Britain must live.

The introduction of automation—the use of machines to superintend the work of other machines—and of nuclear energy for industrial power are two of the principal adjustments that British industry must make. Each will involve labor layoffs and shifts in working population. These are important and difficult processes, and with the Communists on hand to paint them in the darkest colors there will have to be common sense, tolerance, and good will on the part of both management and labor. In particular, the rank and file of British industry must be made aware how important the changes are to the average worker and his family. There is little use in publishing pamphlets, however admirable, if the man for whom they are intended will not stir from in front of the television set.

A comparison of some of the long-range economic plans laid down by successive governments, Socialist and Tory, with the general attitude of the man in the street leads to the conclusion that, whereas government has been "thinking big," the governed have, in the main, been "thinking small." There is in Britain little recognition of or admiration for the truly impressive program for industrial use of nuclear energy. By 1965 Britain expects to have nineteen nuclear power stations in operation. These will be capable of generating between 5,000 and 6,000 megawatts, or about a third of the annual requirement for generating capacity. It is estimated that the operation of these nineteen stations can save the country eighteen million tons of coal each year.

In addition to this basic program, the Atomic Energy Authority will build six more reactors to produce plutonium for military purposes and power for civil purposes. The total cost of the basic program alone will be about £400,000,000 ($1,120,000,000) a year in the early 1960's.

The leaders of both Conservative and Labor parties believe that the program is vital to Britain. Indeed, the foresight, imagination, and ambition of the men at the top on both sides is one of the reasons why the British economy, despite all its present weaknesses and future difficulties, is a good bet to pull through. What is lacking is the ability of any leader or party to evoke from the country the energetic response necessary to meet and defeat the weaknesses and difficulties.

One instance of this lethargy on the part of either employers or the industrial working class is their failure to respond to wider educational advantages, especially in the field of technical knowledge. Recognizing the necessity for greater technical education, the government intends to spend £100,000,000 ($280,000,000) on technical education from 1956 to 1961. Will the government and the people get their money's worth in the present atmosphere?

Industrial research is on a much smaller scale in Britain than in the United States. For years British industries thought it was cheaper to buy patents abroad than to do their own research. As a

result, British technicians were lured abroad. Even today many
industries are indifferent if not openly hostile to the idea of "expensive" industrial research.

The attitude of the new working class to education, technical
or otherwise, has been described earlier in this book. The boys, in
the eyes of their parents, need no more schooling than that given
them before they can leave school and go to work in the factory.
The girls need a little more if they are to graduate into the ranks of
clerical workers, but many girls, attracted by the independence
offered by jobs in mill or factory, leave school with their brothers.

Let me sum up some conclusions about the British economy:

*The drive for exports is not a passing economic phase but
a permanent condition. If wages and prices cannot be held down,
Britain will be priced out of her markets, and the standard of living
of the working class and of all other classes will fall.*

*The ability of the country to meet the adjustments made
necessary by the revolution in the sources of industrial power and
by the introduction of new industrial techniques is gravely endangered by the restrictive practices of both employers and labor, by
interunion bickering often arising from these practices, and by the
prolonged and vicious Communist attack on the trade-union structure.*

*Neither among the middle class nor among the working
class is there sufficient awareness of the critical situation in which
Britain finds herself.*

This is a somber picture. It is relieved, I think, by our knowledge that the British are a surprising people. They are going through
a period of change in their society and of adjustment to their society's place in the comity of nations. The very fact that they are
changing argues for them. The Britain of 1938 could not exist in
the modern world. The Britain of 1958 can be at the top.

Granted the indifference of the working class to politics and
its fierce reaction against anything that seems to threaten its newly
won ease, granted the middle class's penchant for the past, its out-

worn ideas—these are still a great people, tough, energetic, at heart politically mature. And they believe in themselves perhaps more than they are willing to admit. Their character, more than coal or sea power or fortuitous geographical circumstances, made them great in the past. It can keep them great in the future.

XI. *The British Character and Some Influences*

I am a great friend to public amusements, for they keep people from vice.

SAMUEL JOHNSON

I have never been able to understand why pigeon-shooting at Hurlingham should be refined and polite while a rat-catching match in Whitechapel is low.

T. H. HUXLEY

OBVIOUSLY there is great deal more to British society than political and economic problems, although a casual visitor might not think so. Visiting pundits find themselves immersed in the profundities of the Foreign Office or following the ideological gymnastics of Socialist intellectuals. Consequently, they depart firmly convinced that the British are a sober, rather solemn people. These islanders, as a matter of fact, are an exceptionally vigorous and boisterous lot and have been for centuries. Their interest in diplomacy, politics, and commerce is exceeded only by their devotion to cricket, beer, and horse racing. Nor should we allow the deadening background to bemuse us about the essential character of the British. The misty mournfulness of the English countryside, the bleak inhospitality of a Midland city, the eternal sameness of suburbia have failed to tame the incorrigible robustness of the national character.

To know the British today one must know not only their government and politics, their industry and commerce, but other aspects of life through which the national character is expressed. The press, the schools, the military services, sports and amusements, pubs and clubs all are part of the changing British world. Each has been affected by changes in the class structure. Each, in its way, is important to Americans and their understanding of Britain. Opinion about the United States in Britain is based largely on what Britons read in their newspapers. And, whether or not Americans admire the class distinctions inherent in the public-school system, perhaps a majority of the leaders with whom the United States will deal in the future will be products of that system.

THE PRESS:
THE THUNDERER AND THE TIN HORNS

A graduate of Smith, home from a stay in London, asked: "How can you read those London newspapers? Nothing but crime and sex—I couldn't find any news." Years ago Webb Miller, the great United Press correspondent, advised me: "Read *The Times* every day, read all of it, if you want to know what is going on in this country and the world." Both Webb and the young lady from Smith were right: the British press contains some of what is best and a great deal of what is worst in daily journalism.

Most Americans and many Britons, when they speak of the press, mean the London daily and Sunday newspapers. The London papers concern us most because they are national newspapers circulating throughout Britain and influencing and reflecting opinion far beyond the boundaries of greater London. One newspaper published in the provinces, the *Manchester Guardian,* may be said to have national—indeed, world—standing. One of the most influential, interesting, and well-written newspapers, it can also assume on occasion a highly irritating unctuousness.

There are a large number of provincial newspapers—about a hundred morning and evening dailies and Sunday papers, and about eleven hundred weeklies. Many of them are read far more thoroughly than the London "national" paper that the provincial family also buys.

Not long ago a British cabinet minister who represents a constituency in the western Midlands told me his constituents "got their news from the BBC, their entertainment from the London dailies, and their political guidance from the principal newspaper in a near-by provincial city." Other politicians have referred to the same pattern.

Because most London daily and Sunday newspapers circulate all over the British isles, circulation figures are high by American standards. The *News of the World,* a Sunday newspaper that built its circulation on straight court reporting of the gamier aspects of British life, had a record circulation of about 8,000,000 copies. Recently its circulation has dropped slightly, a development that puzzles Fleet Street, for there is no lack of sex, crime, or sport— or interest in them—in Britain.

Of the London dailies, the largest in circulation is the *Daily Mirror,* a tabloid whose circulation average between January and June of 1955 was 4,725,122. The *Daily Express,* the bellwether of the Beaverbrook newspapers, had a circulation of just over 4,000,-000 during the same period, and three other London dailies, the *Daily Mail,* the *Daily Telegraph,* and the *News Chronicle,* all boasted circulations of better than 1,000,000.

For every 1,000 Britons, 611 copies of the daily newspapers are sold each day. Compare this with the United States figure of 353 per 1,000. Britain is a good newspaper country, and the London press is lusty, uninhibited, and highly competitive.

American newspapermen working in London customarily divide the press between the popular newspapers, such as the *Daily*

Mirror and the *Daily Mail,* and the small-circulation papers, such as *The Times* and the *Manchester Guardian.* The circulation of *The Times* for January–June 1955 was 211,972 and for the *Guardian* 156,154. Similarly, on Sundays there is a division between the *Sunday Times* (606,346) and the *Observer* (564,307) and such mass-circulation "Sundays" as the *Sunday Express,* the *Sunday Pictorial,* and the *People.*

The distinction is not based primarily on circulation. *The Times* and the *Manchester Guardian* and the *Daily Telegraph* on weekdays and the *Sunday Times* and the *Observer* on Sundays print more news about politics, diplomacy, and world events than do the mass-circulation papers. They are responsible and they are well written. The *Daily Telegraph,* which has a circulation of over 2,000,000, is the only one in this group whose circulation is in the "popular" field. But it has given few hostages to fortune: its news columns contain a considerable number of solid foreign-news items as well as first-class domestic reporting.

The shortage of newsprint (the paper on which newspapers are printed) has curtailed the size of British papers since 1939. Almost all newsprint is imported, and with the balance of payments under pressure the expenditure of dollars for it has been restricted. But the situation has improved slowly and the London papers are fattening, although they remain thin by New York standards.

Considering this restriction, the responsible newspapers do a splendid job. Day in and day out the foreign news of *The Times* maintains remarkably high standards of accuracy and insight. The anonymous reporters—articles by *Times* men are signed "From Our Own Correspondent"—write lucidly and easily. *The Times* has never accepted the theory that involved and complicated issues can be boiled down into a couple of hundred words with the nuances discarded. News is knowledge, and no one has yet found a way to make it easy to acquire knowledge.

But *The Times,* often called "*The Times* newspaper," is a good deal more than a report on Britain and the world. It is an institution reflecting all British life. By reading its front page entirely devoted to classified advertising one can get a complete picture of upper-class and upper-middle-class Britain. In the left-hand columns are births, deaths, marriages, and memorial notices. If an American wants to understand how unstintingly the British upper classes gave their sons and brothers and fathers to the First World War, let him look at the memorial notices on the anniversary of the Battle of the Somme. If he wants to see how hard-pushed these same classes are today, let him read the painful, often pathetic admissions in the columns where jewelry, old diplomatic uniforms, and the other impedimenta of the class are offered for sale.

The editorials of *The Times*—the British call editorials "leaders" or "leading articles"—are, of course, one of the most important features in journalism. *The Times* is independent politically, but it does its best to explain and expound the policies of the government of the day. Over the years since the war it has supported individual measures laid down by Conservative and Labor governments and it has assailed the policies of both the left and right when this has been conceived of as the duty of *The Times*. The editorial writing in *The Times* often attains a peak of brilliance seldom achieved in any other newspaper. For a time, especially in the period before World War II, "The Thunderer," as it was once called, had become a whisperer. Recently *The Times* has spoken on national and international issues with its old resonance and sharpness.

The influence of *The Times* among politicians, civil servants, and diplomats is extraordinary. It is, I suppose, the one newspaper read thoroughly by all the foreign diplomats in London. As recently as the spring of 1956 an editorial in *The Times* discussing a reconsideration of Britain's defense needs sent the German Ambassador scurrying to the Foreign Office to inquire whether the editorial reflected government policy. It did.

This influence is the result of *The Times*'s special position in British journalism. The editorial-writers and some of the reporters of *The Times* often are told things that are hidden from other reporters. Also, they are members in good standing of that important, amorphous group, the Establishment, which exists at the center of British society; they know and are known by the politicians, the key civil servants, the ministers. Occasionally *The Times* is used to test foreign or domestic reaction to a measure under consideration by the government. By discussing the measure in an editorial, *The Times* will provoke in its letter columns a wider discussion into which various sections of public opinion, left, right, and center, will be drawn.

No other newspaper in the free world has a letter column comparable to that of *The Times*. The first letter may be a sharp analysis of government policy in Persia and the last the report by a Prime Minister that he has seen a rare bird on a walk through St. James's park. Some of the letter column's discussions touch on matters of national interest. Others deal with the Christian names given to children or the last time British troops carried their colors into action.

The *Manchester Guardian,* with a smaller circulation and a smaller foreign staff, still manages to make its influence felt far beyond Manchester. Its policies are those of the Liberal party and, as the Liberal Party is now in eclipse, the *Guardian* brings to the discussion of national and international affairs a detached and refreshing sharpness. Where *The Times* occasionally adopts the tone of a wise and indulgent father in its comments on the world, the *Guardian* speaks with the accents of a worldly-wise nanny. When the *Guardian* is aroused, its "leaders" can be corrosive and bitter. It is less likely to support the foreign policy of the government of the day than is *The Times*. Consequently, the *Guardian* is liable to be more critical than *The Times* in dealings with the United States and American foreign policy. (The Suez crisis was a notable exception.) But it is well informed about the United States, and so are its readers. In Alistair Cooke and Max Freedman the *Guardian* has two of the best correspondents now writing in the United States for the British press. Their reports are long, detailed, and accurate, and Cooke, in particular, never forgets that what a foreign people sees in its theaters, reads in its magazines, and does on its vacations is also news to the readers at home.

Such great provincial newspapers as the *Yorkshire Post* and the *Scotsman* follow the conservative approach to news adopted by *The Times,* the *Manchester Guardian,* and the *Daily Telegraph.* With the responsible London dailies they serve the upper middle class and are its most outspoken mouthpieces in a period when, as we have seen, that class is being pressed by high taxation, the rising cost of living, and the simultaneous development of a new middle class and a prosperous working class. The *Sunday Times,* for instance, has devoted many columns to the plight of the professional man and his family, and all of these papers have reported at length on the appearance of associations and groups devoted to, or supposedly devoted to, the interests of the middle class and opposition to the unions that represent the new working class.

The cult of anonymity has persisted longer in Britain's responsible and reliable newspapers than in the United States. Although Fleet Street knows the names of *The Times*'s reporters, the public does not. Richard Scott, the Diplomatic Correspondent of the *Manchester Guardian,* has no byline, nor has Hugh Massingham, the brilliant Political Correspondent of the *Observer.* The influence wielded in the United States by columnists still is reserved in Britain almost entirely to the anonymous "leader"-writers of the responsible British newspapers. Working with the editorial-writers are hundreds of industrious, well-educated, experienced reporters. They are good men to talk to and to drink with, and they are tough men to beat on a story.

But they and the newspapers they represent are not a part of the bubbling, uproarious, pyrotechnical world of the popular London dailies. Here is a circus, a daily excitement for anyone who enjoys newspapers. The *Daily Express,* the *Daily Mail,* the *News Chronicle,* the *Daily Herald,* the *Mirror,* and the *Sketch* compete hotly for news and entertainment. Their headlines are brash, their writing varies from wonderfully good to wonderfully bad, and their editorials are written with a slam-bang exuberance that is stimulating and occasionally a little frightening. This is the true, tempestuous world of Fleet Street.

In this world the great names are not confined to the writers and editors. The publishers, called "proprietors" in Britain, tower over all. Of these the most interesting, successful, and stimulating is Lord Beaverbrook, who runs the *Daily Express,* the *Sunday Express,* and the *Evening Standard* with a gusto undiminished by seventy-eight active years.

"The Beaver" occupies a unique place in British journalism and politics. No one has neutral feelings about him. Either you like him or you hate him; there is no middle course. I suppose nothing gives him more satisfaction than knowing that when he arrives in London, men in Fleet Street pubs and West End clubs ask one another: "What do you think the Beaver's up to now?"

Is "what the Beaver is up to" really important? The enmity of the *Express,* which is the enmity of Lord Beaverbrook, can make a politician squirm. But does it really lower his standing with the voters? I doubt it. Lord Beaverbrook is an incorrigible Don Quixote who has tilted at and been tossed by many windmills. He is, incidentally, a more powerful writer than most of his employees. Early in 1957 he was prodding his newspapers to the attack against the government's plans for closer economic association with Europe. The headlines were bold and black, the indignation terrifying. Will the campaign itself alter government policy? I doubt it.

Lord Beaverbrook once remarked that he ran his papers to conduct propaganda. Just before the retirement of Sir Winston Churchill, Lord Beaverbrook was asked why his newspapers were so critical of Sir Anthony Eden, the heir presumptive to the premiership. He replied that Sir Anthony had never supported the policies of the Beaverbrook newspapers. As no other leading politician had thrown his weight that way, this seemed a rather weak reason for attacking the new leader of the Conservative Party. The political affiliation of the *Daily Express* is Independent Conservative.

But the Beaverbrook campaigns perform a real public service

by fixing public attention upon issues. I do not think the editorials convince—I have yet to meet a *Daily Express* reader who confused the "leader" column with pronouncements from Sinai—but they encourage that discussion of public issues which is essential in a democracy. Of course the *Express* newspapers' tactics annoy nice-minded people. But the tradition of a free press includes not only such august journals as *The Times* but the rip-roaring, fire-eating crusaders as well. There is not much chance that the popular press in Britain will model itself on *The Times,* but if it did so, the result would be a loss to journalism and to the nation. And as long as the Beaverbrook tradition survives—as long, indeed, as Lord Beaverbrook himself is around to draw on his inexhaustible fund of indignation—one section of the popular press is bound to remain contentious and vigorous.

The *Daily Express,* the morning paper of the Beaverbrook empire, is technically one of the best newspapers in the world. Its layout is admirable, and its headline-writers often show a touch of genius. In its writing and its presentation of news it has been much affected by such divergent American influences as *The New Yorker* and *Time.*

The *Express* is brightly written (too much so at times), and its tastes in policies and politicians are incalculable. Along with a liberal helping of political, foreign, and crime reporting it offers two of the best features in British journalism: Osbert Lancaster's pocket cartoon on the front page and the humorous column of "Beachcomber" on the editorial page. "Beachcomber" and Lancaster are sharp and penetrating commentators on the daily scene. In many instances their references to the occasional inanities of the British society are more cogent than anything to be found in the editorial columns of the *Express.*

The *Express* successfully caters to the new middle class that has arisen since the war, especially that part of it which is involved in the communications industry. The young advertising manager from the provinces who has "arrived" in London may find *The Times* too verbose and the *Telegraph* too stodgy. The *Express,* with its bright features on the theater or London night life, attracts him. But, oddly, three principal features of the *Express* cater to very different tastes. Osbert Lancaster's subject matter is drawn usually from the upper middle class—his Maudie Littlehampton, after all, is a Lady. The humor of "Beachcomber" appeals to tastes that reject the average in British humor, and Sefton Delmer, the peripatetic foreign correspondent of the *Express,* often writes stories on international issues which are much more involved and adult than would seem suitable for the majority of the newspaper's four million readers.

This divided approach is not so obvious in the *Daily Mirror,* which has the largest circulation of any of the London dailies. This is an important newspaper in that it is the most accurate reflection I know of the tastes and mores of the new working class in Britain. There are many indications elsewhere that Cecil King, its proprietor, and his chief lieutenants have pondered long and earnestly about Britain's problems. The *Mirror*'s pamphlet on trade unions and an earlier pamphlet on Anglo-American relations are solid contributions to the literature on these subjects. But the *Daily Mirror*'s customary approach to policies and issues is as robust and sharp as that of a policeman to a drunk. It is belligerent rather than persuasive; it loves big type.

But the *Daily Mirror*'s handling of certain types of stories, particularly those involving industrial disputes and crime, is excellent. (British crime reporting in general, although circumscribed by the libel laws, is of high caliber.) The *Mirror*'s editorials, with their GET OUT or PASS THIS BILL approach to politicians and measures, may alienate as many as they win, but the editorials are alive, dealing often with problems—such as automation and wage differentials—that are of the keenest interest to the industrial working class.

The *Mirror* is much closer to the thinking of this class than is the *Daily Herald,* usually considered the official Labor newspaper. The Trades Union Congress owns 49 per cent of the stock in the *Daily Herald,* and Odhams Press Ltd. owns the remainder. Once

powerful and well informed on industrial and labor-movement hap-
penings, the *Herald* no longer seems to represent either the movement or the industrial working class that supports the movement.
Its approach is stodgier than that of the *Mirror,* less in keeping with
the tastes of the new working class.

The *Mirror*'s most renowned features are "Cassandra" and
"Jane." The former, written by William Connor, is one of the
hardest-hitting and most provocative features in British journalism.
Connor has evoked the wrath of statesmen of both major parties.
The Communists hate him. He is a deflator of stuffed shirts, a pun-
gent critic, and a stout defender of the British worker.

The *Mirror*'s other salient feature is a comic strip called "Jane."
Jane is a well-proportioned young lady whose adventures nearly
always end in near nudity. She is a favorite of British troops abroad
and their families at home. The information value of this daily
striptease is nonexistent, but a *Mirror* employee once defended the
strip on the grounds that "the bloke that buys the paper to look at
Jane may read Bill Connor or the leader."

The London press enjoys an advantage that does not exist in
the United States. This is the presence of a remarkably well-informed critical opinion in the weekly reviews that are also printed
in London. The *Spectator,* the *New Statesman and Nation, Time
and Tide,* and, occasionally, the *Economist* are careful, if sometimes pecksniffian, critics of the national newspapers. Fleet Street
is one big family (it would be stretching things to call so tumultuous
a community "happy"), and the inner workings of the great dailies
are laid bare to the weeklies often through the agency of dis-
gruntled reporters. Consequently, "Pharos" in the *Spectator* and
Francis Williams in the *New Statesman* are authoritative and
knowledgeable critics of the newspapers and their proprietors.

The weeklies themselves are a valuable supplement to the
newspapers. They have time to reflect and space to discuss. In many
cases they are often slightly ahead of public opinion, more so than
the daily papers, and they are not afraid to criticize tartly such
sacred cows of British journalism as the Crown.

Since the end of the war the tendency among the popular newspapers has been to entertain rather than to inform. This recognizes what I believe to be one of the fundamental truths of the communications business in Britain: the majority of the people get their news from the British Broadcasting Corporation's radio and television services and from the news services of the Independent Television Authority.

Readers of the more responsible London and provincial newspapers listen to the news on the BBC and then turn to their papers for expanded stories and ample interpretative material. But the average reader does not read *The Times* or the *Manchester Guardian* or the *Observer*. When he turns off the radio in the morning and picks up his "popular" newspaper, he is confronted with gossip columns, comic strips, newsless but beguiling stories about the royal family, sports stories, and, in some papers, a dash of pornography.

The "popular" papers do print hard news. Correspondents like Sefton Delmer of the *Daily Express* and William Forrest of the *News Chronicle* send interesting, factual, and frequently important stories from Germany or Russia. But such stories are increasingly rare. The trend even in this sort of writing is toward entertainment.

For example, not long ago a London popular daily, once renowned for its foreign staff, sent a reporter to Communist China. This was an opportunity for objective reporting. Instead the readers got a rehash of the reporter's own political outlook plus a few flashes of description of life in modern China.

This tendency toward entertainment rather than information is deplored by those who believe that a democracy can operate successfully only on the foundation of well-informed public opinion. In Britain, however, newspapers are customarily considered not as public trusts but as business, big business. If entertainment pays, the newspapers, with a few exceptions noted above, will entertain. Unfortunately, the BBC cannot provide the time necessary to give the news that the newspapers fail to print. Obviously the great mass of the British people will become less well informed about the great issues at home and abroad if the present trend continues.

During the thirties the critics of the British press liked to repeat a cruel little rhyme that ran:

> *You cannot hope to bribe nor twist,*
> *Thank God, the British journalist,*
> *But, seeing what the man will do*
> *Unbribed, there's no occasion to.*

Yet, from a knowledge of the type of man who writes for the popular press and a thorough acquaintance with his product, I would say that the blame rests not with the reporter but with the management.

It is certainly within the power of the proprietors of the popular newspapers to change the character of the papers. Some editors in Fleet Street habitually sneer at American newspapers and their practices, although these men are not above adopting some American techniques of news presentation which they think will sell newspapers. But the amount of factual information about national and foreign affairs in many small-town American papers is far greater, proportionately, than that provided by some great "national" newspapers in London.

Those who are interested in the improvement of relations between the United States and the United Kingdom must be concerned about the reporting of American news in the popular press. More space is devoted to news from the United States than formerly, and correspondents for the London dailies travel more widely than they did in the past. Men like the late Robert Waithman of the *News Chronicle* did their best to get out of Washington and New York and see the country. But too often the correspondents devote time and space to the more frivolous aspects of American life. From the standpoint of international relations, the space devoted to the stream of stories about the royal family might be better spent on a frank discussion of why the mass of Americans feel as they do about the Communist government in Peiping.

Some good judges of the national character believe that the great mass of the British working class would not read such information even if the newspapers provided it. They see this group as complacent and politically lethargic, no longer willing to be stirred, as it was a generation ago, by great events in the outside world. If this is true, the future is dark indeed. For more than at any time since the summer of 1940 the British people must take a realistic view of their position in the world. They cannot do this if, beyond a few perfunctory headlines, their newspapers provide only the details of the latest murder or the bust measurements of Hollywood stars. To an observer from abroad, it is only too evident that the great problems of our times are not being brought to the people of Britain by their popular newspapers in a serious manner.

THE OLD SCHOOL TIE

Few institutions in Britain are more difficult for Americans to understand than the public schools. Yet a knowledge of the system, how it works, its influence upon British society, its traditions and customs, even its sports is essential to a knowledge of modern Britain. We are going to hear a great deal about the public schools in the coming years, for one of the great battles between the egalitarian, socialist Britain and the traditional, conservative Britain will be waged over the future of these schools.

The "public school" is in fact a private one. The public-school system includes all the schools of this type in Britain. As an influence on the national character it has been and still is extraordinarily potent. This influence is social and political as well as educational. It is, I think, fair to say that to hundreds of thousands in the upper and middle classes, attendance at Eton is regarded as more important than attendance at Oxford.

There are about two hundred public schools in Britain. They range from old established institutions like Eton, Harrow, Charterhouse, Winchester, Rugby, Haileybury, and Wellington to smaller schools whose fame is local and whose plant, equipment, and teaching staff are little better, and in some cases inferior, to those of the state schools.

What keeps the public-school system alive in an era that has seen the fall of so many bastions of class and privilege? To begin with, the public schools represent a well-established, wealthy, and acute force within British society. Such a force fights to maintain its position against the public criticism and political maneuverings of its enemies. The fight is led by men who are sincerely convinced that the continuation of the public-school system is necessary to the maintenance of Britain's position in the world, and they will devote time, money, and effort to win the fight. One of the mistakes made by the Socialist groups that attack the public-school system is to underestimate the wit and energy of those who defend it.

Yet the existence of a powerful institution is no guarantee of its future life in a country that has changed and is changing so rapidly as Britain. The public schools survive and even flourish because of the conviction widely held throughout the upper and middle classes that such schools provide the best type of education for their boys. Indeed, the conviction goes even deeper in the class structure: it is noteworthy that as new groups move up the economic scale into the middle class, these too seek to send their boys to a public school.

Elsewhere I have mentioned the sacrifices that the old middle class makes to preserve its position in British society. Nowhere are these sacrifices more evident than in the struggle to raise the money to send the son or sons of the family to a public school. The Continental holiday may be given up in favor of two weeks at an English seaside resort. The car must be patched up and run for another year. Father will go without a new overcoat, and mother will abandon her monthly trip to "town" to see a play. But John will go to his father's old school. Why?

At the best public schools the formal education is excellent. But when the middle-class Briton speaks of the education his son gets at a public school he is referring only partially to what the boy learns from books. Principally, he is thinking about the development of the boy's character at the school, about the friends he will make there, and about how these friends and attendance at this old school will help the boy later in life.

Critics of the Foreign Office have often charged that British diplomacy is filled with the products of the public schools and that the representatives of the great mass of the nation are excluded from the Foreign Service because they have not attended public schools. Lord Strang, a former Permanent Under Secretary of State for Foreign Affairs and thus head of the Foreign Office, answered this criticism in his book *The Foreign Office*.

"The Foreign Office," he wrote, "can move no faster towards fully democratic methods of selection than the State as a whole is moving in its educational policies, though it has already moved far at the pace set for it by these wider policies of political evolution. The fact is that the Foreign Service always must and will recruit from the best, in brains and character, that the prevailing educational system can produce."

Note that "character" is coupled with "brains" in this indirect reference to the public schools.

What does the middle-class Briton mean when he says that Eton or some obscure public school in the Midlands will develop his son's character? There is no complete answer. But I would say that he includes in character such traits as willingness to take responsibility, loyalty to the class conception of the nation's interests, readiness to lead (which implies, of course, a belief that he is fit to lead and that there are people willing to be led), truthfulness, self-discipline, a love for vigorous outdoor sports. I have heard all these cited as reasons why boys should go to public schools and why fathers will give up smoking or limit their drinking to a small sherry before dinner to provide the money for such schooling.

In considering the development of character in the public schools it should be remembered that these schools often represent the third phase in the education of a British boy. The boy's first preceptor will be a nanny or nursemaid, often chosen from the rural working class. At eight or nine he goes away to a preparatory school. At twelve or thirteen he is ready for his public school. Because of economic pressure only a wealthy minority can follow this system today, but it was the system that produced the majority of the leaders of the Conservative Party and not a few prominent Labor Party leaders.

Direct paternal influence is much less evident in the education of Britons of the middle class than it is in the United States. One argument for the system maintains that the boy learns self-reliance; when in his twenties he is commanding a platoon or acting as Third Secretary of Embassy in a foreign country he is not likely to be wishing that Mom were there to advise him. This argument implies acceptance of the proposition that people will consent to be led by the public-school boy or that his education and character will fit him for a diplomatic post abroad.

Critics of the public schools charge that the concept of public-school leadership was exploded by World War II. This does not jibe with my own experiences with the British forces from 1939 to 1945. I found that most of the young officers in all three services were products of the public schools and that, on the whole, they provided a high standard of leadership in the lower echelons. Their earlier training had enforced upon them the idea that they were responsible for their men, not only in battle but elsewhere. So they would tramp through the Icelandic sleet to obscure posts to organize amateur theatricals or sweat through an African afternoon playing soccer with their men because this was part of the responsibility. They were told that they had to lead in battle, and they accepted the obligation without doubts.

A great many of them were killed all over the world while sociologists and reformers were planning how to eliminate the public schools. Those who were killed were no more intelligent, no more attractive in person, no more energetic than those they led. But when the time came to lead, they led. These remarks, no doubt, will annoy critics of the public schools and public-school leadership. When I am informed how wars are to be won or nations to be governed without leaders I will be properly contrite.

The public school's place in British society rests basically upon this conviction that a public-school education provides character-training that will equip a boy for leadership in business, in politics, in the military services, and in society. But the system as it appears in British society is composed of much more than formal education and character-building. The public schools also mean a body of traditions and customs often as involved and as unrelated to the modern world as the taboos of primitive man.

The Old School Tie is one. Almost all middle-class and some working-class institutions in Britain have a tie striped with the colors of the institution or ornamented with its crest. There are ties for cricket clubs and associations of football fans, there are ties for regiments and clubs. But the tie that generally means most is the tie that stands for attendance at a public school. It is at once a certificate of education and a badge of recognition.

The phrase "Old School Tie" stands not only for the public schools but for their place in middle-class society. The tie is not merely a strip of silk but all the strange, sometimes incomprehensible customs and traditions that surround the public schools. Slang phrases used at one school for generations. Rugby football rather than soccer because there is more bodily contact in rugby and hence it is a more "manly" game and better suited to character-building. School courses which have very little to do with the problems of the modern world but which supposedly "discipline" the mind.

British public schools, like American universities, have been criticized for developing a type rather than individuals. There is a resemblance among their graduates, and the old Etonian and the old Wykehamist (Winchester) and even the graduate of some small school in Yorkshire have a great deal in common. The public-school graduate will be enthusiastic about sports, rather contemptuous and sometimes shockingly ill-informed about the world outside Britain, well-mannered, truthful, and amenable to discipline. In a crowd, whether it be an officers' training unit in war or an industrial training school in peace, he will seek out other members of the fraternity announced by the tie. He is ready to serve and sometimes idealize the State. He believes in, although he does not invariably personally support, church attendance, *The Times,* the monarchy.

Naturally, there are mavericks. Some of the greatest individualists in recent British history—the influence of the public schools on the nation really became apparent in the middle of the last century when the new mercantile and industrial leaders began to send their sons to them—have been public-school products. By a pleasing coincidence, Sir Winston Churchill, Prime Minister Nehru of India, and Field Marshal Earl Alexander of Tunis are old Harrovians.

Politically, the public schools are conservative in thought, and usually their graduates adhere to the Conservative Party. But there are many exceptions. Hugh Gaitskell, the present leader of the Parliamentary Labor Party, is an old Wykehamist. His predecessor, Earl Attlee, went to Haileybury. Scattered through the ranks of the modern Labor Party are dozens of Old Boys of the public schools. If the Labor movement gradually sheds much of its old extremism, it is certain to attract an increasing number of public-school graduates.

The principal criticism of the public schools voiced by reformers at home and critics abroad is that it perpetuates in Britain a class system that divides society during a period when unity is essential to survival. There is truth in this, so much that it cannot be answered, as supporters of the system do answer it, with the assertion that there were no class differences in Britain until the Labor Party created them. Nor is the argument valid that the masses in Britain like class distinction, like to live their lives within a precise social classification. British society is changing today just as it has changed in the past. It would not have changed without popular pressure. The newly rich manufacturer of cheap cotton who decided to send his boy to a public school a hundred years ago was just as much a part of this change as the Labor Party politician who wants to abolish the public schools even though he himself is a graduate of one.

Another disadvantage of the perpetuation of the public-school system in its present form is that it is unsuited in many ways to modern conditions. It was admirable training for young men who were to rule thousands of untutored natives or maintain the might, majesty, and dominion of the British Empire with a handful of police or administer without deviation the justice of the Crown in smelly courtrooms half a world away. But today the young men are going out to sell Austins or electronic products or to represent a weaker Britain among peoples tipsy with the heady wine of nationalism. At home the old stratifications are breaking up, new groups of technicians and managers are shouldering the once un- challenged leaders of the professional middle class, new indus- tries requiring a high degree of technical training are ousting the old.

In these circumstances the road will be difficult for a man who has been trained to regard himself as a leader, either born or edu- cated to leadership, who has been taught that his caste is auto- matically superior to the industrialists of Pittsburgh or the scientist at Harlow or the excitable politicians of New Delhi and Athens. Certain traits encouraged by the public schools will always be im- portant. But self-discipline, truthfulness, physical courage must be accompanied in the modern world by a broader outlook on that world and a more acute realization of Britain's place in it.

There is a strong movement in Britain for the expansion of technical education. The public schools are not technical schools; their object is the well-rounded product of a general education. While the public schools maintain their social prestige, the new middle class as well as the old will send its sons to them. But the leaders of tomorrow's Britain will be the leaders of the new tech- nology taught in the technical schools. As these schools develop, they may offer a real challenge to the public school's position as the trainer of the governing or leading class.

The indictment of the public schools is that they are educating boys to meet conditions that no longer exist. Yet the public schools are trying to change with the times even while maintaining that what is needed to meet the challenge of modern conditions is not narrow technical education but precisely the comprehensive schooling backed by sound character-training that public schools are supposed to provide.

We should not overlook the role the public schools are playing and will play in the absorption into the middle class of the new groups that have entered it from industry, science, communications, and management in the last decade. Many men in these groups had no public-school education. In fact, a decade ago many of them were among the severest critics of the system. But a surprisingly large number today are sending their sons to public schools. The desire to keep up with the Joneses—the Joneses in this case being the old middle class that sent its sons to public schools as a matter of course—is one reason for this. Another is the recognition that the public schools endow their graduates with certain social advantages.

When change occurs in Britain it often takes place behind a façade that appears unchanged. The battle over the public schools is certain to take place, and, whichever group wins, the schools themselves will be altered by it. It is inconceivable that they will be eliminated from the British scene. It is equally inconceivable that they will not change under the pressure of the times.

In the spring of 1956 I lunched with a wartime friend who said he had given up smoking in order to save money to send young Nigel through Winchester. Someone else at the table muttered that "this public-school business" was a lot of damned nonsense. My friend smiled. "Damn it," he said, "you [the mutterer] are always talking about how well the Russians do things. Well, I read in *The Times* this morning that Khrushchev says they're going to start schools to train leaders. What's good enough for old Khrush ought to be good enough for you pinks down at the London School of Economics!"

THE ARMY, THE NAVY, THE AIR FORCE

"The Army, the Navy, and the Air Force, they always play the game." So sang the girls and boys of careless, complacent Britain in the thirties. The verse symbolizes the middle-class public-school atmosphere of the services' place in British society. Prior to World War II the three services enjoyed a more honored place in British society than did the Army and the Navy in American society.

The commanding officer of a battalion on home service thought himself socially superior to the leading industrialist of the neighborhood, and, in most cases, the industrialist agreed. The retired Navy commander or Army major was a recognized figure in the life of the village or town in which he lived—a figure of fun, perhaps, to the bright young people down from Oxford or Cambridge, and an easy mark for social caricaturists and cartoonists, but also a man of importance in the affairs of the community.

He was also, in many cases, a man of means. Pay in the prewar Army was ridiculously small, and an officer in a "good" regiment needed a private income if he were to live comfortably. Again, the retired officer and the serving officer knew a good deal about the world, a circumstance forced upon him (for he was never especially cordial to foreigners) by the necessity of garrisoning the Empire. He had lived in India or China or Egypt and fought in South Africa or France or Mesopotamia, and he had formed firm conclusions about these countries and their people. These conclusions, often delivered with the certainty of an order on the parade ground, raised the hackles of his juniors and were derided as the reactionary ideas of relics from Poona, the citadel of conservatism in India. There is an old service verse about the "Poona attitude":

There's a regiment from Poona
That would infinitely sooner
Play single-handed polo,
A sort of solo polo,

> *Than play a single chukker*
> *With a chap who isn't pukka.*

After the Second World War had burst on Britain in all its fury and in its aftermath, it occurred to many who had fumed while the ex-officers talked that the Blimps had known what they were talking about. Earlier I noted that the retired officers were right in their predictions about what would happen in India once the British withdrew, and that the politicians and publicists of the left were wrong. I do not suggest that the British should or could have remained. But several hundred thousand lives might have been saved if the withdrawal had been slower.

The services and their officers thus had established themselves as a much more important part of society in Britain than had their counterparts in the United States. They were always in the public eye. The Army and the Air Force fought campaigns on the northwest frontier of India. The Navy chased gun-runners and showed the flag.

Socially, the Army was the more important. The sons of the very best families—which means the oldest and most respectable, not the richest—went into the five regiments of the Brigade of Foot Guards or into the Household Cavalry or into the old, fashionable, expensive cavalry regiments like the 16th/5th Lancers or the Queen's Own Fourth Hussars (which once, long ago, attracted a young subaltern named Churchill). It was the fashion among the intellectuals of pre-war England to laugh at the solemn ceremonials of the Foot Guards and to snicker at the languid young men who protested when their horses were taken away and replaced by armored cars and tanks. (It might be remarked that when the time came there was nothing to laugh at and a good deal to be proud of. The account for the parties at the night clubs and the hunting, shootin', and fishin' of the careless days was rendered and paid in blood. You could see them in France in May and June of 1940 going out with machine guns and horribly antiquated armored cars to take on the big German tanks.)

If the Army was predominant socially, the Navy held military pre-eminence. It was the Navy which was the nation's "sure shield," the Navy which had been matchless and supreme since Trafalgar. It was the Navy which time and again had interposed its ships and men between the home islands and the fleets of Spain, France, and Germany. The naval officer standing on his bridge in the North Sea or off some tropic port was a watchman, a national symbol of security.

As the two senior services were so firmly implanted in the public consciousness, it is easy to see why the Royal Air Force, the youngest of the three, lived on such short commons before the war. Socially it did not count. "He's one of these flying chaps," a young Hussar said at Lille one day in 1939, "but a very decent fellow." It did not attract the young men who entered the Guards or the Cavalry, for the RAF dealt with machines and grimy hangars smelling of grease and oil, and it planned for the future without much hope of governmental financial assistance or any real support from tradition. Whereas the Loamshire Hussars had been fighting since Blenheim, the Secretary of State for War was an ex-officer, and the port at the mess was beyond praise.

Militarily, the RAF meant a great deal more. When the war began, it became the savior of Britain—for a few years the one service through which the country could strike directly and powerfully at Germany. The rise of the RAF to pre-eminence among the fighting services in post-war Britain began with its long, bitter, successful battle against the *Luftwaffe* in the summer of 1940.

The ascent of the RAF to its present position is the first of the changes that have overtaken the services in Britain, which is a martial if not a militaristic nation. Of course, the development of air power as the means of carrying the new nuclear weapons would have ensured an improvement in its position in any case. But the expansion of the RAF during the war, the post-war necessity for continued experimentation in associated fields such as the development of guided missiles, and the creation of a large, highly trained group of technical officers provided an opportunity for the new middle class and the upper levels of the industrial working class, the planners and technicians, to win advancement in what is currently the most important of the services.

The Battle of Britain was won by public-school boys. But the modern RAF, although it has its share of public-school boys especially among the combat units, is increasingly manned, officers as well as the higher noncommissioned officers, by products of the state schools. The RAF needs now and will need increasingly in the future the services of the best technical brains Britain can offer. The main source of supply will be not the officers' training units at the public schools or the universities but the new technical colleges and training courses in Britain.

It follows, then, that in time the military defense of the realm will rest primarily not upon the class who have always considered themselves ordained by birth and education to carry out this task but upon a new group springing from the new middle class and from the proletariat. This is a social development of the first importance.

The change in the character of the officer class is not confined to the RAF, although it is most noticeable there. There has been a change, too, in the composition of the commissioned ranks of the Army.

When World War II ended, the "military families," which for generations had sent sons into the local county regiments, found that the second war, following the terrible blood-letting of the first, had almost wiped them out. Perhaps one son in three or four survived. And he, surveying the post-war Army and the post-war world, was disinclined to follow tradition and devote the remainder of his working life to the service. He might gladly have served another twenty years in the "old" Army with its horses and hunting, its tours of duty in India, its social importance. But now tanks and armored cars had replaced the horses, India was gone, and a bunch of shirking Bolshies from the Labor Party were running things. Above all, the two wars had swept away many of the private fortunes with which young officers eked out their miserable pay and allowances. So the survivor of the military family became a personnel manager in a Midlands factory, and elderly men said to elderly wives: "Do you know that for the first time since '91 there's no Fenwick serving with the Loamshires?"

But the Second World War also raised to officer rank thousands of young men whose social and educational background would not have been considered suitable for commissioned rank in peacetime. They came from the state's secondary schools, from technical colleges, or from the ranks, and they did remarkably well. Many of them are still serving as officers.

At the war's end many of them remained in the service. I was always interested during the maneuvers of the British Army of the Rhine to find how many of the young officers in the infantry and tank regiments had served in the ranks or had come to the Army with a sound education and a proletarian accent from one of the state schools. The technical branches of the Army, such as the Royal Electrical and Mechanical Engineers and the Royal Army Ordnance Corps, draw an increasing number of their officers from the noncommissioned officers and from among the graduates of technical schools.

Nowhere is the middle class's ability to assimilate new groups and thus perpetuate itself more striking than in the Army. The officers from the ranks or from a state school assume the social coloration of the established officer class. Manners, accent, turns of phrase, and dress alter to conform with those of the old officer class. At present the new group is in a minority. There naturally are many members of the old officer class still serving. With the return of prosperity the upper middle class has resumed the tradition of sending its sons into the Army as a matter of course.

The general officers of the old school, which in this case means the old public school, vehemently defend the middle class as the only proper breeding-ground for service officers. They assert that only men from a certain class, by which they mean their own, and from a certain background, by which they mean a public school, will accept the responsibility and provide the leadership necessary in war. A general told me: "It's really very simple. Men who drop their *h*'s won't follow an officer who also drops his *h*'s. They don't think he'll take care of them as well as some young pipsqueak six months out of Eton but with the correct accent."

This will strike Americans as ridiculous. Certainly it ignores the high quality of leadership exercised by sergeant pilots of the RAF Bomber Command. But the general cannot be dismissed as unrealistic. The correct accent *does* count in Britain. The public-school boy *has* been trained to look after others. The idea of an officer class may offend us as contradictory to democratic equality. But it can and does work. Nowhere in the world is the officer caste better treated than in the proletarian society of Soviet Russia.

The Army and the Navy will continue to assimilate into the commissioned ranks of their services an increasing number of men of working-class origin. Science's invasion of the military art, long established but tremendously accelerated since 1945, makes it inevitable that the sharp young technician, "without an *h* to his name" as the middle class says, will continue to rise to commissioned rank. It also seems relatively certain that as he rises he will assume some of the social patina of the middle class.

The old conception of military leadership as a prerogative of the aristocracy died hard. It took the blunders and casualties of the Crimean War, the Boer War, and the First World War to kill it. During World War II the British services produced a large number of outstanding leaders: Alexander, Brooke, Dill, Montgomery, Slim, Wavell, Leese, Horrocks in the Army, Cunningham, Fraser, Vian, Mountbatten in the Navy, Portal, Harris, Tedder, Slessor, Bowhill in the RAF. With the exception of Alexander and Mountbatten, all were products of the old middle class. But in a changing Britain the authority of this class in the field it made particularly its own is being undermined both by new techniques of war and by the shifts in internal power which have occurred in Britain since 1940.

Those officers and ex-officers who recognize this are not greatly concerned for the survival of their class leadership; most are convinced that it will survive. They are concerned, however, lest in this rapidly changing century the traditions that their class perpetuated and, in some cases, changed into fetishes should perish. Regimental traditions, some of which stretch back three centuries into military history, will, they insist, be as important in the era of guided missiles as they were in the days of the matchlock.

It is argued that the sense of continuity, the conviction that men before them have faced perils as great and have survived and won is essential if Britain is to continue as a military power. The composition of the Army, Navy, and Air Force officer groups may change. But the new men will have to rely quite as much on the service and regimental traditions as did the men who fought at Minden, Waterloo, or Le Cateau.

WORKER'S PLAYTIME

The leisure activities of the British people in the present decade offer a revealing guide to the changes that have overtaken their society. One can learn a great deal by comparing a rugby crowd at Twickenham and a soccer crowd at Wembley. The rise in popularity of some forms of entertainment, notably television, testifies to the new prosperity of the working class. The slow decline of interest in some sports and the shift from playing to watching illustrate other changes in the make-up of Britain.

Television is the greatest new influence on the British masses since the education acts of the last century produced a proletariat capable of reading the popular press, a situation capitalized by Lord Northcliffe and others. And the mass attention to "what's on television," like every other change in Britain, has social connotations. Among many in the middle class and the upper middle class it is close to class treason to admit regular watching of television. "We have one for Nanny and the children," a London hostess said, "but we never watch it. Fearfully tedious, most of it."

Significantly, the middle class, when defending its right to send its sons to public schools, emphasizes that the working class could send its sons to the same schools if it were willing to abandon its payments for television. This may reveal one reason for the middle-class dislike for this form of entertainment. Television sets are expensive, and possibly the cost cannot be squeezed into a budget built around the necessity of sending the boy to school.

The spread of television-viewing in Britain has had far-reaching economic and social effects. A sharp blow has been dealt the corner pub, by tradition the workingman's club. Since the rise of modern Britain, it is to the pub that the worker has taken his sorrows, his ambitions, and his occasional joys. There over a pint of bitters he could think dark thoughts about his boss, voice his opinions on statesmen from Peel to Churchill, and argue about racing with his friends. "These days," a barmaid told me, "they come in right after supper, buy some bottled ale—nasty gassy stuff it is, too —and rush home to the telly. In the old days they came in around seven, regular as clockwork it was, and didn't leave until I said 'Time, gentlemen, please.' "

Television also has affected attendance at movies and at sports events. The British have never been a nation of night people, and nowadays they seem to be turning within themselves, a nation whose physical surroundings are bounded by the hearth, the television screen, and quick trips to the kitchen to open another bottle of beer. My friends on the BBC tell me this is not so; television, they say, has opened new horizons for millions and is the great national educator of the future. It is easy to forgive their enthusiasm. But how can a people learn the realities of life if what it really wants on television is sugary romances or the second-hand jokes and antics of comedians rather than the admirable news and news-interpretation programs produced by both the BBC and the Independent Television Authority? The new working class seems to be irritated by attempts to bring it face to face with the great problems of their country and of the world. Having attained what it wants—steady employment, high wages, decent housing—it hopes to hide before its television screens while this terrible, strident century hammers on.

The view that the British have become a nation of spectators has been put forward with confidence by many observers, British as well as foreign. It is valid, I believe, only if one takes the view that the millions who watch soccer (which the British call football), rugby football, field hockey, and other sports on a Saturday afternoon in autumn are the only ones who count. But there are hundreds of thousands who play these sports. Some few hundred are professionals playing before thousands, but many thousands more are amateurs. Stand in a London railroad station any Saturday at noon and count the hundreds of young men and young women hurrying to trains that will take them to some suburban field where they will use the hockey sticks, football shoes, or cricket bats they are carrying.

Neither soccer nor rugby football is so physically punishing as American football, although both demand great stamina. So the British play these games long after the American college tackle has hung up his cleats and is boring his friends at the country club with the story of how he blocked the kick against Dartmouth or Slippery Rock. An ex-officer of my acquaintance played cricket, and pretty good cricket, too, until he was well into his forties. On village cricket grounds (the British call them "pitches") on a Sunday afternoon one can see sedate vicars and husky butchers well past fifty flailing away at the ball.

If one adds to these the thousands who take a gun and shoot or a rod and fish, and the tens of thousands more who cycle into the countryside spring, summer, and fall, the picture reveals a nation which does not rely solely on watching sports for its pleasure but which still gets enormous fun out of playing them.

Sports of all sorts, either spectator or participant, occupy an important, even a venerated, place in British society. Kipling's warning against the damage that "the flanneled fool at the wicket and the muddied oaf at the goal" might do to the nation's martial capacity was never taken very seriously. After all, Britons have been told interminably and mistakenly that Waterloo was won on the playing-fields of Eton. The Duke of Wellington, who commanded the British forces in that notable victory, could recall no athletic triumphs of his own at Eton save that he had once jumped a rather wide ditch as a boy. The Duke's pastimes were riding to hounds and women, neither of which was in the Eton curriculum at the time he matriculated. Nevertheless, the tradition remains.

When an American thinks of British sport, he automatically thinks of cricket. But cricket is a game that can be played in Britain only during the short and frequently stormy months of late spring and summer. In point of attendance, number of players participating, and national interest, *the* game is soccer. Soccer, the late Hector McNeil loved to emphasize, is "the game of the people." It is also the game of millions who have never seen a game but who each week painfully fill out their coupons on the football pools, hopeful that *this* time they will win the tens of thousands of pounds that go to the big winners. The football pools are an example of a diversion that has moved upward in the social scale. The British, almost all of them, love to gamble, and the retired colonial servant at Bath finds as great a thrill in winning on the pools or even trying to win as the steel worker at Birmingham does. These days the steel worker has a little more money to back his choices.

To many Americans soccer is a game played by national groups in the big cities and by high schools, prep schools, and colleges too small or too poor to support football. Soccer, actually, is an extremely fast, highly scientific game whose playing evokes from the crowds very much the same passions that are evident at Busch Stadium or Ebbets Field. There is no gentlemanly restraint about questioning an official's decision in soccer as there is in cricket. The British version of "ya bum, ya" rolls over the stadium on Saturday afternoons. Once I heard a staid working-class housewife address a referee who had awarded a free kick against Arsenal as "Oh, you bloody man!" The English can go no further in vituperation.

Although soccer is principally the game of Britain's working masses, there are some among the middle class who find it entrancing. But the great game of this class in the autumn and winter is rugby football.

Here we encounter a social difference. Rugby was popularized at a public school and is pre-eminently the public-school game. The "old rugger blue" is as much a part of the rugby crowd as the ex-tackle from Siwash in the American football crowd. The games, incidentally, have a good deal in common and require similar skills. There is no blocking or forward passing in rugby, but the great backs of rugby football would hold their own in the American game.

In the middle class it is good form to have played rugby or to watch rugby. At the big games at Twickenham just outside London one will see a higher percentage of women than at the major soccer matches. The difference between the classes watching the two sports is emphasized by the difference in clothing. Twickenham costumes are tweeds, duffel coats, old school ties, and tweed caps. At Wembley there are the inevitable raincoat (usually called a "mac"), the soft gray hat, and the decent worsted suit of the industrial worker on his day off.

Rugby crowds are as partisan as soccer crowds but less vociferous. A bad decision will occasion some head-shaking and tut-tutting, but there will be little shouted criticism—with one exception: the Welsh.

The people of the Principality of Wales take their rugby as the people of Brooklyn take their baseball. In the mining valleys and the industrial cities rugby, not soccer, is the proletarian sport. The players on an English team in an international match with Wales will include university graduates, public-school teachers, and law students. The Welsh side will boast colliery workers, policemen, and teachers at state schools. More than a sport, rugby is a national religion. Consequently, the invasion of Twickenham by a Welsh crowd for an international match is very like the entry of a group of bartenders and bookmakers into a WCTU convention. The Welsh feel emotionally about rugby, and they do not keep their feelings to themselves. They are a small people but terribly tough. My happiest memory of the 1956 international at Twickenham is of a short, broad Welsh miner pummeling a tall, thin Englishman who had suggested mildly that Wales had been lucky to win.

There is another break in the pattern of middle-class allegiance to rugby. A game called Rugby League, somewhat different from the older and more widely played Rugby Union, is played in the North of England. It is definitely a working-class game and a professional one, whereas Rugby Union is, by American standards, ferociously amateur. The English feel badly when one of their players succumbs to the financial lure of Rugby League and leaves the amateur game. The Welsh feel even worse, not because the player is turning professional but because "Look, dammit, man, we need Jones for the match with England."

There are survivals of the old attitude toward professionals in sport in the English (but not the Welsh) attitude toward rugby football. Soccer football, like baseball in America, began as an amateur game and at one time was widely played by the middle class. But middle-class enthusiasm and support dwindled as the game became professionalized. Of late there has been a revival of interest in the amateur side of the sport, but basically the game is played by professionals for huge crowds drawn from the industrial working class. However, thousands in the crowds also play for club and school teams.

Yet here we encounter another contradiction. Cricket, considered the most English of games, is played nowadays mostly by professionals, as far as the county teams (the equivalent of the major-league teams in baseball) are concerned. But many English approach cricket with something akin to the Welshman's attitude toward rugby. Professionalism is no longer looked down upon, and the old distinctions between Gentlemen and Players are slowly vanishing.

John Lardner once mentioned how difficult it was to explain the extraordinary ascendancy that baseball assumed over Americans in the last half of the nineteenth century. It is equally difficult to explain the hold that cricket exercises today on a large section of Britain. More people watch soccer, but that game does not seem to generate the dedicated, almost mystic attitude displayed by cricket enthusiasts. Cricket is an extraordinarily involved, delicate, and, at times, exciting game. But it cannot be merely the game itself which brings old men doddering to Lord's and rouses whole families in the chill cold of a winter morning to listen to the broadcast of a match played half a world away in the bright sunshine of Melbourne.

Part of the hold may be explained by cricket's ability to remind the spectators of their youth and a richer, greener England. To that nation, secure, prosperous, and powerful, many thousands of the middle class return daily in their thoughts. Cricket—village cricket or cricket at the Oval or Lord's, twin sanctums of the game—represents that other England. For a time they can forget the taxes, forget the unknown grave in France or Libya, forget the industrial wasteland around them, and return to the village green and the day the Vicar bowled (struck out) the policeman from the next village.

It is a peaceful game to watch. The absence of the noise, the strident criticisms and outbursts, of the baseball game has been noted by enough Americans. In addition, there is a soporific atmosphere about cricket. Men sit on the grass and watch the white figures of the players make intricate, shifting patterns against the bright green of the grass. Their outward show of enthusiasm is confined to an "Oh, well hit, well hit indeed, sir" or applause when a player makes fifty runs or is bowled. There is no need to hurry or to worry about anything more important than saving the fellow who is on. The pipe is drawing nicely, and later you can meet old So-and-so at the club, or the pub, for a chat about the match. "I go out on a summer evening to watch them play," a Londoner said. "Sort of rests me, it does."

The influence of cricket on the middle class that follows the game has been and is remarkable. Cricket terms have become part of the language of this class. Such phrases as "hit them for six" and "batting on a sticky wicket" pepper the speeches of politicians. As cricket was played originally by amateurs who were presumed to be gentlemen, it assumed an aristocratic tone. Anything that was "not cricket" was not gentlemanly.

Many Britons in World War II showed a tendency to think of the war in terms of cricket. This was discouraged by the tougher-minded commanders on the sensible grounds that war is not cricket.

But no one could stop Field Marshal Montgomery from promising his troops they were about to "hit the Germans for six." This introduction of a sporting vocabulary into a fight for survival is one of the reasons why many Continentals regard the English as a frivolous race. I remember still the look, compounded of awe and disgust, on the face of a Norwegian, lately escaped from his homeland, when in the summer of 1940 he found that the newspaper-sellers on the street corners were writing the results of each day's fighting in the Battle of Britain in cricket terms. "Here they are," he said, "fighting for their lives, and I see a sign reading 'England 112 Not Out.' I asked the man what it meant, and he said: 'We got 112 of the ——ers, cock, and we're still batting.' A strange people."

If soccer is primarily a working-class sport and cricket the central sporting interest of the middle class, horse racing is the attraction that transcends all class distinctions. In Britain, as in America, great trouble is taken by those who administer the business to clothe it with the attributes of a sport. But essentially horse racing is a means of gambling, and the British, beneath their supposed stolidity, are a nation of gamblers. I do not recall during my childhood buying a ticket for a sweepstakes on the Kentucky Derby. But in Britain boys and girls of ten and eleven customarily buy tickets in "sweeps" run by their classmates, and the more precocious swap tips on horses.

A tremendous amount is bet each day on racing in Britain, and it is estimated that more money is bet on the Epsom Derby each June than on any other single horse race in the world.

Derby Day at Epsom is one of the best opportunities of seeing contemporary British society, from the Queen at the top to the London barrow boy at the bottom, en masse. Inside the track are the vans of the gypsy fortune-tellers, the stands of the small-time bookmakers, scores of bars and snack bars, carousels and other amusement-park attractions. Across the track are the big stands filled with what remains of the aristocracy and the upper middle class of Britain carefully dressed in morning coats, gray top hats, and starched collars. Its members may envy the great wads of banknotes carried by some of the prosperous farmers and North Country businessmen across the track, but on Derby Day anything goes, and there are champagne and lobster lunches, hilarious greetings to old friends, and reminiscences of past Derbies.

Queen Elizabeth II's love of racing endears her to her subjects. An interest in racing has always been a passport to popularity for monarchs or politicians. Sir Winston Churchill, who divined the wishes and thoughts of his countrymen with uncanny ability during the years of crisis between 1939 and 1945, had few interests in common with the people he lectured and led. He cared little for soccer or cricket. But when, after the war, he began to build up a racing stable, he acquired a new popularity with the people. Naturally, this was the last thing in Sir Winston's mind. He had made some money, he was out of office, and racing attracted him.

Racing is an upper-class sport in the sense that only the rich can afford it. But the true upper-class sports that survive are fox-hunting, shooting, and fishing, known in upper-class parlance as "huntin', shootin', and fishin'." Shooting is bird-shooting—pheasant, grouse, partridge. Fishing is for salmon or trout. As Britain's sprawling industrialization has gobbled up land, the field sports have become more and more the preserve of the rich or at least the well-to-do. George Orwell once noted the dismay of British Communists who learned that Lenin and other revolutionary leaders had enjoyed shooting—shooting birds, that is—in Russia, a country teeming with game. They thought it almost treasonable for the Little Father of the masses to engage in a sport that in Britain was reserved for the capitalists.

Fox-hunting, chiefly because of its close connection with the cult of the horse, takes social precedence over shooting and fishing. But here again we encounter a change. Death duties, taxes on land, and income taxes have impoverished a large number of rural aristocrats who formerly supported local hunts. Their places have been taken by well-to-do farmers and professional men and women from near-by towns. Some of the better-established hunts, such as the

Quorn and the Pytchley, try to maintain the old standards of exclusiveness.

The attention paid the cavalry regiments in the old Army, the middle-class conviction that children must be taught to ride because it is a social asset, the aristocratic atmosphere of fox-hunting and show jumping are all expressions of the cult of the horse which flourishes in one of the most heavily industrialized nations in the world. This, too, may express an unconscious desire to return to the past and a secure Britain. Here, too, we see the newly emerging middle class sending its sons and daughters to riding schools where they will meet the sons and daughters of the established middle class.

Golf and tennis are two games that Britain spread around the world. Golf is every man's game in Scotland and a middle-class game in England. I well remember my first trip to St. Andrews in 1939 and my delight at watching a railroad worker solemnly unbutton his collar, take off his coat, and play around one of the formidable courses there in 89. The incongruity was made more marked by the foursomes of expensively outfitted English and Americans who allowed the Scot to play through.

Tennis in Britain, like tennis in America, retains aristocratic overtones. But today it is a middle-class sport; membership at the local tennis club is ranked below membership in the local yacht club or the local hunt.

In both games British representatives in international competitions are at a disadvantage because there is not in Britain the urgent drive to develop players of international ability which exists in the United States and Australia. British cricket and rugby football teams, on the other hand, have enjoyed a number of brilliant successes in competition with Commonwealth teams since the war, and English soccer football, after some lean years, has begun to climb back to the top of the international heap.

In this land of paradox which was the birthplace of the modern "sporting" attitude, the original home of "the game for the game's sake," we find that the most popular sport is soccer football played

for money mainly by professionals; that rugby football can be a
middle-class game in England and a working-class game one hundred miles away in Wales; that cricket through the years has acquired the standing not of a sport but of a religion among one
important class in society; and that shooting and fishing, two proletarian pastimes in both the United States and the Soviet Union, are
the domain of the wealthy, the well-bred, and the middle class in
Britain.

PUBS AND CLUBS

Long ago one of my bosses advised me to spend less time listening
to people in pubs. Had I taken his advice, which fortunately I did
not, I would be richer by many pounds but poorer in both friends
and information.

Although writers have contended otherwise, the public house
is not a unique British institution. Frenchmen gather in *estaminets*
to drink, to argue, and to write interminable letters. Americans
meet at bars and taverns. The Spaniard patronizes his café. The
unique aspect of the British pub is its atmosphere.

The pub is a place where you can take your time. In city or
country it is a refuge. A man may enter, drink three or four pints
of beer in moody silence, and depart refreshed. Or he can come in,
drink the same amount of beer, debate the state of the nation and
the world with other drinkers and the barmaid, and play darts.
Dart-playing, of course, is a national sport, and there are enthusiasts who claim it has more devotees than tennis or golf. Dart
leagues flourish throughout the country, to the delight of the publicans, who reap a rich harvest from each match.

Pubs come in all shapes and sizes. Recently many of the old
London pubs have been modernized. Plastics and neon lights have
taken the place of huge glass walls engraved with advertisements
for gin and beer and old-fashioned glass-shaded electric lights. In
their efforts to meet the competition of television at home and milk
bars or soda fountains down the street, many pubs have adopted

new and, to a purist, disgusting attractions. The news that a pub in
Cambridge intended to sell ice cream convinced many serious
thinkers that this *was* the end of the Empire. Similarly, a friend told
me in shocked tones that when he was served a pint of beer in a
suburban pub the barmaid handed him "a damned doily" to put
under the glass. He informed her, he reported, that he had given up
spilling his drinks at the age of three and a half.

Despite the inroads of the milk bars and the trend toward
bottled beer bought in the pub and drunk before the television set,
draught beer is still the mainstay of British drinking. "Beer and
beef have made us what we are," said the Prince Regent. (His
friend, the Duke of Wellington, somewhat surprisingly, thought the
Church of England was responsible.)

English beer has a bad name in the United States. The GI
invading the country in 1942–5 found it weak, warm, and watery.
During the war years it was indeed both weak and watery. Today,
however, it has regained its old-time potency.

In addition to the standard beers and ales, the British brew
small quantities of special ales that, as the old saying goes, would
blow a soft hat through a cement ceiling. The Antelope, in Chelsea,
had managed to hoard some bottles of this liquid as late as the
autumn of 1940. After two bottles apiece, three Americans walked
home through one of the worst nights of bombing exclaiming happily over the pretty lights in the sky.

The merits of the brews in their respective countries are a
favorite topic for conversation between Britons and Americans.
The tourist will find that his host holds no high opinion of American beer, considering it gassy, flavorless, and, as one drinker inele-
gantly described it, "as weak as gnat's wee." The British are continually surprised by American drinking habits. They consider that
the GI who hastily swallows three or four double whiskies is asking
for trouble, and that the object of a night's foray in the pub is not
to get drunk but to drink enough to encourage conversation and
forget your troubles. Prohibition, gone these many years, is still a
black mark against Americans in the minds of the pundits in the

pubs. They regard it as a horrible aberration by an otherwise intelligent people.

It should not be assumed that the British drink only beer. When they are in funds or when the occasion calls for something stronger, they will drink almost anything from what my charwoman once described as "a nourishing drop of gin" to champagne. During the war they drank some strange and weird mixtures and distillations that, if they did not kill the drinker as did some Prohibition drams, at least made him wish he were dead the next morning.

But the pub's importance, let me repeat, is due to its place as a public forum as much as to its position as a public fountain. There questions can be asked and answers given which the average Briton would regard as impertinent if the conversation took place in his home or his office. There interminable public arguments will probe the wisdom of the government's policy on installment buying or Cyprus or, with due gravity, will seek to establish the name of the winner of the Cambridgeshire Handicap in 1931.

The atmosphere of discussion and reflection of the English pub thus far has been proof against the juke box, the pinball machine, and the television set. But the fight is a hard one. These counterattractions to the bar are making their appearance in an increasing number of pubs each year. At the same time, publicans are giving more thought to the catering side of their business. The bar, which was the heart of the pub, has become merely an adjunct to the "attractions" and the restaurant.

The spread of restaurant eating is itself a novel change in British habits. Until the Second World War the great majority of the working class and the middle class ate their meals at home. Even today, in the New Towns, the industrial worker prefers to return home for lunch. But the shortage of servants, the difficulties of feeding a family on the weekly rations, the need to get away from the drabness of chilly, darkened homes during the war and immediate post-war years combined to send millions of Britons out to eat.

This has changed the character of a large number of pubs. It has also improved restaurant cooking, especially in the provinces.

British cooking is a standard music-hall joke, but the comedians are somewhat behind the times. It has improved steadily since the war, largely because the British had to learn how to cook in order to make their meager rations palatable. The squeeze on the established middle class forced the housewives of that group to study cookery. Dinners in that circle are shorter and less formal than before the war, but the cooking is vastly improved.

Décor in modern pubs varies from the overpoweringly new to the self-consciously old. Tucked away in the back streets of the cities, however, or nestling in the folds of the Cotswolds one can still see the genuine article. There the political arguments flourish as they have since Bonaparte was troubling the English. There on a Saturday night you can still hear the real English songs—"Knees Up Mother Brown" or "Uncle Tom Cobley and All."

A sense of calm pervades the rural bars. The countryman is a long-lived, tough person. At the Monkey and Drum or the Red Dragon or the Malakof (named for a half-forgotten action in the Crimean War) the beer is set out for wiry ancients in their seventies and eighties, masters of country crafts long forgotten by the rest of the population. The sun stays late in the sky on a summer evening. From the open door you can see it touching the orderly fields, the neat houses. It is difficult, almost impossible in such surroundings to doubt that there will always be an England. Yet this is precisely the England that is and has been in continuous retreat for a century and a half before the devouring march of industrialization.

The pub is the poor man's "club"—in the sense that it is a haven for the tired worker and a center of discussion. The actual British clubs are another singular institution. There are, of course, men's and women's clubs throughout the West, but only in Britain have they become an integral and important part of social life. Like the pubs, they are changing with the times. But they still retain enough of their distinctive flavor to mark them as a particularly British institution.

London's clubs are the most famous. But throughout the

islands there are other clubs—county clubs in provincial capitals, workingmen's clubs that compete with the pubs. There are women's clubs, too, but the club is mainly a masculine institution in a nation whose society is still ordered for the well-being of the male.

"Do you mean to tell me that these Englishmen go to their clubs for a drink after work and don't get home until dinnertime?" a young American matron asked. She thought it was "scandalous." Her husband, poor devil, came home from work promptly at six each night and sat down to an early dinner with his wife and three small children. I suppose he enjoyed it.

London's clubs cater to all tastes. There are political clubs such as the Carlton, the Conservatives' inner sanctum. There are service clubs: the Cavalry or the Army and Navy. On St. James's Street are a number of the oldest and best: White's, Boodle's, Brooks's, the Devonshire.

The same American matron asked me what a club offers. The answer is, primarily, relaxation in a man's world. Like the pub, the club is a place where a man can get away from his home, his job, his worries. If he wishes, he can drink and eat while reading a newspaper. Or he can stand at the bar exchanging gossip with other members. He can read, he can play cards, he can play billiards. If he wants advice, there may be an eminent Queen's Counsel, a Foreign Office official, a doctor, or an editor across the luncheon table. There is the same atmosphere of relaxed calm which marks the best pubs.

Because for centuries the clubs have been the refuges of the wealthy or the aristocratic or the dominant political class they have exerted considerable political influence. Feuds that have shaken great political parties have begun before club bars and, years later, been settled with an amicable little dinner party at the club. In politics, domestic and foreign, the British put great faith in the "quiet get-together" where an issue can be thrashed out in private without regard for popular opinion.

During the worst days of the debate over the future of Trieste a Foreign Office official remarked to me that "all these conferences" complicated the situation. "There's nothing that couldn't be settled in an hour's frank talk over a glass of sherry at White's," he said. Foolish? Old-fashioned? Perhaps. But how much progress has been made at full-dress international conferences where national leaders speak not to one another but to popular opinion in their own and foreign countries?

The clubs are centers in which opinion takes form. As the opinion of many who are leaders in Britain's political and economic life, it is important opinion. For instance, it was obvious in the clubs, long before the failure of the Norwegian campaign brought it into the open, that there was widespread dissatisfaction in the middle class over Neville Chamberlain's direction of the war. Similarly, stories of the aging Churchill's unwillingness to deal with the pressing domestic economic problems of his government were first heard in the clubs.

The high cost of maintaining the standards of food, drink, and service required by most members has hurt the clubs. There are in every such institution a few staff mainstays whose remarks become part of club lore. But the Wages and Catering Act has made it difficult to staff clubs adequately.

The food in clubs is man's food. Its emphasis on beef, lamb, fish, and cheese would upset a Mamaroneck matron. But some of the chefs are as good as any in Britain, and the food can be accompanied by some of the finest wines in the world.

Essentially, the club remains man's last refuge from the pressures of his world. He can talk, he can listen, he can drink a second or even a third cocktail without the slight sniff that betokens wifely censure. The latest story about the Ruritanian Ambassadress or the government's views on the situation in Upper Silesia will be retailed by members. The taxes may be high, the world in a mess, the old order changing. Here by the fire with his drink in his hand he is his own man. "Waiter, two more of the same."

XII. *Britain and the Future*

I will not cease from mental fight,
Nor shall my sword sleep in my hand,
Till we have built Jerusalem
In England's green and pleasant land.

WILLIAM BLAKE

Those who compare the age in which their lot has fallen
with a golden age which exists only in imagination, may
talk of degeneracy and decay; but no man who is correctly
informed as to the past, will be disposed to take a morose
or desponding view of the present.

THOMAS BABINGTON MACAULAY

IS THE long story of British greatness nearly done? That is the question we must ask ourselves as we survey the real Britain, the changing Britain of today.

The question is a vital one for Americans. Our generation faces a challenge that dwarfs those offered by Germany in 1917 or by Germany, Japan, and Italy in 1941. Communist dominion stretches from the Elbe to the Pacific, from the arctic to the jungles of Indochina. Nearly a thousand million people serve tyrannical systems of government. Behind the barbed wire and the empty-faced guards at the frontiers we can hear the explosions of devastating weapons of war, we can discern the ceaseless effort to achieve the world triumph of Communism.

To the leaders of all these millions, the United States is the enemy, the people of America their principal obstacle in the march to world power. As the most successful capitalist state, the United States is now and will be in the future the principal target for the diplomatic intrigues, the political subversion, and the economic competition of the Communist bloc. The avenues of attack may be indirect, the means may differ from place to place. But the enmity does not vary. America is the enemy today, as it was yesterday, as it will be tomorrow.

Living at the apex of power and prosperity, it is easy for Americans to be complacent, it is natural for them to fasten on hints of Russian friendship. But it is folly to believe that the world situation is improving because Nikita Khrushchev jests with correspondents in Moscow or because a delegation of visiting farmers from the Ukraine is made up of hearty extroverts. For the Communist challenge, as it has developed since the death of Stalin, is as real as that which produced the cold war of 1945–53. But because it is expressed in terms superficially less belligerent than blockades and riots, violent speeches and editorials, and overt instant and implacable opposition to Western policies, the current challenge is far more insidious. Concepts and policies developed to meet a purely military challenge will not suffice to defeat it.

For a decade the United States has been busy "making" allies all over the world. But you cannot "make" allies as you make Fords. You cannot buy them as you buy bread at the baker's. Of course, in war, or at war's approach, threatened nations will hurry for shelter under the protecting wings of Uncle Sam. But we are facing a situation in which every effort will be made to lure our friends away with protestations of peaceful intent. Our real allies will be those who share common interests and believe in the same principles of government and law. Among these the British stand pre-eminent.

There was a wise old general commanding the United States Army in Germany at the height of the cold war. At this time, early in 1951, no one was sure what the next Russian move would be. Some of the general's young officers were playing that engaging game of adding divisions of various nationalities to assess Western strength. In the unbuttoned atmosphere of after-dinner drinks they conjured up Italian army corps and Greek and Turkish armored divisions. After ten minutes of this, the idea that the Soviet Union might even think of a war seemed downright foolish.

The general surveyed them with a wintry eye and then spoke. They were, he said mildly, playing with shadows. If "it" came, the only people to count on were the four divisions of British troops up on the left flank. These are the only people on our side, he added, who think the way we do and feel the way we do. These are the people who, in war or in peace, in good times and bad, are going to stick.

This identity of broad political outlook is essential in American assessments of Britain. It is more important in the long run than concern over the power of the Trades Union Congress or competition for overseas markets.

But, granting this identity of outlook and aims, we have the right to ask ourselves if Britain remains a powerful and stable ally of the United States in the leadership of the Western community. I believe that the answer is in the affirmative, that with all her difficulties and changes Britain will continue to play a leading role in the affairs of the world, that she will not decline gradually into impotent isolation.

Let us be quite clear about the future outline of British power. The Empire is gone or going. The British know that. But the endurance, the resolution, the intelligence that transformed a small island off the coast of Europe into the greatest of modern empires is still there. Beneath the complacency, the seeming indifference, it re-

mains. The best evidence is the series of social, economic, and political changes that has transformed British life.

These changes, whatever individual Britons or Americans may
think of them, are not signs of complacency or indifference. They
are rather proofs that the society has not lost its dynamism, that
its leaders admit and understand their losses in political influence
and economic power and are determined to build a stronger society
on the foundations of the old.

Admittedly, the British make it difficult for their friends or
their enemies to discern the extent of change. They cling to the old
established forms. This is a characteristic that is almost universal
in mankind. When the first automobiles appeared, they were built
to resemble horse-drawn carriages. Men cling to the familiar in the
material and the mental. Think of our own devotion, in a period
when the nation has developed into a continental and world power,
to a Constitution drafted to suit the needs of a few millions living
along the eastern fringe of our country.

The changes in Britain have taken place behind a façade of
what the world expects from Britain. The Queen rides in her car-
riage at Royal Ascot, the extremists of the Labor Party cry havoc
and let slip the dogs of political war, the Guards are on parade, and
gentlemen with derbies firm upon their heads walk down St. James's
swinging their rolled umbrellas. Literature, the stage, the movies,
the appearance of the visiting Englishman in every quarter of the
globe has implanted a false picture firmly in the popular mind.

"Mad dogs and Englishmen go out in the noonday sun." They
also play cricket and drink tea to the exclusion of other entertain-
ments, live on estates or in tiny thatched cottages, say "by Jove" or
"cor blimey." Their society is stratified, their workers are idle, their
enterprise is negligible. Britain itself is a land of placid country villages, one large city (London), squires and lords, cockney humor-
ists and rustics in patched corduroy.

This is Britain as many Americans think of it. It is also, as I
have mentioned earlier, the Britain to which many of its inhabitants
return in their daydreams. But it is not contemporary Britain.

The real Britain is a hurrying, clamorous, purposeful industrial nation. Its people, with a sense of reality any nation might envy, are carrying out major changes in the structure of the national economy and in the organization of society. The Welfare State may be considered a blessing or a curse, according to political taste, but the nation that first conceived and established it cannot be thought deficient in imagination or averse to change.

The human symbol of modern Britain is not John Bull with his country-squire clothes or the languid, elegant young man of the West End theater, but an energetic, quick-spoken man of thirty-five or forty. He is "in" plastics or electronics or steel. He talks of building bridges in India, selling trucks in Nigeria, or buying timber in Russia. In the years since the war he has been forced to supplement his education—he went to a small public school—with a great deal of technical reading about his job. His home is neither an estate nor a cottage but a small modern house. He wants a better house, a better car in time. Indeed, he wants more of everything that is good in life. He recognizes the need for change—and his own pre-eminence in the economy of the nation is a sign of change. But by tradition he opposes any change so rapid and revolutionary that it shakes the basis of his society. Politically, he is on the left wing of the Conservative Party or the right wing of the Labor Party. When in 1945 he left the Army or the Navy or the Air Force his views were well to the left of their present position. The thought that Britain's day is done has never entered his head.

The moderation of his political outlook expresses an important trend in British politics. This is the movement within both major parties toward the moderate center and a reaffirmation of the national rather than the party point of view. The antics of the extreme left and the extreme right in British politics are entertaining and occasionally worrying. But under present conditions neither group represents a dominant doctrine, although in London, as in Washington, governments must make gestures in the direction of their more extreme supporters.

This movement toward the center seems to express two deeply

felt national attitudes. One is that further experimentation in transforming British society should be postponed until the changes that took place in World War II and the decade that followed it have finished their alteration of that society. There will be—indeed, there must be—further alterations in the industrial economy, and these, of course, will affect society. But I do not believe the British people are now prepared for further sweeping, planned changes in their life or would support such changes if they were to be proposed by either political party.

The second attitude is a growing determination to face up to the national danger. Successive governments have attempted to drive home the lesson that Britain's economic peril is very real and that it is not a transient matter; that exports and dollar balances and internal consumption will be matters of great importance for years to come. As the memories of pre-war Britain fade, and as a new generation that has never experienced the national economic security of imperial Britain gains power, awareness of the nation's real problems should take hold. And because the British are a sensible people bountifully endowed with courage and resource, they should be able to meet and defeat the problems.

But at the moment the percentage of those who understand the national position is too small. They must eternally contend against two psychological factors in working-class opinion which we have already encountered. One is the political lethargy of the new industrial worker who, after centuries of shameful treatment, has emerged into the sunlight of full employment, adequate housing, high wages, strong industrial organization, political representation, amusements, clothes and food that for decades have been out of the reach of Britain's masses. This new working class has shown itself capable of great self-sacrifice on behalf of its class interests and, let us never forget, on behalf of its country in the last fifty years. But now, having reached the home of its dreams, it has hung a "Do Not Disturb" sign on the gate. Apparently it has done with sacrifice and realism.

To a certain extent this attitude is encouraged by the big national newspapers. The emphasis on sport, crime, the royal family, and the trivia of international affairs leaves inadequate space for the grim realities of the long politico-economic struggle with Russia, and the new working class remains uninformed about its real problems. A Prime Minister or a Chancellor of the Exchequer may expound the realities of the national position in a speech, but if people are not interested enough to listen or to read, what good does it do?

Such a state of mind in an important section of the populace seriously impedes national progress. When dollar contracts are lost because of union squabbles there is something radically wrong with the leadership exercised by the trade unions. Would the contracts be lost, one wonders, if the union leaders had given their followers a clear explanation of the importance of such contracts not only to one factory in one industry but to the entire nation?

Admittedly, there are plenty of others in Britain who do not understand the importance of the economic situation or the changes that have taken place. But the attitude of a retired colonel in Bedford or a stout matron in Wimbledon is not so important to the nation's welfare as that of the members of the working class.

The second factor affecting the response of this class to the nation's needs is the effect upon it of the economic depression of the years between the two world wars. Again and again we have seen how the memory of unemployment, of the dole, of endless empty days at labor exchanges, of hungry children and women's stricken eyes has colored the thinking of the working class. It is too ready to see the problems of the 1950's in terms of its experiences of the 1930's. Consequently, it adopts a partisan attitude toward political development and a reactionary attitude toward industrial innovation.

There are those who argue that these attitudes will change as the working class becomes more accustomed to its new condition of life and place in the national pattern. This may prove true. But can Britain afford to wait until the union leaders understand that each new machine or industrial technique is not part of a calculated plan by the bosses to return the workers to the conditions prevailing in South Wales in 1936?

This partisan approach to economic problems is as important a factor as complacency and lethargy in obstructing adoption by the working class of a national viewpoint toward the British economic predicament. The British political system is a marvelously well-balanced one. But the balance is disturbed now and has been for some years by the tendency of organized labor to think almost exclusively in terms of its own rather than national interests. Labor can with perfect justice retort that when the middle class dominated British society it thought in terms of its own interests, too. This is true, of course. The difference is that the present national position is too precarious for blind partisanship.

Much is made in public speeches of the educational side of trade-union work. It would seem that the great opportunity for the unions now is in this field. Someone or some organization that enjoys the respect of the workers must educate them out of their lethargy and out of their memories of the past. The popular newspapers will not or cannot do it—and, naturally, as largely capitalist, they would be suspected by many of those most in need of such education. But the job must be done if Britain is to benefit fully from the enterprise and ingenuity of her designers and engineers.

Certainly the educational process would work both ways. A traveler in Britain in the period 1953–6 would notice that in many cases there was a difference between the TUC leaders' views about what the workers thought and what the workers themselves thought. Many of the unions have become too big. Contact between the leaders and the rank and file is lost. The Communists take advantage of this.

Can the working class awaken to the necessities of Britain's position and sublimate its agonizing memories and fierce hatreds in a national economic effort? This is the big "if" in Britain's ability to meet the economic challenge of today. I do not doubt that the working class will respond again, as it has in the past, to a national emergency that is as real, if less spectacular, than the one which faced the nation in 1940. This response, I believe, will develop as firmly, albeit more slowly, under a Conservative government as under a Labor government because it will be a development of the trend, already clearly evident, in the new middle class to take a national rather than a class outlook on Britain's problems. But the response must come soon.

We have seen how the present political alignment in Britain has developed out of the political and economic circumstances of the years since 1939. What of the future?

The Conservative government since the end of 1955 has been engaged in a gigantic political gamble. It has instituted a series of economic measures to restrict home spending. These measures are highly unpopular with the new working class from whom the party has obtained surprising support in recent elections. At the same time the Tory cabinet has not provided as much relief from taxation as the old middle class, its strongest supporters, demanded and expected after the electoral triumph of May 1955. These are calculated political risks. The calculation is that by the next general election, in 1959 or even 1960, the drive to expand British exports will have succeeded in establishing a new prosperity more firmly based than that of the boom years 1954 and 1955.

To attain this objective the Conservative government will have to perform a feat of political tightrope-walking beyond the aspirations of ordinary politics. The new prosperity can be achieved successfully, from the political point of view, only if the measures taken to attain it please the old middle class without offending Conservative voters in the new middle class and the new industrial working class. This will mean budgets in 1957 and 1958 that will relieve financial pressure upon the first of these groups without alienating the other two, whose interests are mutually antagonistic. It will mean that Britain's defense commitments must be reduced and adjusted to the extent that the savings will cut taxation of the old middle class but not to the extent that the reduction of defense construction will affect the employment of either the new middle class or the industrial working class.

This book was completed before the government's course was run. If its policy succeeds, then Harold Macmillan must be accorded a place in history not far below that of the greatest workers of political miracles.

Had there been a general election in the winter of 1956–7, the Labor Party would have won, although its majority would probably not have been so large as its enthusiastic tacticians predicted. The party should be able to appeal to the electorate at the next general election with greater success than in 1955, providing certain conditions are met.

The big "if" facing the Labor Party concerns not abstruse questions of socialist dogma but the oldest question in politics: the conflict between two men. The men are Hugh Gaitskell, the leader of the Parliamentary Labor Party, and Aneurin Bevan.

Nye Bevan remains a major force in British politics. He is the only prominent politician who is a force in himself, a personality around which lesser men assemble. Like the young Winston Churchill, he inspires either love or hate. Untrammeled by the discipline of the party, he can rally the left wing of the Labor movement. Simultaneously he can alienate the moderates of the party, the undecided voters, and the tepid conservatives who had thought it might be time to let labor "have a go." If the next general-election campaign finds Bevan clamoring for the extension of nationalization in British industry, beckoning his countrymen down untrodden social paths, lambasting Britain's allies, and scoffing at her progress, then the Labor Party will be defeated.

I have known Aneurin Bevan for many years. For the weal or woe of Britain, he is a man born to storm and danger. A sudden war, a swift and violent economic reverse would brighten his star. In a crisis his confidence, whether that of a born leader or a born charlatan, would attract the many.

Barring such catastrophes, a reasonable stability in government is to be expected. The Conservative majority in the House of Commons after the 1955 election probably was a little larger than is customary in a nation so evenly divided politically. Despite the rancor aroused by the Suez crisis, there seem to be reasonable grounds for predicting the gradual disappearance of Tories of the old type and of the belligerent Labor leaders surviving from the twenties. The development of a national outlook by both parties seems probable.

Americans need not be concerned over the fission of the British political system into a multi-party one capable of providing a government but incapable of government. Stability means, of course, that British governments will know their own minds. In the complex, hair-trigger world of today this is an important factor. It is equally important in charting the future course of Britain. Nations that know where they want to go and how they want to go there are not verging on political senility.

This political stability is vital to Britain in the years of transition that lie ahead. For it is in British industry that the greatest changes will take place.

Britain is moving in new directions, economically, politically, and socially. The base of this movement is industrial—a revolution in power. The world's most imaginative, extensive, and advanced program for the production of electricity from nuclear power stations is under way. This magnificent acceptance of the challenge of the nuclear age is also an answer to one of the key questions of 1945: how could British industry expand and British exports thrive if coal yearly became scarcer and more expensive to mine? The answer is nuclear energy, 5,000 to 6,000 megawatts of it by 1965.

The program for constructing twenty nuclear power stations in Britain and Northern Ireland is the most spectacular part of the power program. As coal will be vital to the economy for years to come, more economic and more efficient mining methods also are regarded as a matter of national urgency.

Throughout the nation's industrial structure there is an air of purpose and enthusiasm. Five huge new steel plants will be started in 1957. An ambitious program of modernizing the railroads and the shipbuilding industry is well under way. The new industries that have developed since 1945 and old industries now delivering for the export markets are pushing British goods throughout the world: radar, radioactive isotopes, electronic equipment, sleek new jet aircraft, diesel engines, plastics, detergents, atomic power stations. All are part of Britain's response to the challenge of change.

To fulfill present hopes, production and productivity must rise, management must grasp the changed position of Britain in the world. From the courted, she has become the courter, competing for markets with Germany, Japan, Sweden, and the United States. Such competition existed in the past, but now, with the cushion of overseas investments gone, such competition is a true national battle. There is plenty of evidence that a portion at least of industrial management in Britain fails to understand these conditions. Such complacency is as dangerous to the export drive as the unwillingness or inability of the industrial worker to grasp the export drive's importance to him, to his factory, to his union, and to his country.

Due emphasis should be given to such failings. But we must not forget that the British are a great mercantile people, eager and ingenious traders ready, once they accept its importance, to go to any length of enterprise to win a market. It is also wise to remember that, although circumstances have made the British share of the dollar market the criterion of success, the British do extremely well in a number of important non-dollar markets.

The attitude of the industrial working class to wage increases is a factor in the drive to boost the exports on which the nation lives. The modernization of British industry to meet the requirements of the nation's economic position, alterations in management and sales practices, higher production and productivity will not suffice to win export markets if the wage level in industry continues to rise. A steady rise will price Britain out of her markets. Should this occur, the question of whether organized labor is to take kindly to automation will become academic. The country cannot live without those markets.

Early in September of 1956 when the world was worrying over

the Suez Canal, *The New York Times* carried a news item from Brighton, the English seashore resort, that surely was as important to Britain as anything Premier Nasser or Sir Anthony Eden or Mr. Dulles might say.

The Trades Union Congress, the dispatch said, had rejected the Conservative government's plea for restraint in pressing wage claims. The final paragraphs of a resolution passed unanimously at the eighty-eighth annual conference said that the TUC ". . . asserts the right of labor to bargain on equal terms with capital, and to use its bargaining strength to protect the workers from the dislocations of an unplanned economy.

"It rejects proposals to recover control by wage restraint, and by using the nationalized industries as a drag-anchor for the drifting national economy."

These phrases reveal the heart of the quarrel between the TUC and the government. The Conservatives are belabored for not carrying out a Socialist policy—i.e., a planned economy—but restraint on wages is rejected.

The resolution represented a serious check in progress toward a national understanding of the country's economic position. It ensured, I believe, another round of wage demands by the unions, protracted industrial disputes, and, eventually, higher costs for industry and higher prices for foreign buyers.

The constant bickering between union and union, between unions and employers, and between the TUC and the government should not divert us from the qualities of the British industrial working class. It is highly skilled, especially in the fields of electronics and the other new industries now so important to the export trade. Its gross production and productivity are rising. It is, once aroused, intelligent and energetic. The nation is essentially homogeneous. There is obviously a wide gap between worker and employer in Britain, but it seems less wide when we compare it with the French worker's hostility toward his boss.

But of course the industrial worker is only one unit of the industrial system. Working with him are hundreds of thousands of engineers, technicians, planners, and managers—men of high quality, imaginative, daring, and resourceful. Together these two groups operate industries that are rapidly recovering from the effects of the war and the frantic post-war period in which all machines had to run at top speed, regardless of repairs, if Britain was to make enough to live.

If Americans understand that in a smaller country industry will be on a smaller scale than in the United States, they must concede that the steel plants in Wales and the North, the hydroelectric power system built in the fastnesses of the Scottish Highlands, the new nuclear-energy power stations now nearing completion are impressive industrial installations. British industry in the physical sense is not a collection of obsolete or obsolescent factories and rundown mills; new plants and factories are appearing with greater frequency every year, and the emphasis is on the future.

A journey through the busy Midlands provides the proof. Everywhere one sees new construction for industrial production. The rawboned red brick factories, relics of Victorian England, are silent and empty; many have been pulled down. The main problem for Britain is not the modernity of her industrial system but the lack of modernity in the outlook of her industrial workers.

The judgment may seem too harsh. It is manifestly unfair to place the entire burden of progress toward a healthier economy on one element in the economic situation. Certainly British capital in the past and to some extent in the present has been singularly blind to the country's new situation and unenterprising in seeking means of adjusting itself to this situation. The price rings and monopolistic practices have sustained inefficient factories and restricted industrial enterprise.

Nevertheless, it is my conclusion that today the industrial owner and manager understands the nation's situation and the union leader does not. The TUC has attained great influence in the realm. The industrial worker has won living standards undreamed of a generation ago. Nonetheless, there is a dangerous lack of tolerance in labor's approach to management. This carries over into labor's approach to government. It is a highly unrealistic attitude in which organized labor clamors for the adoption by a Conservative government of a system of economic planning which that government was elected to end.

As we have seen, thousands of the Tories' strongest supporters are angry because they regard the government they elected as pseudo-socialist.

This contest between labor and capital is involved and sharply partisan. Viewed from the outside, it may seem an insurmountable obstacle to British progress. But to accept that view is to ignore the most important, the most enduring of all the country's resources: the character of the British people.

From the time of Charles II on, visitors to Britain have been struck by the way in which the character of the British people has allowed them the widest latitude for internal differences, often carried to the very edge of armed conflict, and has yet enabled them to maintain their political stability.

There is a lesson in recent history. Imposing forces within the kingdom reached a pitch of fanatic fury over the Ulster question shortly before World War I. Great political leaders took their positions. The Army was shaken by rumors of disaffection. Officers were ready to resign their commissions rather than lead their troops into action against the turbulent Ulstermen. The Germans and others watching from the Continent concluded that the heart of the world empire was sick. Yet what was the outcome? Finally aware of the magnitude of the challenge presented by German aggression in Belgium, the country united instantly. The leaders composed their differences. The Army closed its ranks. The officers went away to fight and die at Mons and Le Cateau.

The lesson is that the British, because of their essential homogeneity, can afford a higher pitch of internal argument than can other nations. Indeed, the very fury of these arguments testifies to the vitality of the nation. It means a country on the move, in contrast to the somber, orderly, shabby dictatorship of Spain or the somnolent French Republic where the great slogans of the past have been abandoned for the motto "We couldn't care less."

Those who admire the British accept British character as one of the strongest arguments for their nation's survival as a great power. But before we go too far in endorsing this view we must note that there are bad characteristics as well as good ones. We know that the British society is changing. Is it not possible that in the process of change some of the characteristics which made the nation great are disappearing?

Mr. Geoffrey Gorer tells us that the British have become a law-abiding nation dwelling in amity and honesty under British justice. In some aspects of civil relationship this is true. Visitors to Britain only a century ago were alarmed by the behavior of British mobs. The cockneys of London pulled the mustaches of a visiting Hungarian general and shouted rude remarks at their Queen and her Prince Consort. From medieval times the British working classes have been long on independence and short on respect. The uprising of the *Jacquerie* in French history is balanced in British annals by the dim, powerful, and compelling figures of Wat Tyler and John Ball.

Has all this changed so much? Have the turbulent, violent British really become a nation of sober householders indifferent to their rights or to those at home or abroad who threaten them? Superficially the answer may be yes. Basically it is no. The present strife between organized labor and the employers is only a contemporary version of a struggle which has gone on throughout its history and which is world-wide. It is when this struggle is submerged that it is dangerous. Despite all the damage it is doing now to the British economy, dissension in the House of Commons and in the boardrooms of industries is preferable to wild plots laid in cellars.

When we consider the heat with which these debates are conducted we must also take notice of one sign of British stability: partisan passions, either in industrial conflict or in political warfare, never reach the point where the patriotism of the other party is impugned. The Conservatives do not label the Socialists as the party of treason. The patriotism of Hugh Gaitskell is not questioned by

Harold Macmillan. Ultimately we come round to the realization that, despite the bitterness of debate, the central stability of the state remains.

Much of this stability may result from the existence of the monarchy at the summit of British affairs. All public evidence indicates that the Crown is nearly powerless in modern Britain, yet it represents an authority older and higher than any other element in the realm. It may be the balance wheel, spinning brightly through the ages, that insures stability.

"At the heart to the British Empire there is one institution," Winston Churchill wrote twenty years ago, "among the most ancient and venerable, which, so far from falling into desuetude or decay, has breasted the torrent of events, and even derived new vigor from the stresses. Unshaken by the earthquakes, unweakened by the dissolvent tides, though all be drifting the Royal and Imperial Monarchy of Britain stands firm."

It can be argued that the excessive interest of the British people in the monarchy and the expense and labor involved in its upkeep are characteristics ill suited to Britain in her present position. This interest reflects the national tendency to dwell fondly on the past, to revere institutions for their historical connections rather than for their efficiency or usefulness under modern conditions. Serious criticism of this well-defined trait comes not only from Americans but from Australians, Canadians, and other inhabitants of newer nations. We look forward, they say, and the British look back.

There is some justice in the criticism, but perhaps the error is not so grave as we may think. Obviously, it is impossible for a people living in a country that has known some sort of civilization from Roman times not to be impressed by their past. A tendency in the same direction marks contemporary American society. Just as we are struck by the Londoner's interest in Roman relics dug up in the heart of his city, so European visitors note that an increasing number of Americans are turning to their own past. All over the East the fortresses of the French and Indian and Revolutionary wars are being reconstructed and opened to tourists. National attention is given to attempts in the Far West to re-create for a day or a week the atmosphere of a frontier that passed less than a century ago. Half-forgotten battles and generals of the Civil War are rescued for posterity by the careful labor of scholarly biographers and military writers. This does not mean, however, that the United States is looking back in the field of science or invention.

Similarly, British preservation of old castles or folkways is not a sign that the nation has turned its back on the twentieth century. The boldness with which the British accepted the challenge of the nuclear era in industrial energy is a better guide to their temper than their respect for the past. What is damaging is not reverence for the past of Nelson or Gladstone, but the tendency of some of the middle class to mourn the recent past, the dear dead days before the war when servants were plentiful, taxes relatively low, and "a man could run his own business." These mourners are temporarily important because their resistance to needed change infects others. But the life whose end they bewail has been disappearing in Britain for half a century, and the generation now rising to power will not be plagued by these memories to the same extent. To those who matured in war and post-war austerity, modern Britain is a prosperous land.

The trappings of British society are much older than our own. But their interest in maintaining an unchanged façade should not mislead Americans into believing the British are returning to the hand loom. Reverence for the past is often advanced as one reason for the lethargic attitude of Britons toward the present. Certainly an awareness of history, its trials and triumphs, gives an individual or a people a somewhat skeptical attitude about the importance of current history. But in Britain those who know and care least about the nation's great past are the ones most indifferent to the challenge of the present. They are the industrial working class, and their indifference results from other influences.

Talking to the planners, technicians, factory bosses, communications experts, salesmen, and senior civil servants, one finds less complacency and more enterprise than in most European countries. In fact, it sometimes seems to the outsider that British society is a little too self-critical, too contentious. Obviously, it must change to meet the altered world, but self-criticism pushed to the maximum can ultimately crush ambition.

If we turn to modern British writing, we find sociologists, economists, anthropologists, and politicians pouring forth a steady stream of books analyzing the nation's social, economic, and political problems. One of the great men of the modern Labor Party, Herbert Morrison, thought it well worth while to devote his time to the writing of *Government and Parliament*. The intellectual leaders of Britain have turned increasingly to a minute assessment of their nation and what is right and wrong about it.

This preoccupation with the state of the realm is healthy. The complacency that was once the most disliked characteristic of the traveling Briton is vanishing. The British are putting themselves under the microscope. Nothing but good can come of it.

We hear from the British themselves confessions of inadequacy to meet the modern world and flaming criticisms of aspects of their society. As a nation they are fond of feeling sorry for themselves; indeed, someone has said that they are never happier than when they think all is lost. Such British statements should not be taken as representing the whole truth. The reforming element is very strong in the British character. Without its presence, the social reforms of this century could not have been accomplished.

Anyone who frequents political, business, and journalistic circles in Britain will hear more about mistakes and failures than about success. (The most notable exception to this enjoyment of gloom is the popular press, which since the war has made a specialty of boosting British achievements.) Similarly, any discussion of British character with Britons is sure to find them concentrating on negative rather than positive traits. Perhaps this is because they are so sure of their positive characteristics. In any case, the latter constitute a major share of the national insurance against decline.

Over the years the British trait that has impressed me most is toughness of mind. This may surprise Americans who tend to regard the British as overpolite or diffident or sentimental—aspects of the national character which are evident at times and which hide the essential toughness underneath.

Although they bewail a decline in the standards of courtesy since the war, the British are a polite race in the ordinary business of living. From the " 'kew" of the bus conductor or the salesgirl to the "And now, sir, if you would kindly sign here" of the bank clerk they pad social intercourse with small courtesies. However, when an Englishman, especially an upper-class Englishman, desires to be rude he makes the late Mr. Vishinsky sound like a curate. But it is an English axiom that a gentleman is never unintentionally rude.

With some notable exceptions, the British are seldom loudly assertive. They will listen at great length to the opinions of others and, seemingly, are reluctant to put forward their own. This does not mean they agree, although foreigners in contact with British diplomats have often assumed this mistakenly. The British are always willing to see both sides of a question. But they are seldom ready to accept without prolonged and often violent argument any point of view other than their own.

They are a sentimental people but not an emotional one. Failure to distinguish this difference leads individuals and nations to misjudge the British.

Sentimentalists they are. Their eyes will glisten with tears as they listen to some elderly soprano with a voice long rusted by gin sing the music-hall songs of half a century ago. As Somerset Maugham has pointed out, they revere age. The present Conservative government and the Labor front bench are unusual in that they contain a large percentage of "young men"—that is, men in their fifties. Sir Winston Churchill did not truly win the affection of his countrymen until he was well into his seventies, when the old fierce antagonism of the working class was replaced with a grudging admiration for "the Old Man."

On his eightieth birthday the leaders of all the political parties in the House of Commons joined in a tribute that milked the tear

ducts of the nation. When, six months later, Sir Winston retired as
Prime Minister there was another outbreak of bathos. But when two
months after that a new House of Commons was sworn under the
leadership of Sir Anthony Eden, some of the young Conservative
Members of Parliament who owed their offices and, in a wider sense,
their lives to Sir Winston pushed ahead of him in the jostling throng
making for the Speaker's bench. It was left to Clement Attlee, his
dry, thoughtful foe in so many political battles, to lead Sir Winston
up ahead of his eager juniors. Sentiment, yes; emotion, no.

For many reasons the British as a people are anxious to find
formulas that will guide them out of international crises, to avoid
the final arbitration of war. The appeasement of Neville Chamberlain and his associates in the late thirties was in keeping with
this historically developed tendency. One has only to read what
Pitt endured from Napoleon to preserve peace, or the sound, sensible reasons that Charles James Fox offered against the continuation of the war with the First Empire, to understand that this island
people goes to war only with the utmost reluctance.

One reason is that in 1800, in 1939, and in the middle of the
twentieth century the British have lived by trade. Wars, large or
small, hurt trade. Prolonged hostility toward a foreign nation—
Franco's Spain, Lenin's Russia, or Mao's China—reduces Britain's
share in a market or cuts off raw materials needed for production
at home. In this respect we cannot judge Britain by the continental
standards of China or Russia or the United States. This is an island
power.

Because they are polite, because they are easily moved to sentimental tears—Sir Winston Churchill and Hugh Gaitskell, who
otherwise have few traits in common, both cry easily—because they
are diffident, because they will twist and turn in their efforts to
avoid war (although at times, for reasons of policy, they will present the impression of being very ready for war), the British have
given the outside world a false idea of their character. Beneath all
this is toughness of mind.

I recall landing in England in April of 1939. It was then

obvious to almost everyone in Europe that war was on the way. On the way to London I talked to a fellow passenger, a man in his late twenties who had three small children and who lived in London. "The next time Hitler goes for anyone, we'll go for him," he said casually, almost apologetically. He conceded that the war would be long, that Britain would take some hard knocks, that going into the Navy and leaving his wife and children would be tedious. But he had made up his mind that there was no other course. The thing had to be done.

After the war—and, indeed, during it—many Americans ridiculed the British reaction to the war. They found exaggerated the stories of the cockney who said: " 'arf a mo', Adolph" while he lit his pipe, the women who shouted "God bless you" to Winston Churchill when he visited the smoking ruins of their homes. This was a serious error. In those days, the most critical that had ever come upon them, the British acted in a manner which made one proud to be a member of the same species.

But that was a decade and a half ago, and the circumstances were extraordinary. Nations change—compare the heroic France of Verdun with the indulgent, faithless France of 1940. Have war and sacrifice, austerity and prolonged crisis weakened Britain's mental toughness? I think not.

The prolonged conflict between employers and employed and among the great trade unions is the most serious friction within British society. Its critical effect upon Britain's present and future has been emphasized. I do not believe, however, that in the long run the men on both sides who hold their opinions so stoutly will be unable to compromise their difficulties in the face of the continuing national emergency. In the twenties and thirties such great convulsions in industrial relations as the General Strike were harmful but not catastrophic. The British economy was buttressed by overseas investments and by the possession of established export markets throughout the world. That situation no longer exists. Anything approaching the severity of a General Strike could break Britain. In the end, I believe, the extremists of both sides will realize this and will find in themselves the mental toughness—for it takes a hard mind to accept an armistice short of final victory in exchange for the promise of future benefits—to compose their differences and move toward a national rather than a partisan solution.

Of course, Britain's difficulties are not confined to the home front. But I have consciously emphasized the importance of her internal problems because they reflect the nation's present position in the world and help to determine how Britain will act abroad.

Just as the last decade has seen drastic changes in industrial direction in Britain, so the coming decade will witness changes equally great in the development of Britain's international position. Britain cannot, and would not if she could, build a new empire. But it is evident that the country intends to replace the monolithic concept of power with a horizontal concept. We will see, I am confident, a steady growth of Britain's ties with Europe and the establishment of Britain as a link between the Commonwealth nations and Europe.

The British have fertile political imaginations. They are adroit in discussion and debate. After years of uncertainty a number of politicians of great influence are moving toward closer association with Europe. At the moment the Grand Design (a rather grandiose title for the British to use) is endorsed by Prime Minister Harold Macmillan, Foreign Secretary Selwyn Lloyd, Defense Minister Duncan Sandys, Chancellor of the Exchequer Peter Thorneycroft, and President of the Board of Trade Sir David Eccles. Given a change in government, I think we can assume that the idea would be supported, although enthusiasm would be somewhat less great, by the leaders of the Labor Party.

What is the Grand Design? It is the concept of a Europe co-operating in fields of economy and politico-military strategy. It goes beyond the Europe of Western European Union or the North Atlantic Treaty Alliance and thinks in terms of a general confederation into which the Scandinavian and Mediterranean nations would be drawn. Existing organizations such as the Organization for European Economic Co-operation would be expanded to include new members. At the top would be a General Assembly elected by the parliaments of each member nation. There would be a general pooling of military research and development.

The establishment of such an association of European states is at least ten years in the future. The British do not think it should be hurried. Careful, rather pragmatic, they advocate methodical progress in which new international organizations could be tested against actual conditions. Those that work will survive. Those that do not will disappear.

Is the Grand Design a new name for a third force to be interposed between the Sino-Russian bloc in the East and the United States in the West? The British say emphatically not. They see it as a method of strengthening the Atlantic Alliance by uniting Europe. Naturally, they believe their flair for diplomacy and politics, their industrial strength, and, not least, Europe's distaste for German leadership will give them an important role in the new Europe. Obviously, that role, as spokesman for both a united Europe and a global Commonwealth, will be more suitable and, above all, more practical in the world of 1960 than the obsolete concept of Empire.

The development of British action toward the accomplishment of the Grand Design will be accompanied by the gradual transformation of what is left of the Empire into the Commonwealth. Ghana, established as an independent member of the Commonwealth in March 1957, will be followed by Singapore, Malaya, Nigeria, Rhodesia, and many more. Since 1945 Britain has given self-government and independence to well over 500,000,000 souls (at the same time the Soviet Union was enslaving 100,000,000) and the process is not over. Certainly there have been shortcomings and failures—Cyprus is one. But it seems to me that a people prepared on one hand to abdicate power and turn that power over to others and at the same time ready to conceive and develop a new plan for Europe is showing an elasticity and toughness of mind the rest of the world might envy. We are not attending the birth of a new British Empire but watching the advent of a new position for

Britain in the world—one less spectacularly powerful than the old, but important nonetheless. The speed of its development is inextricably connected with an expanding and prosperous economy at home.

Bravery is associated with tough-mindedness. But bravery is not the exclusive possession of any nation. The British are a courageous people, certainly. As certain classes are apt to combine courage with the national habit of understatement, the bravery of the British has an attraction not evident in the somewhat self-conscious heroism of the Prussians. Of course, it can be argued that the apparent unwillingness of the British to exploit the fact that Pilot Officer Z brought his plane back from Berlin on one engine or that Sergeant Major Y killed thirty Germans before his morning tea is a form of national advertisement more subtle and sure than that obtained by battalions of public-relations officers.

Although they revere regimental traditions, the British seldom express their reverence openly. In war they are able to maintain an attitude of humorous objectivity. During the fighting on the retreat to Dunkirk I encountered two Guards officers roaring with laughter. They had learned, they said, that the popular newspapers in London had reported that the nickname of the Commander in Chief, General the Viscount Gort, was "Tiger." "My dear chap," said one, "in the Brigade [of Guards] we've always called him 'Fat Boy.' "

Coupled with tough-mindedness is another positive characteristic: love of justice. This may be disputed by the Irish, the Indians, the Cypriotes. But it is true that in all the great international crises in which Britain has been involved, from the War of Independence onward, there has been a strong, sometimes violent opposition to the course that the government of the day pursued. Beginning with Burke, the Americans, the Irish, the Indians, the Cypriotes have had defenders in the House of Commons, on political platforms, and in the press.

This is not the result of partisan politics, although naturally that helps. Englishmen did not assail the Black and Tans in Ireland because of love for Irishmen. Indian independence did not find a redoubtable champion in Earl Mountbatten because of his particular fondness for Indians. The impulse was the belief that justice or, to put it better, right must be done.

It is because a large section of the nation believes this implicitly that the British over the years have been able to make those gestures of conciliation and surrenders of power which will ever adorn her history: the settlement with the Boers after the South African war, the withdrawal from India, the treaty with Ireland.

The British people suffered greatly during both world wars. Yet any ferocious outbreak of hatred against "the Huns" was promptly answered by leaders who even in the midst of war understood that the right they were fighting to preserve must be preserved at home as well as abroad.

It was this belief in justice, a justice that served all, incorruptible and austere, which enabled a comparative handful of Britons to rule the Indian subcontinent for so long. It was this belief in justice, interpreted in terms of social evolution, which moved the reformers of the present century in the direction of the Welfare State. The British concept of justice is inseparably bound to the strong reformist element within the British people. As long as that element flourishes, as it does today, we can expect that British society will continue to change and develop.

Tough-mindedness, a quiet form of bravery, a love of justice; what else is there? One characteristic I have noted earlier: a living belief in the democratic process. The British know the world too well to believe that this delicate and complex system of government can immediately be imposed upon any people. They themselves, as they will admit, have trouble making it work. But neither fascism nor communism has ever made headway. Any political expert can provide long and involved reasons for this. I prefer the obvious one: the British believe in democracy, they believe in people. Long ago, as a young man entering politics, Winston Churchill, grandson of a Duke of Marlborough, product of Harrow and a fashionable

Hussar regiment, adopted as his own a motto of his father's. It was simply: "Trust the People."

The actual practice of democracy over a long period of years can be successful only if it is accompanied by a wide measure of tolerance. Despite all their vicissitudes, this virtue the British preserve in full measure. The British disliked Senator McCarthy because they thought he was intolerant; they were themselves slightly intolerant, or at least ill-informed, about the causes that inflated the Senator. In their own nation the British tolerate almost any sort of political behavior as long as it is conducted within the framework of the law. Communists, fascists, isolationists, internationalists all may speak their pieces and make as much noise as they wish. There will always be a policeman on hand to quell a disturbance.

Toleration of the public exposition of political beliefs that aim at the overthrow of the established parliamentary government implies a stout belief in the supremacy of democracy over other forms of government. Even in their unbuttoned moments, British politicians will seldom agree to the thesis, lately put about by many eminent men, that complete suffrage prevents a government from acting with decision in an emergency.

Early in 1951 I talked late one night with a British diplomat about the rearmament of Germany. He was a man of wide experience, aristocratic bearing, and austere manner. During our conversation I suggested that the British, who had suffered greatly at the hands of the Germans in two world wars, would be most reluctant to agree to the rearmament of their foes and that the ensuing political situation would be made to order for the extremists of the Labor Party.

"I don't think so," he replied. "Our people fumble and get lost at times, but they come back on the right track. They'll argue it out in their minds or in the pubs. They'll reject extreme measures. The Labor Party and the great mass of its followers will be with the government. The people, you know, are wiser than anyone thinks they are."

Tolerance is coupled with kindness. British kindness is apt to be abstract, impersonal. There is the gruff, unspoken kindness of the members of the working class to one another in times of death. The wealthy wearer of the Old School Tie will go to great lengths to succor a friend fallen on evil days. He will also do his best to provide for an old employee or to rehabilitate an old soldier, once under his command, who is in trouble with the police. This is part of the sense of responsibility inculcated by the public school. Even in the Welfare State it persists. "I've got to drive out into Essex this afternoon," a friend said, "and see what I can do for a sergeant that served with me. Bloody fool can't hold onto a farthing and makes a pest of himself with the local authorities. Damn good sergeant, though."

I remembered another sergeant in Germany. He was a man who had felt the war deeply, losing a brother, a wife, and a daughter to German bombs. When it was all over and the British Army rested on its arms in northern Germany he installed his men in the best billets the neighboring village could provide. The Germans were left to shift for themselves in the barns and outbuildings. Within a week, he told me, the situation was reversed. The Germans were back in their homes. The soldiers were sleeping in the barns. I told a German about it afterward. "Yes," he said, "the British would do that. We wouldn't, not after a long war. They are a decent people."

It is upon such characteristics, a basic, stubborn toughness of mind, bravery, tolerance, a belief in democracy, kindness, decency, that British hopes for the future rest.

Any objective study of Britain must accept that, although there has been a decline in power at home and abroad, the national economy has recovered remarkably and the physical basis of the economy has improved. Far from being decadent, idle, and unambitious, the nation as a whole is pulsing with life. The energy may be diffused into paths that fail to contribute directly to the general betterment of the nation. But it is there, and the possession of the important national characteristics mentioned above promises that eventually this energy will be directed to the national good.

In the end we return to our starting-point. Although there is a cleavage between the working class and the middle class, it is not deep enough to smash the essential unity of the people. No great gulfs of geography, race, or religion separate them. The differences between employer and employed are serious. But there is no basic difference, nurtured by the hatred of a century and a half, as there is between revolutionary France and conservative France. The constant change in the character of the classes, the steady movement of individuals and groups up the economic and social ladders insures that this will never develop. From the outside the society seems stratified. On the inside one sees, hears, feels ceaseless movement of a flexible society.

The long contest with Russia has induced Americans to follow Napoleon's advice and think about big battalions. But national power and influence should not be measured solely in terms of material strength. By that standard the England of the first Elizabeth and the Dutch Republic of the seventeenth century would have been blotted out by the might of Spain just as our own struggling colonies would have been overcome by the weight of England. The character of a people counts.

So it is with Britain. The ability of the British people to survive cannot be measured only in terms of steel production. The presence of grave economic and social problems should not be accepted as proof that they cannot be solved by people of imagination and ability. The existence of external class differences should not blind observers to the basic unity of political thought.

It is natural that in their present position Britons are far more aware of the ties that bind them to the United States, ties that include a common language, much common history, dangers shared, and enemies overcome, than the people of the United States are aware of the ties that bind them to Britain. But Americans must guard against the easy assumption that, because Britain is weaker than she was half a century ago, because she has changed rapidly and will change further, Britain and the British are "through."

It is often said in Washington that the leading politicians of the Republican and Democratic parties and the chief permanent officials of the Treasury, State Department, and other departments did not recognize the extent to which Britain had been weakened by World War II. It is hard to understand why this should have been so. The sacrifice in blood was written large on a hundred battlefields. The cost in treasure was clearly outlined in the financial position of the United Kingdom in 1945.

Americans should not fear political differences between the United States and the United Kingdom on foreign policies. As long as the British are worth their salt as allies they will think, and occasionally act, independently. What would be dangerous to the future of the alliance in a period of crisis would be the growth in Britain of a belief that Britain's problems, internal or international, can be blamed on the United States. A similar belief about Britain existed in France in 1940. Verdun occupied the position in French minds that the Battle of Britain does today in some British minds, that of a great heroic national effort that exhausted the nation and left it prey to the post-war appetite of its supposed friend and ally. If this concept were to be accepted by any sizable proportion of the British people, then the alliance would be in danger. The possibility that this will happen is slight. The British retain confidence in themselves, undaunted by the changes in the world.

The United States can help sustain this confidence. It is difficult to see why the political, industrial, and social accomplishments of the British since 1945 are so casually ignored in the United States and why Americans accept so readily the idea that Britain's day is done.

Certainly many Americans criticized the establishment of the Welfare State. Certainly ingorance led many to confuse socialism in Britain with communism in the Soviet Union. Certainly the achievement of power by the great trade unions has alienated those Americans who still decry the powerful position of organized labor in the modern democratic state.

But it is folly to expect that even our closest friends and truest allies can develop economically and politically along paths similar to those trod by the people of the United States. It is time that we looked on the positive side of Britain's life since the end of World War II. We must remember that this is a going concern. The new nuclear power stations rising throughout Britain are part of the general Western community which we lead. British advances in the sciences or in any other field of human endeavor should not be thought of as the activities of a rival but as the triumphs of an ally that has in the past given incontrovertible proof of her steadfastness in adversity, her willingness to do and dare at the side of the United States.

There they are, fifty millions of them. Kindly, energetic, ambitious, and, too often, happily complacent in peace; most resolute, courageous, and tough-minded in the storms that have beaten about their islands since the dawn of the Christian era.

What is at stake in the relationship between the two nations is something far greater than whether we approve of Aneurin Bevan or the British approved of Senator McCarthy. The union of the English-speaking peoples is the one tried and tested alliance in a shaky world. Three times within living memory its sons have rallied to defeat or forestall the ambitions of conquerors. To understand Britain, to share with her the great tasks that lie before the Western community is much more than a salute by Americans to common political thought, a common tongue, or common memories. It is the easiest and most certain method by which we in our time can preserve the freedom of man which has been building in all the years since King and barons rode to Runnymede.

INDEX

i

A NOTE ON THE TYPE

The text of this book was set on the Linotype in a face called TIMES
ROMAN, *designed by* STANLEY MORISON *for* The Times *(London), and
first introduced by that newspaper in the middle nineteen thirties.*

*Among typographers and designers of the twentieth century,
Stanley Morison has been a strong forming influence, as typographical
adviser to the English Monotype Corporation, as a director of two
distinguished English publishing houses, and as a writer of sensibility,
erudition, and keen practical sense.*

*In 1930 Morison wrote: "Type design moves at the pace of the
most conservative reader. The good type-designer therefore realises
that, for a new fount to be successful, it has to be so good that only
very few recognise its novelty. If readers do not notice the consummate
reticence and rare discipline of a new type, it is probably a good letter."
It is now generally recognized that in the creation of* Times Roman
Morison successfully met the qualifications of this theoretical doctrine.

Composed, printed, and bound by H. WOLFF, *New York. Paper
manufactured by* S. D. WARREN CO., *Boston.*

A NOTE ABOUT THE AUTHOR

DREW MIDDLETON *was born in New York City in 1913. After being graduated from Syracuse University, he went into newspaper work, and in 1938 became a foreign correspondent. Since then he has been chief of* The New York Times *bureaus in England, Russia, and Germany. In 1940, during the Battle of Britain, he was in London covering the operations of the Royal Air Force, and he later sent his dispatches from Supreme Headquarters of the AEF. In the decade since the war, Mr. Middleton's reporting and interpreting of the Cold War struggle between East and West have earned him a wide and respectful audience both here and abroad. His earlier books include* The Struggle for Germany *(1949) and* The Defense of Western Europe *(1952).*